The Politics
of
Future Citizens

NEW DIMENSIONS
IN THE POLITICAL SOCIALIZATION
OF CHILDREN

Richard G. Niemi
and Associates

THE POLITICS
OF FUTURE
CITIZENS

 Jossey-Bass Publishers
San Francisco • Washington • London • 1974

THE POLITICS OF FUTURE CITIZENS
New Dimensions in the Political Socialization of Children
by Richard G. Niemi and Associates

Copyright © 1974 by: Jossey-Bass, Inc., Publishers
615 Montgomery Street
San Francisco, California 94111
&
Jossey-Bass Limited
3 Henrietta Street
London WC2E 8LU

Library of Congress Catalogue Card Number LC 73-21074

International Standard Book Number ISBN 0-87589-225-6

Manufactured in the United States of America

JACKET DESIGN BY WILLI BAUM

FIRST EDITION

Code 7421

The Jossey-Bass
Behavioral Science Series

Preface

Political scientists have only recently begun systematic studies of political learning among children. Barely a decade has passed since the first major studies were carried out and the results published. As in any field of study, changes in focus and improvements on earlier studies follow immediately on the heels of the first tentative steps. New methods of study are devised; new findings lead to new theories; new interpretations are made of earlier findings.

The contributors to *The Politics of Future Citizens* have followed this course in expanding current perspectives on political socialization. They have tested new methods and have made discoveries that sometimes contradict the conclusions of earlier studies. They have added to cross-sectional questionnaire data their findings from structured and unstructured interviews and from panel studies. They have extended the focus on white middle-class American children to children of several American minority groups and to children of other countries. And they have gone beyond the compilation of facts by emphasizing the processes of socialization as well as the utility and implications of their findings.

Students of political socialization—at any stage in their studies—will find in *The Politics of Future Citizens* an illumination of past studies and encouragement to expand still further on these findings and methods. To the professional, these chapters speak for themselves, though I have written an introductory chapter which indicates my interpretation of some of the findings and of their place in the political socialization literature. The other chapters are all original research reports. Though a few have been presented in earlier forms at conferences and meetings, almost none of what is reported here has been previously published. Students will probably find the book most meaningful when used in conjunction with Greenstein (1965a), Hess and Torney (1967), or one of several texts or collections of previously published material.

I would like to thank the contributors for their considerable efforts in writing and rewriting their chapters. They deserve the credit for their individual contributions; I hope that in the editing process I have made marginal improvements in their products. I would also like to thank Roman Hedges, who freely contributed his capacity for critical reading. The secretaries at the University of Rochester, Peg Gross and Janice Brown, did their usual excellent job.

Lastly, I like to think that this volume itself proves that pre-adult socialization is not entirely determinative of adult behavior, but that it does play some part in structuring adult roles. That seven of twelve contributors are women indicates that their early socialization to passive, domestic roles was not entirely successful, to the benefit of the readers. That I would comment on this indicates the continuing effects of socialization and other factors on the role of women in the professions and in academic disciplines in particular.

I dedicate this book to my parents.

Rochester, New York   Richard G. Niemi
January 1974

Contents

Contributors

PAUL ALLEN BECK, *Department of Political Science, University of Pittsburgh*

MARILYN BROOKES, *Eagleton Institute of Politics, Rutgers University*

CHRISTINE BENNET BUTTON, *Department of Secondary Education, University of Florida*

GUNNEL GUSTAFSSON, *Department of Political Science, University of Umea, Sweden*

DEAN JAROS, *Department of Political Science, University of Kentucky*

JEANNE N. KNUTSON, *The Wright Institute, and Department of Psychiatry, Ross-Loos Medical Group, Los Angeles*

KENNETH L. KOLSON, *Department of Political Science, Hiram College*

JAMES W. LAMARE, *Department of Political Science, University of Texas at El Paso*

SARAH F. LIEBSCHUTZ, *Department of Political Science, State University of New York at Brockport*

RICHARD G. NIEMI, *Department of Political Science, University of Rochester*

ROBERTA S. SIGEL, *Department of Political Science, Douglass College, Rutgers University*

PAULINE MARIE VAILLANCOURT, *Department of Political Science, McGill University*

The Politics
of
Future Citizens

NEW DIMENSIONS
IN THE POLITICAL SOCIALIZATION
OF CHILDREN

I

Political Learning

RICHARD G. NIEMI

Some years ago Peter Rossi (1959) introduced a collection of articles on voting behavior by observing, among other things, that the virtues of earlier research became the vices of later work (p. 54). What he meant, of course, was that the earliest studies represented bold new developments in the literature on voting behavior, but that later studies—building on the foundations of the older ones—represented substantial improvements on and additions to the original work. It is the same in the field of political socialization. The major studies of children and politics remain the New Haven study of Greenstein (1965a) and the "Chicago" study of Hess and Torney (1967) and Easton and Dennis (1969). These studies were masterpieces of new ideas; along with Hyman's compendium (1959), they opened up a whole new subfield in political science.

For all their virtues, however, these initial studies were severely limited. In one sense the limitations were strictly methodological. The research relied largely on mass-administered questionnaires. It was conducted almost exclusively with white, mostly urban, American children in a narrow historical period. Cross-section designs were employed to the exclusion of panel studies. Little could be said with confidence about the relationship between early learning and adult behavior. And application of the findings was usually

1

not even considered. But always methodological limitations were closely linked to substantive concerns. Sigel (1966), for example, points out in a convention paper that the use of questionnaires rather than personal interviews might seriously bias researchers' assessments of young children's attitudes toward political authorities. Similarly, the rise in black consciousness has illuminated the biasing effects of the exclusion of minority groups from research designs.

New studies were clearly needed to fill in the gaps in previous research and to expand upon the foundations of the initial work. The following chapters represent some of these new studies. Each of the chapters involves a research design that differs in some important respects from those of the New Haven and "Chicago" studies. Depth interviewing, panel studies, studies of minority groups, curriculum applications, and non-American studies are all represented here. But the point of each chapter is substantive and usually theoretical to a degree impossible in the first studies.

Several of the chapters focus on the socialization of minority group children. In each case, however, the authors do more than simply indicate that the attitudes of minority group children are different from those of white Americans. Jaros and Kolson, for example, contrast the views of political authority figures held by Amish children with the views of whites and blacks living in the same area. Their purpose is not merely to document the attitudes of a rather unusual group on the American scene, but rather to use the sharply contrasting viewpoints of these three groups to test alternative explanations of the source of children's ideas. They conclude that the general environment in which children are raised is more important than the specific environment of the family.

Lamare studies a minority group which has received little attention in the past—Mexican-Americans. He too is not content to simply describe their attitudes, but looks for the source of their attitudes in the language environment of family and friends. He concludes that language is more important in creating awareness of political objects than in influencing evaluations of political matters.

Liebschutz and I test two conflicting hypotheses about the development of black children's attitudes. In addition, we investigate a program designed to influence young blacks' attitudes in the early elementary grades; while the program had an effect on its participants, the effects appeared to be completely erased within a few years after the children left it.

The chapter by Knutson is based on in-depth interviews of young children. Knutson investigates the prepolitical ideology of children—intrapsychically generated pervasive attitudes which she argues are a basis for later political beliefs and behavior. With interviews she shows that young children have a more integrated, even if simplistic, prepolitical view of the world than questionnaire data indicates. Moreover, children's views of political authority are not as benevolent as previous research suggests.

Two of the chapters are based on the ever-suggested, seldom-undertaken panel-study method. Sigel and Brookes show how even young children's attitudes are strongly influenced by governmental performance. Children's views are not based on universal cognitive characteristics; they are enormously altered in only a few years by governmental actions. This does not, however, seem to diminish youngsters' overall affect for the political system. Using another panel study, Vaillancourt and I show that party identification in children is somewhat unstable—a more halting, wavering process than the usual stereotype indicates. We observe widespread, though moderate changes over a six-month period.

Each of these panel studies has a unique methodological component. The Sigel and Brookes chapter includes a grade-across-time comparison. They interviewed fourth, sixth, and eighth graders, then reinterviewed them two years later, and thus interviewed the current group of sixth and eighth graders. This allowed them to look at changes in particular individuals (the panel component) as well as changes in the attitudes of sixth and eighth graders two years apart (the grade-across-time component). The chapter which Vaillancourt and I wrote is based on a three-wave panel, which aids in sorting out true change from measurement error.

The addition of a comparative focus is another extension of the early socialization research. In the chapter by Gustafsson the focus is on the transmission of political attitudes between generations in Sweden. As in the chapters on minority groups, however, she is not content simply to present new data in a setting different from those studied before. Instead, her emphasis is on the effect made on this transmission by the surrounding environment. She compares areas in Sweden which have a high growth rate to those with a relatively stable population and those with a declining population. Adults and children in these different areas have quite different perspectives on the political world, but most importantly, population growth and decline affect the transmission of political ideas to growing children. The similarity of parents', teachers', children's, and their peers' attitudes varies with the surrounding environment.

Efforts have begun recently to apply research findings from the political socialization field to precollegiate curriculum development. This work is represented here in the chapter by Button. She devised and tested a curriculum designed to teach political efficacy. The experiment was successful, although the results were not always as expected. Most interestingly, political efficacy among black students, and to a lesser degree among Mexican-Americans, was increased not by giving them a false sense of confidence in the government, but by increasing their political cynicism. They became increasingly aware of difficulties encountered in the political world by minority groups, but at the same time they discovered ways that the political system itself could be used to overcome or remove these problems. Though her emphasis is on curriculum development, Button makes use of equal numbers of white, black, and Mexican-American young people. She finds that the extent or quality of course influence often varies by the race or sex of the student. Though the effects vary, the course can nonetheless be said to "work" for all groups.

Finally a problem that has characterized nearly all socialization work is the presumed connection between childhood learning and adult attitudes and behavior. It is typically presumed that there is an intimate connection between the two, but theoretical specification of this connection and data relevant to it are seldom produced. Beck confronts this problem directly in proposing a theory to show how generational changes help account for the periodic "critical elections" in American history. While his paper is theoretical, it draws on empirical work in electoral behavior and ties in closely with the work which Vaillancourt and I did. Beck argues that the weakest link in the intergenerational flow of partisanship is the preadult years, and that this link is most likely to be broken during the transition between childhood and full adulthood. Socialization in childhood is not thus deemed unimportant; there simply is no one-to-one correspondence between childhood socialization and adult attitudes. Deviation from childhood socialization is most likely to occur at a particular time in the life cycle as well as under the historical circumstances surrounding the onset of critical elections.

Another contribution of the Beck paper is that it suggests an important linkage between political socialization and aggregate properties of the adult electorate. Whereas most studies of socialization try to describe and understand the socialization process itself, Beck treats the important question of what socialization means for some important characteristics of the adult political system.

A significant feature of this book is that most of the chapters are multiple contributions. For example, the chapters by Knutson, by Sigel and Brookes, and by Vaillancourt and me all concern innovative or underutilized methodologies. In each case, however, the emphasis is on substantive results rather than on the methodology itself. Similarly, the Jaros and Kolson and Button chapters present contrasting data on minority groups, but the emphasis is not on minority groups; theories of socialization and a curriculum study occupy the focus. The chapter by Liebschutz and me emphasizes black children's political attitudes, but also considers the effects of a specially designed curriculum. Most of the papers present data from the late 1960s or the early 1970s, a useful contrast with data collected in the late 1950s and early 1960s by Greenstein (1965a), Hess and Torney (1967), and others.

If an underlying theme could be said to run through many of the chapters, it seems to be an emphasis on the narrowly individual and broadly environmental factors in the socialization process. The early work on socialization focused largely on descriptions of children's attitudes at different age levels, matching them with the attitudes of parents, teachers, and occasionally other adults and the children's peers. The work here takes a less simplistic view of a direct relationship between child-adult attitudes and behavior, recognizing instead the unique contribution of each child in his or her own socialization and the role of the surrounding environment apart from particular agents such as family, school, and friends.

The emphasis on the uniqueness of the child is found in Knutson's focus on the idiosyncratic nature of some aspects of political learning. Her research suggests the importance of each individual's interpretation and internalization of political lessons, compared with global similarities and differences among age groups. Even young children do not merely reflect the viewpoints of adults around them, but adapt what they see and are told according to their own interpretive frameworks.

The importance of the surrounding environment is apparent in a number of the chapters. Jaros and Kolson perhaps make this most explicit, as they show that the general information conditions in which people live seem to be more important than specific directives from the family. Surrounding environment is also one of the major themes of Gustafsson's chapter. She does not conclude that the family and school are unimportant but that their apparent impact on children varies with the character of the larger environment. The Sigel and Brookes chapter directly reflects this theme by emphasizing how sensitive children's views are to political events. Lamare emphasizes the language environment in which children are raised; the family is a major element in determining the language environment, but the important point is that it is the general background which is crucial and not specific communications from parents. Beck takes a more explicitly generational point of view, emphasizing the importance of the surrounding environment, but observing that its effect is most noticeable at certain regular intervals in history.

Taken together, these two themes expand upon the viewpoint expressed in the last chapter of a recent book that Jennings and I wrote (1974). Much of the emphasis in that book is on the contribution of family, school, and friends to the socialization process, but in the last chapter we argue that family and school factors do not account in full for the political dispositions of late adolescents. The political context in which children grow up and the role of the individual as an independent, mediating influence in the socialization process help determine the political outlook of the new adult. The following chapters expand upon and reinforce both these points—the importance of the individual and especially of the surrounding political environment.

II

Prepolitical Ideologies: The Basis of Political Learning

JEANNE N. KNUTSON

Political socialization research today mirrors the fluctuation of thinking by political scientists generally at this time (Easton, 1969). The study of political socialization began with an inherently conservative bias, as Plato and then Aristotle examined the means of developing a character structure supportive of the ideal polity. Slowly at first, and then rapidly through the impetus of behavioralism, socialization research next attempted to examine and measure the fit between individual characteristics and systemic needs. Today, however, questions are arising about the continuing utilization of the traditional socialization model (Greenberg, 1970d). This model could perhaps be termed *a model of successive approximations,* in which the individual's development increasingly approximates the needs of the political system. Today this model is often described as politically conservative and intellectually limiting.

I would like to express appreciation to James C. Davies, Fred I. Greenstein, and M. Brewster Smith for their thoughtful reviews of a draft version of this chapter.

7

Yet, in spite of the questions which have been raised about value orientations in the study of politicization, most current research efforts (Niemi, 1973) continue to employ the traditional model, which underlies such statements as the following: "Political socialization . . . is essentially a conservative process facilitating the maintenance of the *status quo* by making people love the system under which they are born" (Sigel, 1965a). This model is also the foundation of the major effort at theoretical analysis of political socialization by Easton and Dennis (1969). However, the predominant emphasis in socialization research on the systemic viewpoint of the traditional model appears to be unfounded because it rests on a view of the politicization of the members of a polity as inevitably purposeful, goal-oriented, rational, and organized, and it precludes an understanding of individual differences in ability and willingness to learn. This view contradicts the accumulated evidence.

In place of a systemic (and rather uniformly received) process, I propose here a view of politicization as a process through which individuals (in Piaget's terms) both accommodate to *and assimilate* (make their own) the generalized themes of their political culture. Further, in the model employed here, the maturing citizen assimilates political learning in conformity with a nonverbally acquired (and therefore preexisting) *Weltanschauung*, or "prepolitical ideology," which is integral to his personality. This model thus opposes the view of the citizen-to-be as a tabula rasa who systematially (perhaps at his own pace) acquires the values, beliefs, and attitudes necessary for the preservation of the political system of which he is a member (even if such orienting responses were uniformly and purposefully taught by elements of the political system).

Thus I adopt here the definition of political socialization put forth by Easton and Dennis (1969, p. 9), without accepting their emphasis on socialization as a system response. In their terms, political socialization is perceived "simply as a developmental process through which orientations and patterns of behavior are acquired." The emphasis in this chapter is on this process as one which is idiosyncratic to the person and which begins with his prepolitical ideology. A major dimension of political learning through which the process of socialization will be examined is that of views toward authority. By employing projective techniques to explore this dimension, we accomplish an additional task: an examination of the degree to which previously gathered paper-and-pencil responses about perceptions of authority have been shaped by the constraints of the methodology employed.

Process of Political Learning

Within every polity a process of political socialization occurs. To put the matter baldly: the adults in each polity possess politically relevant information and orientations not possessed by new members of that culture or (in its entirety) by adult members of other cultures. Much socialization literature simply assesses attitudes and information at different stages of an individual's development and compares the quantity of this data with the quantity of similar attitudes and information possessed by adult subjects. Such quantitative analysis offers certain satisfactions by illustrating the general influence of a culture on its members.

It does not, however, provide a systemic analysis *or* an analysis of the differential impact of the socialization process. A systemic analysis requires a specification of the parameters of the system (as opposed, say, to the society in which it functions), as well as some analysis of the functional relationships between parts of the system. Systemic analysis further requires an understanding of a purposive, causal, system-preserving role played in the socialization process by specific institutions—a definitively different matter from illustrating the existence of diffuse, culturally supported learning patterns. An analysis of the differential impact of the socialization process, however, necessitates consideration of developmental stages and intrapsychic components and thus is inherently related to individual personality variables. (See Hess and Torney, 1967, pp. 19–22; Connell, 1970, 1971.) It might appear that the frequent quantitative analyses of the development of political ideology deal with more psychological than social explanations. Yet, as Connell (1969, 1970) points out, analysis of aggregate responses distorts and avoids the individual personality differences it purports to capture. The analysis of socialization as an individual process requires assessment at the individual level.

The emphasis here on socialization as an individualized process is emphatically not synonymous with psychological reductionism. Individual-level analysis, rather, emphasizes the *interaction* between intrapsychic and extrapsychic factors in producing political effects. Thus, by declining a systemic emphasis as an inaccurate view of reality, I attempt here to avoid the equally invalid view of socialization as intrapsychically determined. Instead, this chapter focuses on political learning as a process in which the interaction of social and intrapsychic constraints determines outcomes.

The model for this interactional process is shown in Figure 1. This model, as detailed elsewhere (Knutson, 1973b), emphasizes two important concepts. First, it views behavior as multidetermined—by personality needs; social, cultural, and situational constraints; and the interaction among these factors. Thus this examination of the linkages between personality factors and political behavior must be regarded as a necessarily limited aspect of the large problem of understanding and predicting political behavior. Second, this model illustrates the hypothesized existence of a prepolitical ideology which influences formal political learning. This prepolitical ideology combines a person's view of himself, of others, and of causality with his idiosyncratic coping and expressive patterns; it thus exhibits politically important individual proclivities (which, however, allow nomothetic analysis).

Personality and Politicization

Unfortunately for the development of political socialization, researchers have made little effort to include personality variables in their designs. The reported research generally measures the politicization process in relation to specific demographic variables, particularly those of age, sex, socioeconomic status, and intelligence (Niemi, 1973; Sears, forthcoming). While the evidence is fragmentary, however, it does suggest how personality factors, integrated within a holistic personality theory, such as Maslow's need-hierarchy theory (1954), can illumine the study of the process of political learning. A study by Zellman and Sears (1971) supports the utility of an interactional model in which personality predispositions mediate political socialization. The authors report on the disparity in children (fifth through ninth grades) between general expressions of demo-

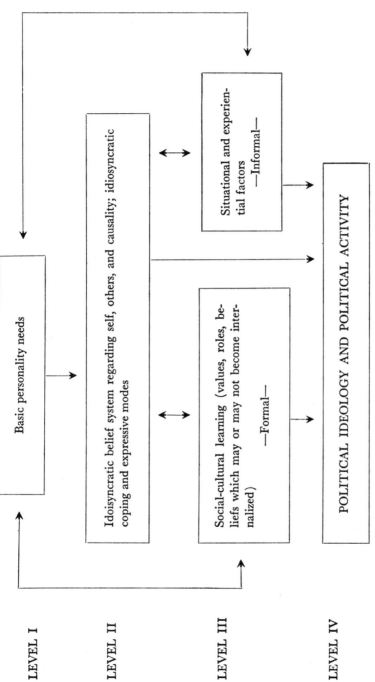

FIGURE 1. Linkages between personality and politics. Adapted from Knutson (1973b, p. 40).

The figure contains the following elements:

LEVEL I — Basic personality needs

LEVEL II — Idoisyncratic belief system regarding self, others, and causality; idiosyncratic coping and expressive modes

LEVEL III — Social-cultural learning (values, roles, beliefs which may or may not become internalized)
—Formal—

Situational and experiential factors
—Informal—

LEVEL IV — POLITICAL IDEOLOGY AND POLITICAL ACTIVITY

cratic tolerance and specific expressions of intolerance—a phenomenon well-documented among adult subjects (Stouffer, 1955; Prothro and Grigg, 1960). They note that the intolerance which their subjects expressed was largely the subject's antagonism to a particular, threatening group (such as the Communists). Furthermore, they found that children from elite groups, like adult elites, were likely to be much more tolerant than the rest of the children in their sample. Zellman and Sears also report—as do Hess and Torney (1967)—that subjects with higher socioeconomic status and intelligence had more advanced knowledge of abstract information (in this case the general rule of free-speech tolerance).

Of considerable importance here, Zellman and Sears report that expressed tolerance was significantly related to self-esteem in general, but most closely related to a variable which they call *divergent-thinking self-esteem*. This relationship held with intelligence controlled. They also report that tolerance was related to the intention to go to college and that self-esteem did not wholly account for this relationship. Finally, they note that although tolerance in specific situations was related to their general index of ethnocentrism, this relationship was generally weak.

A good deal of evidence indicates that acceptance of others is closely related to acceptance of self (Fey, 1955). Thus a holistic personality model (Maslow, 1954; Knutson, 1972a) is congenial to data illustrating that subjects with higher self-esteem are most likely to be tolerant of others and unthreatened by divergency—characteristics which Maslow labels as evidence of self-actualization, which develops as esteem needs are met (Davies, 1963, 1965; Knutson, 1973d). In the Zellman and Sears study, ethnocentrism, like intolerance in specific situations, probably would have been consistently and significantly related to low esteem, if the ethnocentrism measured related to ethnic groups of intrapsychic relevance and social significance for the subjects (such as blacks, Chicanos, and Orientals in the Sacramento area). Finally, families who can afford to send their children to college (and encourage them to do so) are probably the same families who both meet a growing child's basic intrapsychic needs and inculcate the value of tolerance. In addition, the probable degree of psychological selectivity in the educational process suggests that children whose basic needs are most adequately met are most likely to continue in school (Knutson, 1972a).

Tolerance is a dimension of political learning that is particularly likely to be mediated by personality needs. Gough (1951) reports a study of 271 high school seniors which focused on intolerance (measured by the Adorno E and F scales and the Levinson-Sanford antisemitism scale). Gough found a significant relationship between intolerance and (a) low socioeconomic status, (b) lack of sociability and participation in extracurricular activities, (c) "uneasiness and discomfort in social situations," (d) "tendency to complain of personal dissatisfactions, problems, and annoyances" and "feelings of victimization and exploitation," and (e) four types of antidemocratic attitudes, summarized by Gough (1951, p. 245) as: "(1) narrowness of outlook in regard to national and international affairs, (2) debunking attitude toward questions of political-social ideals and goals, (3) antagonism toward many outgroups, not just some particular outgroup, (4) emphasis on nationalism, chauvinism, and conservatism."

These findings suggest that teen-agers may have a fairly coherent personalized ideology which mediates the school's attempts to inculcate democratic values. Thus it appears that Easton and Dennis would make their argument more useful by distinguishing between agreement with general system-supportive views and the maintenance of specific beliefs (regarding the nature of causality, of self, and of others) which make a democratic, participatory process viable and constrain the actualization of generalized views.

That holistic personality needs mediate the educational process is also supported by a study (Knutson, 1967) using the entire senior class of a rural Oregon high school, plus one senior English class at a nearby high school (N = 125). The students were categorized on the basis of Maslow's (1954) need hierarchy in terms of major intrapsychic needs. They were also categorized as school activists or not, on the basis of their reported activities, and their attitudes were assessed in a number of politically relevant dimensions. Personality needs proved to be useful in differentiating students along political dimensions. For example, in answer to the "textbook" question designed to measure political efficacy ("If an average citizen has a gripe about the decisions our government makes, will it help to get together with others of the same opinion and pressure the government to change its decision?"), every one of the group designated as "psychologically deprived" (motivated by physiological, safety, affiliative, or esteem needs) said that it *would* help. When the matter was made personal on another question ("If you were out of school and our national government did something which really bothered you—passed a very high tax you had to pay, entered a war you really objected to, would it do any good if you tried to get the government to change its decision?"), personality differences were clearly differentiating in identifying a sense of competence (see Table 1).

Table 1.

PSYCHIC NEEDS VS. EFFICACY

	Will Help	Won't Help	Total
Physiological needs	2.3%	10.1%	7.2%
Safety-affiliative needs	2.3	11.4	8.0
Esteem needs	4.7	8.9	7.2
Low self-actualizers	44.2	52.9	48.8
High self-actualizers	46.5	16.7	28.0

Source: Adapted from Knutson (1967, p. 10).

Furthermore, degree of extracurricular activity was clearly related to level of psychic competence. Equally highly active—as was found among adults (Knutson, 1972a)—were the esteem and high self-actualizer groups. Yet the esteem group's participation was accompanied by a jaundiced view of the environment they attempted to influence. They tended to perceive their high school experience as "unhappy" and to feel that school administrators didn't care about them. A number of undemocratic attitudes also related to personality needs. For example, generalized intolerance (as measured by a version of the F scale) was significantly correlated with psychic deprivation. Indeed, knowledge of the existence of psychic deprivation proved to be a better indicator of authoritarianism than whether the student was categorized as a school leader or was a member of the student council—an important finding in view of the training for democracy which such leadership is assumed to provide. Psychological deprivation was also related to lack of faith in people, as measured by Rosenberg's well-known scale (1956).

A study by Simpson (1971) extends and confirms the relationship between Maslow's need hierarchy and the learning of democratic values in a sample from two San Francisco high schools and an all black school in Georgia. While the relationships were usually stronger in the total sample than in the individual schools, the following trends were statistically significant. Psychic deprivation (needs for physiological satisfaction, safety, affection, and esteem) was related to lack of faith in human nature, to perceiving causality as external—in Rotter's sense (1966)—to dogmatism, intolerance, and manifest anxiety.

Studies of the effect of personality variables continually show a relationship between psychic competence and social and academic status, thus underlining the interlocking, hierarchical nature of society, in which advantage in one sphere is inevitably correlated with advantages in other spheres. Thus a position on one indicator (for example, socioeconomic status or intelligence) may both partially determine and provide knowledge of the person's position on a different indicator (such as physical or mental health). For example, Langton (1969, chap. 4) reports data on a national sample of high school seniors which suggests that status differences in socialization effects may reflect basic areas of motivation and personality needs. He found that college-bound students were already more knowledgeable about politics and more efficacious, interested, and tolerant than the rest of the high school students. Langton also reports that black subjects were less efficacious and less tolerant, but —surprisingly—they were not more cynical.

Other personality effects on political learning can be indirectly inferred from the massive study of elementary school children reported by both Hess and Torney (1967) and Easton and Dennis (1969). One of the major findings of this study, which replicates a finding by Greenstein (1965a, pp. 94–99), is that there is little range in the expression of system approval and belief in a citizen's duty but a great deal of variation in psychic ability to utilize these beliefs. Further, this range in psychic ability (measured in this study by efficacy) develops rather early in children; it is measurable by at least the third grade. (Minority students were specifically excluded from the Chicago study, however, and race was not a variable in the Greenstein study.)

Such an early disparity between acquiescence with norms and the psychic ability to put such acquiescence to use illustrates that while the school may be able to instill verbal agreement with general rules—as Zellman and Sears (1971) showed—it cannot similarly inculcate subsequent political participation because such behavior is apparently mediated by intrapsychic feelings of competence, which develop in preschool years. Further, while one might suggest that it makes small political difference, given widespread norm acceptance, that many future citizens are unlikely to participate politically, research with adult subjects has frequently shown a clear relationship between lack of efficacy and various undemocratic values and attitudes (Stokes, 1962; Agger, Goldstein, and Pearl, 1961; Horton and Thompson, 1962; Thompson and Horton, 1960; Hastings, 1954, 1956; Knutson, 1972a). Since small children with no political experience show a range in feelings of efficacy similar to that displayed by adults (in which this variable has been shown to relate to participation), it seems likely that intrapsychic competence limits the degree to which formal learning can cultivate participation.

A second finding by the Hess and Easton study (1960) is that for children—as for adults (Milbrath, 1965; Mussen and Wyszynski, 1952)—participation in nonpolitical groups clearly relates to political interest and participation. Here it is likely that both relational needs and interpersonal competence help determine first whether a young person participates in extracurricular school activities and later whether, as an adult, he participates in social and political activity. Hess and Torney (1967, p. 121) found, for example, that social participation is closely related to attitudes involving overt political behavior: "*Students who join groups express more interest in political affairs, are more actively involved in conversations about politics and current events, and are more likely to defend their opinions on those issues.* High school participators were more likely to feel that individual political activity is efficacious. The differences between high- and low-participation groups was most extreme in their reported political activities."

A third finding of the Hess and Easton study was that intelligence and socioeconomic status have little relationship to variables such as progression from abstract to concrete and positive attachment to the political system, although intelligence usually indicates a greater ability to abstract and to differentiate (which is also related to age) (Hess and Torney, 1967, pp. 223–224). A major exception, which illustrates the interlocking hierarchies discussed previously is that political efficacy is directly related to intelligence and to socioeconomic status, with intelligence differences more marked than socioeconomic status (p. 149). Further, participation in political discussion, degree of political activity, and concern with political issues were also related to intelligence and socioeconomic status (pp. 154, 165). Finally, intelligence was related to basic political orientations (p. 159):

> Perhaps their [the high-intelligence group's] basic confidence in the processes is such that they do not see change as threatening. In contrast, children in the low-intelligence group are more inclined to be oriented toward the status quo; they think of government as representing benign and competent operations needing no change. Social class differences that appeared in this item were in the same direction—high-status groups were inclined to see a candidate's motivation as desire for change, while the low-status groups tended to perceive candidates as wanting to maintain the status quo.

It is well-known that intelligence is not a pure measure of native ability but is confounded by cultural experiences and personality factors (such as motivation to achieve and test-taking anxiety). I suggest that both the intelligence and socioeconomic variables here point to—and partially determine—restrictive personality needs because of their general (and intrapsychically uniform) relationship to efficacy, activity and a conservative view of political activity.

While the above evidence is fragmentary, it suggests that the process of political learning is far from uniform but appears to be mediated by factors within the child which can be located by using socioeconomic status, intelligence, or—it is suggested here—most parsimoniously, holistic personality needs. This mediation process makes political learning much more complex than does the view which sees children approximate, with great uniformity, adult political attitudes and beliefs in a developmental pattern that flows as smoothly as the process of physical maturation. Awareness of this mediation process impells an assessment of the prepolitical ideology and personality needs of the child which developmentally proceed the formal learning process—intrapsychic factors which show considerable stability and which will constrain political responses throughout life (Knutson, 1973a, 1974).

Individual Political Learning

In order to assess the validity of the assumptions detailed above, a pilot study was carried out in November 1971 at a predominantly middle-class and upper-class elementary school in southern California. In compliance with California law, permission slips were given to all third ($N = 99$) and sixth ($N = 107$) graders to bring home for parental approval of their participation in the study. As usual, at this age, many slips never went home; a random selection was made from those returned (twenty-two at the third-grade level, thirty-two at the sixth-grade level). According to the principal, the resulting group of seven boys and seven girls from each of the grades ($N = 28$) reflected the range of economic levels, scholastic aptitude, and behavioral stances in this school.

Each of the subjects was interviewed for approximately two hours with the use of a large battery of projective materials. First, the students were asked to tell stories to the ten-picture series of the Political Thematic Apperception Measure (PTAM) (discussed in Knutson, 1973c). Presentation was standard for Thematic Apperception Test administration; interviewer comments were limited to "and then what happened?" (for the initially shy) and "How does the story end?" (for the incessantly inventive).

Second, the students were given ten cardboard-backed pictures taken from magazines: (1) an American flag, (2) a group of pickets carrying illegible signs, (3) a picture of a man behind bars, (4) a picture of President Nixon, (5) a policeman in traffic uniform, (6) hands of a man and a woman held through bars (of a jail), (7) a general (unfortunately identifiable as Patton), (8) two very long-haired, casually dressed youth, (9) a prison guard looking down from a catwalk on a group of cells and prisoners, and (10) a group of soldiers carrying a wounded or dead companion. The subjects were handed the cards in order and were asked not to tell any more stories but just to say anything that the picture reminded them or or made them feel. On picture nine, the subjects were asked what the guard was feeling, as a follow-up question.

Third, the children were asked to give the meaning of some political concepts, such as *government, Democrat, democracy, laws, poor people,* and *citizen.* After *poor people,* the child was asked, "Do you have any idea why some people are poor?" After *citizen,* he or she was asked, "Do you know what *good citizen* means?" The children were next requested, as the basis of deeper psychodiagnostic assessment, to draw a picture of a person and then another picture of a person of the opposite sex, during which time a clinical impression of the subject was written.

Each child was then asked, "If there was one thing that you could get our government to do, what would it be?" Next (assuming here that his answer to the first question was "end pollution"), "If you were grown up and wanted very much to have our government *end pollution,* what is the very best thing that you could do to get our government to do this?" Finally (assuming here that his answer to the second question was "write a letter to the President"), the subject was asked, "If you were grown up and wanted very much to have our government *end pollution* and if you did *write a letter to the President,* what good do you think that this would do in *ending pollution?*"

Each of the projective responses was scored blindly, without knowledge of the subject's identity or of his or her other responses. In reporting the results, I focus on individual differences in prepolitical orientations and on indications that past use of survey methodology has restricted understanding of children's beliefs (Greenstein and Tarrow, 1970; Knutson, 1972b).

In order to illustrate the range of politically crucial perspectives through which young children perceive their world, we begin with a general overview of data from the PTAM and from the "efficacy" series at the end of the battery. Next, we present a statistical summary of some of the interrelationships between responses which suggest the organization of prepolitical ideology. Finally, to support and illustrate the organized nature of our subjects' perspectives, two case summaries are reported. Because of the small size of the sample, its nonrandom nature, and the heuristic concerns which guided this initial study, significance levels were inappropriate and qualitative materials were considered of primary importance. As the statistical materials suggest, however, the methods are amenable to aggregate analysis and rigorous quantification.

Each PTAM card was designed and scored to assess certain critical themes of political psychology. The validity of the analysis is limited by the extent to which the methodology accurately taps these themes; the validity of the analysis here is supported by the statistical interrelationships which occured and the points of similarity between these findings and those of previous investigations.

The theme of card one is "legalized force"; the card depicts two male figures involved in verbal interaction; one is in a suit, the other is in an official's uniform. In the background, a couple is walking by. At each grade level, two children saw only two friends or acquaintances interacting. At each level, two other children saw "the policeman" solely as a helper. The largest group of children, however, perceived "the policeman" enforcing either a vague or specific law, with the action resulting in some type of punishment. Of this group, three third graders and one sixth grader were ambivalent about whether the "policeman" was acting in a punitive or facilitative manner. Several older children perceived in this card an example of the maintenance of social order through a citizen's aiding authority. Finally, while no one saw the "policeman" as brutal, one sixth grader perceived him as unjust. "They're walking on the sidewalk, and there's a doctor crossing the street. A police officer got out of a car and told him that he used narcotics illegally. "No, I didn't," goes the doctor . . . and he was innocent, I guess. [How does your story end?] He was arrested in the state prison for no less than five years and no more than ten years" (Subject 21).

The theme of card two is "human nature." In this picture a small head and raised arm are shown far out in the ocean, while in the foreground several figures are verbally interacting with apparent excitement, with one figure both pointing toward the water and shouting toward someone down the beach. The theme of this picture is basic to political (as well as prepolitical) ideology: the belief that human beings are essentially cooperative is crucial to democracy. Only one third grader avoided the hazard and conflict in this anxiety-provoking picture; the rest of the subjects recognized it as a crisis situation. By far the largest group of responses were concerned with a cooperative attempt to save a drowning person, with the following results (parentheses show first the number of third graders, then the number of sixth graders): failure (1,1), success by appeal to authority figure (3, 9), success by united effort (4, 1); success, means unspecified (2, 1). One sixth-grade response saw an authority figure saving the drowning person on his own (with considerable ambivalence about the power of the authority figure as a helper), while another sixth-grade response depicted human nature as basically uncooperative, authority as weak, and help as inadvertent: "A guy was playing in the water and a big tide came up and he can't swim. Everyone's calling but nobody's doing anything about it. Everyone cares about it, but not enough to do anything themselves. A guy goes and tells the lifeguard. He goes in and swims into the tide and gets washed out because the tide's so heavy. So another guy goes in and saves him" (Subject 20).

Thus somehow, to most children, a person in trouble can be helped, and, furthermore, authority figures are usually available and efficacious when called upon. Yet, for a few children, authority figures are unavailable or lacking in power, human beings are basically unconcerned about each other, and, when one is in trouble, the world is a threatening place.

Card three has the theme "authority" and shows a man sitting at a desk behind a nameplate and another man standing in front of the desk with his hand on a chair, facing the first man. All the children saw this authority figure as distant; they described no affective flow between the two figures. Again younger children were more uncertain of the benevolence of authority than were older children (3, 0). Both grade levels were equally likely to see the authority figure as judgmental (2, 2), the relationship as indecisive (4, 3), and the authority as expert only—providing knowledge, not help (2, 2). The most noticeable age difference occurred in the view of authority as facilitative and helpful (3, 7). An important subtheme of many responses (particularly those from sixth graders) was that authority, at least initially, doesn't always have the right answer.

> A man came to the doctor because he was having stomach cramps. The doctor examined him and couldn't find out what he had. He said it was just probably regular stomach cramps, and if it happened again, he should come in and they'd try to find out what's wrong with him. The man kept getting stomach cramps, and the doctor couldn't find out what's wrong with him. The doctor took a blood test and decided that it was something that the man had eaten. Finally, the doctor comes to the decision that it was his tap water. And so the man got a distiller to put under his sink, and he didn't have any more stomach cramps [Subject 22].

Thus authority, even from the viewpoints of young children, is not always seen as infallible or necessarily regarded with positive affect. The impersonality and indecisiveness that these children generally saw here contradict the compulsive positive affect for authority checked so frequently in paper-and-pencil studies of socialization.

The theme of card four is "leader and followers"; a central male figure is surrounded by a crowd of semidistinct figures. Interestingly (and surprisingly), the largest category of responses (5, 5) were stories about the group against the individual (or central) figure. As one third grader saw it: "Wow! A lot of people are ganging up on this one man, and this man is looking up and wondering — Wow! What's happening! Maybe they get in a fight or something. Maybe they start talking before— I guess that's what happened. It probably ended like he got beat up or something" (Subject 03).

As elsewhere in their responses, these young children gave disturbing evidence of hostile ingroup conformity, which has so often been seen to typify "middle America." Other children (3, 2) did not perceive an individual-group distinction, while additional responses granted the central figure authority based on his expertise (2, 3) and variously saw him as helpful, different, or somehow interacting with the group to accomplish a group goal.

The theme of card five is "security in society," and, like card two, this picture is anxiety-provoking. It shows a street at night with a figure in the background walking away from the observer and a figure in the foreground emerging from underground steps and looking back toward the first figure. While a number of the subjects (3, 5) avoided the conflict theme explicitly, a hint of interpersonal conflict and threat exists in their stories: "It looks like this man just came out of his house, and he saw this other man, and he thought it looked like one of his friends, and he comes out and he walks up to him and it's not one of his friends" (Subject 07).

Most of the children who acknowledged the interpersonal conflict, saw the conflict solved. For some, interpersonal conflict was solved by authorities (3, 4) or by authorities with citizen aid (2, 1). For those who saw the conflict as one between an offender and a societal rule, the person was punished by authorities but with the assistance of citizens (4, 1). Few subjects (1, 3) saw the conflict as unsolved. Thus to most children who admit the existence of interpersonal conflict (in which they uniformly identify with the victim) or of the breaking of societal rules, authorities are available to protect and to punish. Furthermore, the child frequently sees himself as necessary to the maintenance of social order—personal action which likely stems from the anxiety experienced by young children when social order is threatened.

The theme of card six is "youth." In this picture, an adult man is walking past a store and is looking, in passing, at a group of younger figures. The intention of this card is to elicit politically relevant intergenerational attitudes, but for these young subjects such a theme is apparently not relevant. Instead (similar to the responses of card four), the outstanding response was that of the group against the individual (8, 7). About half of these responses were from the viewpoint of the group; the other half were from the viewpoint of the individual. A particularly poignant expression of the individual's view was given by one of the two black children in the study, a sixth-grade girl.

> There was a gang of teen-agers and they belonged to a neighborhood, and a new kid moved into the neighborhood. When he was walking down the street going to the store, he knew what they were doing. He heard they

were planning a party. He said to himself that he was going to the party to make friends. When he got there, the gang was in a corner of the room huddled up whispering. We walked up to them and they asked who he was, and he said he was new and wanted to make friends. So they invited him in, and one of the girls had a needle and she stuck it in his arm; and he asked what it was and she said dope. And then a couple of minutes later he started acting strange, and his eyes looked like they were going to come out of the sockets. He ran out . . . and just went crazy. He went into his bedroom to see if he could get over the trip. But when his parents came home, they found him just lying there. He couldn't make it through the trip [Subject 18].

Not only does this story give further evidence of the debilitating effects of being black in America (and being a black child in a predominantly white school), but also the power of the hostility felt by the outsider suggests that to this girl certain political alternatives will never seem viable, and others will seem deeply necessary to build a wall against the hatred of the group.

Some of the subjects perceived no group-individual relationship (2, 3). Others saw the individual helping to control the group or to judge it (1, 3). Finally, three of the third graders saw the individual as a member of the group, alienated by disinterest in the group's goals. Thus this card generally elicited feelings of conformity versus alienation and was suggestive of the likelihood of various future avenues of political involvement, such as level of group activity, degree of ingroup feeling, and amount of optimism that the majority will be amenable to the individual's needs and views.

The theme of card seven is "locus of control." The picture— a visual representation of the work of Rotter, DeCharms and Seeman—shows two figures sitting in the foreground, one leaning on the second, the second holding his hands over his eyes; a third, tattered person is walking away in the distance. In the middle ground of the picture are some apparent ruins. The theme taps a sense of efficacy, a belief that problems are solvable by human effort, that life is manageable. The theme was clearly perceived by all but one subject. All the others described it as people solving a problem

(5, 6); an overwhelming and unsolved problem (5, 6); a problem ending with no individual efforts (2, 2); the problem's solution avoided (1, 0). A typical example of a problem solution is: "Some of these old-time people who were in a desert in a oasis, and they were going around getting their crops; and the oasis went dry and a sandstorm came, and the sand got in their eyes and there was no water for two weeks. Then the water came back, but it was mud water so they couldn't drink it. Then finally there was water they could drink but the crops needed it, so they decided to take their crops to a better oasis" (Subject 02). As other studies have indicated, these responses show that young children can be differentiated by the degree of efficacy which they possess, and this, I submit, is an important factor in a prepolitical ideology that mediates a good deal of later political learning.

Card eight has the theme "group and individual"; it depicts three figures leaning over a table and a fourth figure opening a door and approaching them. In its focus on affiliative needs, this card (like card two) relates to the subject's view of human nature, as well as to his ability to join with others in group activities. Here the responses exemplify the wide range of viewpoints through which even young children approach human interaction. Several children (3, 2), described the group accepting the individual's approach. In other children's stories, the group rejected or harmed or threatened the individual (3, 4). Some children saw no interaction or relationship between the individual and the group (2, 2). Some perceived the individual helping the group (3, 1), while others saw the individual as an authority figure from whom positive affect had been blocked (3, 1). Only three sixth graders perceived in the picture a theme of group interaction producing misdeeds which were then punished by authority figures who were not part of the scene. Finally, one sixth grader saw the individual rejecting the group's code. (It should be apparent that all of these stories give evidence of the psychic needs of the subjects, as well as their political attitudes.)

The theme of the ninth card is "poverty"; it shows a draped adult figure holding an emaciated figure of a child; the adult figure is squatting next to a wall and a box. In the background, a receding figure and car can be seen. This card also taps views of locus of control and of human nature; its purpose is to elicit the degree of the subject's social awareness of problems, as well as his understanding of the causes of the problems. The responses fell into several initial categories (some of which, as elsewhere, were combined for statistical analysis): misery is solved by beneficence (5, 4); misery is solved by a person's own efforts (2, 2); misery is unsolved or help comes too late (3, 2); misery is solved inadvertently (3, 0); misery is part of a larger social problem and is solved by social effort (0, 6). Only third graders felt disturbed enough about the existence of misery that when a solution did not come to mind, the problem was solved inadvertently—suggesting again their larger concern with the maintenance of an orderly, caring world. In line with the work of Adelson and O'Neil (1966), it is also of note that only sixth graders adopted what these authors call a *sociocentric* viewpoint—a predominantly communal, rather than individual-level, orientation. (For the theoretical analysis of these distinctive changes, see Piaget, 1932.)

Finally, card ten, with the theme "systemic loyalty," portrays a guard figure marching in front of a fence (carrying a gun), while two nonuniformed figures watch him. Although the political relevance of this card is to elicit feelings about patriotism and system support, the children again utilized this card to express their concern with authority figures, as follows: authority is successfully evaded (4, 0); authority is unsuccessfully evaded (3, 2); rules are followed and authority lets figures in (2, 2); no interaction occurs (3, 2); authority is successfully evaded but punishment follows (2, 1). These concerns with authority cover the responses of the third graders. However, half of the sixth graders saw the picture from a sociocentric perspective, with the following themes: people protest the social utility of the base and lose (1); people admire the social utility or prominence of the guard (4); people look down on the social role of guard (1); and people are themselves accepted as authority figures and dislike roles (1). Besides illustrating the development of a sociocentric perspective, the responses to this card again underline these children's lack of a monistic view of authority.

In the children's choices of the one thing that they would most like the government to do, by far the overriding concerns of all the children were, first, to stop the war in Vietnam and, second, to end pollution. Thus, for most of the children there existed meaningful political issues.

As Hess (1968) has so clearly shown, however, American schools emphasize content rather than process; few of these children also comprehended viable channels of political pressure. While the third graders frequently suggested pressures to be directed against the government that they probably use to influence their parents, even sixth graders showed little understanding of what it means for citizens to be *actively political* rather than merely passively obedient (which was uniformly the perceived meaning of *good citizen*).

Additionally, and most disheartening to those who see a sense of efficacy as a basic foundation of a participant democracy, the majority of the children did not feel that even if they *were* adult and *had their choice of methods,* imperative personal and societal goals could be achieved through political action. The box score for efficacy is: efficacious feelings (5, 4), ambivalence about results (4, 3); clear lack of feelings of competence (5, 7). These data suggest a frustrated generation of students who, on the one hand, hear continually about the dangers of a polluted environment and the evils of war, but who, on the other hand, are not taught how to utilize political power to reduce societal ills. Thus their understanding of the importance of solving issues does not match their understanding of the processes by which solutions may be effected. Equally important, even young children, whose knowledge of politics is not dimmed by negative experience in influencing the system, do not feel sanguine about the power of adult citizens to move the political system toward valued political goals. One can but speculate how the opportunity to engage in political activity will affect their perspectives.

Interrelationships between the subjects' answers indicate that their responses represent an integrated, personalized view of the world relevant to political concerns. First, on a number of items there is a clear, differential tendency to recognize and rely on authority; this tendency *increases* significantly with age and correlates with other responses made by these children. For example, subjects who perceived the official on card one as an authority figure who enforces rules tended—on Card Nine—to see misery as a social and

solvable problem (see Table 2). It is likely that these subjects'
dominant responses to card nine represent a problem-solving rather
than a humanitarian orientation, for in response to the picture of
the hands joined through bars, authority-oriented subjects tended
not to be empathic. Further, in their definitions of the causes of "poor
people," these authority-oriented subjects were likely to see poverty
as due either to individual failure or to external circumstances, while
subjects who were not authority-oriented tended to be less simplistic
in their views and to give answers exemplifying more cognitive com-
plexity, as Table 2 illustrates.

The manner in which subjects view authority on card three,
where the authority is *non*official, was not closely related to the authority dimension in the responses to card one. Still, however, the

Table 2.

CARD ONE: OFFICIAL AUTHORITY DIMENSION

	Not Authority-Oriented, 43%		*Authority-Oriented,* 57%	
A. *Vs. card nine, poverty*				
Unsolved, or solved by own effort	42%	(5)	25%	(4)
Social problem; solvable	58	(7)	75	(16)
	100%		100%	
B. *Vs. "hands" picture*				
Empathic	50%	(6)	13%	(2)
Neutral	25	(3)	56	(9)
Nonempathic	25	(3)	31	(5)
	100%		100%	
C. *Vs. causes of "poor people"*				
Individual failure	8%	(1)	31%	(5)
Individual failure and external circumstances	67	(8)	13	(2)
External circumstances	25	(3)	56	(9)
	100%		100%	

nonofficial view of authority indicates politically relevant dimensions (see Table 3). Children who saw no clear authority relationship or who saw the authority as of uncertain benevolence on card three responded most negatively to the "policeman" picture. Furthermore, the subjects who did not perceive any authority relation on card three tended to be empathic to the "hands" picture, suggesting (as on card one) a correlation between humanitarian responses and responses that are not authority-oriented—as the Berkeley authoritarianism study predicted long ago (Adorno and others, 1950). Finally, while few of the subjects gave patriotic responses to the picture of "General Patton," those who did saw authority on card three as clearly commanding: helpful and expert or judgmental. Antiwar responses tended to come from those who did not see authority relationships on card three.

Paper-and-pencil tests of children's political attitudes have consistently found children highly likely to agree with positive affective statements about nonspecific political figures. Thus, the use of projective techniques here suggests that a "positivity effect" has occurred when objective methods of data gathering are used. One possible explanation is that paper-and-pencil methods are likely seen as "tests" in which the "right" (socially approved) answer is requested. For example, in the massive Chicago study (Easton and Dennis, 1969, p. 234), the sentence stem for the policeman—"He is my favorite"—received the following obviously nonveridical replies. Thirty-one percent of the third graders checked that the policeman was "my favorite of all," 29 percent found him "my favorite almost of all," and 16 percent checked "my favorite more than most." The corresponding statistics for sixth-grade responses are 19 percent, 24 percent, and 23 percent. (It should also be noted that such positive response patterns likely additionally reflect the range of subjects employed and the time periods during which the data were gathered.)

In our pilot study (see Table 3), only 32.1 percent of the children gave positive responses to the "policeman" picture when the responses were cued *solely* by a stimulus picture. (These positive responses cannot be equated affectively with choosing the policeman as favorite above all others). When the children were asked to define the concept *police*—bringing their performance closer to a test

Table 3.
CARD THREE: NONOFFICIAL AUTHORITY DIMENSION

	No Authority Relation, 25%	Helpful or Expert, 43%	Benevolence Uncertain, 18%	Judgmental, 14%
A. Vs. policeman's picture				
Positive, 32.1%	29% (2)	33% (4)	20% (1)	50% (2)
Neutral, 14.3%	0 (0)	33 (4)	0 (0)	0 (0)
Enforcer punitive, 53.6%	71 (5)	33 (4)	80 (4)	50 (2)
	100%	99%	100%	100%
B. Vs. "hands" picture				
Empathic	57% (4)	17% (2)	0 (0)	50% (2)
Neutral	43 (3)	66 (8)	20 (1)	0 (0)
Nonempathic	0 (0)	17 (2)	80 (4)	50 (2)
	100%	100%	100%	100%
C. Vs. general's picture				
Patriotic	0 (0)	25% (3)	0 (0)	25% (1)
Neutral	29% (2)	50 (6)	100% (5)	50 (2)
Antiwar	71 (5)	25 (3)	0 (0)	25 (1)
	100%	100%	100%	100%
D. Vs. definition of police				
Helping, 57.1%	57% (4)	33% (4)	100% (5)	75% (3)
Ambivalent, 7.1%	0 (0)	17 (2)	0 (0)	0 (0)
Enforcer negative, 35.7%	43 (3)	50 (6)	0 (0)	25 (1)
	100%	100%	100%	100%

situation—57.1 percent saw the policeman as helping. Further, the subjects who were uncertain about the benevolence of authority or perceived authority as judgmental or saw no authority relationship on card three were most likely to express a more positive view of the police in this more cognitive and structured response suggesting that positive verbal expressions about powerful authority may involve psychic defense. (See Table 3.)

Attitudes toward authority appear relatively consistent (see Table 4). For example, those who expressed positive regard for the men in prison were likely to see the police as punitive or only enforcing rules, and those who saw the police in positive terms tended to be positive or neutral toward the prison guard. Additionally, those who defined *police* as helping tended to be proauthority in other respects, as the responses to the "systemic loyalty" theme on card ten attest. Certainly, on a prepolitical level, our subjects typify the breadth of alignments on an authoritarian-humanitarian dimension on which more political and ideologically sophisticated adults have previously been comfortably placed.

In addition to the authority dimension, the group-individual dimension also appears to help organize a child's perspective of his

Table 4.

FURTHER AUTHORITY CORRELATES

A. *Guard picture vs. definition of police*	*Helping*	*Ambivalent*	*Enforcer/ Negative*
Positive to guard, 64%	61% (11)	6% (1)	33% (6)
Neutral, 18%	80% (4)	20% (1)	0 (0)
Positive to men, 18%	20% (1)	0 (0)	80% (4)

B. *Card X vs. definition of police*	*Helping*	*Ambivalent*	*Enforcer/ Negative*
No interaction, 18%	60% (3)	40% (2)	0 (0)
Antiauthority, unsuccessful 29%	37% (3)	0 (0)	63% (5)
Antiauthority, successful, 25%	57% (4)	0 (0)	43% (3)
Proauthority, 29%	75% (6)	0 (0)	25% (2)

world. Table 5 shows that subjects who saw the violence on card
five solved by citizen's aid, or who perceived conflict as being unsolved tended to express negative views of the police on the "policeman" picture, while those who saw violence solved by authorities
tended to react positively to the policeman image. Further, those
positive to the leader on card four tended, to see the group rejecting
the individual on card eight, while those who were hostile to the
leader tended to see positive interaction between the individual and
the group. Finally, those who perceived no clear relationship between
the group and the leader on card four tended to see the individual
as alienated from the group on card eight. Thus there is a suggestion
of two competing mechanisms at work: one is proauthority and ingroup conformist; the other is antiauthority and stresses group co-
operation. While some of these relationships may mirror age-specific
attitudes regarding self and important others, it is likely that they
also reflect the intrapsychic determinants elucidated in the Berkeley
study of authoritarianism (Adorno and others, 1950).

A brief sketch of two protocols illustrates the psychological
integrity of each child's total responses and supports the view that
children do possess a prepolitical ideology which shapes their political learning. The first child is a third-grade boy from a professional family which includes a foreign-born father. According to his
principal, this child is above average in ability (although no intelligence score has been taken), and his adjustment is "very good." His
protocol is of interest not only because it suggests the seeds of possible future personality disturbance but also because his antiauthority impulses may be the basis of either future radicalism or, given
a different set of extrapsychic constraints, of a reaction-formation
pattern of harsh authoritarianism. I shall call him Saul.

In response to the pictures of the PTAM Saul consistently tells
stories about stealing impulses which are controlled only with difficulty, if at all. Interwoven with these impulses is a clear antiauthori-
tarian bias and a decided ambivalence about the helping and pro-
tective nature of authority.

[Card one.] That policeman stops that man probably because these two people he tried to rob them or
something. He's going to go to jail. . . . The police-

Table 5.
GROUP-INDIVIDUAL DIMENSION

A. Card V vs. picture of policeman	Positive	Neutral	Enforcer/ Punitive
No conflict, 32%	33% (3)	33% (3)	33% (3)
Conflict unsolved, 14%	0 (0)	25% (1)	75% (3)
Solved by authorities, 25%	71% (5)	0 (0)	29% (2)
Solved with citizen's aid, 29%	12% (1)	0 (0)	88% (7)

B. Card IV vs. card VIII	Group Rejects Individual	Individual Alien. from Group	Positive Interaction
No clear relation, 36%	20% (2)	50% (5)	30% (3)
Group positive to leader, 29%	63% (5)	12% (1)	25% (2)
Group hostile to leader, 36%	0 (0)	40% (4)	60% (6)

man probably thought he did something, but he really
didn't. The policeman is going to take him to court—
and then to a higher court, and they'll probably say that
he's not guilty.

[*Card three.*] Probably that's a banker and that
man has found a check of someone else's money and he's
going to the bank to get someone else's money. Probably
when he gives him the money, it will probably bounce
like. Then he'll probably be like a robber and say "Stick
um up and give me all the money" and then he'll go to
court and go to jail. After a few years, when he gets out,
he takes some drugs and starts stealing things and he's
like a kleptomanic and doesn't know it and they put him
in jail and where he gets out, he still has the check and
he goes to get the money and the banker tells how he
looks and they found he was taking drugs and they put
him to jail and he stayed in jail.

[*Card six.*] Well, probably these people are all in
line for a movie but that person is a spy for that person
because he saw him stealing and handcuffed him and he
went to court but they had to let him go and in the next
town he stole much more money and ran into this the-
ater and turned his projector on the spy and the spy became bald—I mean blind—and he had to get someone
else to do it and the people are bending over because he
shot someone—but no one was hurt. He went to court
for twelve years and then probably he came out and died
of old age.

[*Card seven.*] Well, probably here this was their
house and these three men lived in it and they were very
old so they had enough food to last until they died and
one man started a fire and burned the house down and
the one man took a knife and killed him and the other
two . . . [eventually] went to the United States and
never came back. [And then they started hijacking air-
planes] but they came back and didn't kill, but they
really did kill the other man.

These five stories indicate the themes of antiauthority, lack of im-
pulse control leading to disaster, and blindness that thread their way

through Saul's stories. Saul's responses to the issue-related picture cards express similar themes in political terms:

[*Demonstrators.*] The people were against the king and they were putting these signs all over Persia and they caught the king and cut off his head and they were trying to get a very bad king out of their country.

[*Man in jail.*] When I was watching a program about a black man and they thought he was guilty because of his color but he really wasn't guilty, he was innocent.

[*Policeman.*] [long pause] Probably about when a man who made the policeman laugh and the policeman thought he was friendly and he stole something from the policeman and finally he stole his gun and shot the policeman.

[*Hands.*] Probably when a man was in jail because he stole something but his wife thought he was innocent and she was right.

Again, in the (more factual and less personality-revealing) definitions, Saul continues his themes. Here, however, their statement is subdued and the value of employing a projective measure is clear. Saul says that police "helps stop like if people are being robbed or someone just took the TV set or robbed. Helps people." He believes that people are poor because they "gamble and get robbed," and that a good citizen is "someone who doesn't steal, who drives carefully, who doesn't rob." If he had one choice of government activity, it would be to "probably try to have it stop pollution." His means: "probably protest"; his estimate of his success as an adult: "not very far." He draws a figure of a boy, and the boy wears glasses (Saul doesn't) because he hurt his eye.

Saul is obviously a problemed boy who possesses considerable anger against those in authority and (while psychoanalytic discussion is beyond the scope of this chapter), his desire to steal and to look and his accompanying needs to be jailed and blinded suggest the nature of his hostility, its origin and dynamics. In political terms, Saul is also a boy who is oppressed and accused, but—in his heart —innocent. By nature he chooses protest as his means of political

activity. Like the other third graders, his political ideas are but partially formed, and his ideology is incomplete. His prepolitical ideology, however, seems meaningful in terms of his needs, internally
consistent, and predictive of future political behavior and beliefs.

The protocol of the second boy, a sixth grader whom I shall
call Laurence, is radically different from that of Saul. Like Saul,
Laurence is a bright, well-dressed (indeed, overly "mod"), articulate boy. He also comes from a professional family; the principal
describes his father as successful but strict and his mother as a liberal. He has never been a behavior problem. Laurence is ambivalent
about authority:

> [*Card one.*] That looks like a policeman stopping
> a guy from doing something wrong, and it looks like the
> guy's saying he didn't do anything. And it looks like he's
> pointing at a kid and saying he did it. And there's some
> people watching—looks like they're wondering what's
> happening. [And the end?] The policeman gets it all
> straightened out with this guy and he walks away.
>
> [*Card two.*] It looks like there's a party or some-
> thing on the beach and they look out and see somebody
> drowning and they call the lifeguard and it looks like
> there's one guy about to run and get something. I don't
> know whether the lifeguard heard him or not and they
> finally get him and he comes in the nick of time and
> saves the guy.

Yet, as the responses on cards three and ten indicate, he also ad-
mires and identifies with authority:

> [*Card three.*] It looks like it's a high school and
> this guy that's standing up looks like he's done something
> wrong or didn't understand something, and he was called
> into the office just to get it straightened out and he
> leaves the office and now he's happy because he knows
> what he's doing now.
>
> [*Card ten.*] This guy he's in the army. He's a
> guard and there's kid's houses around this place where
> he used to guard. He like kids and he was always talking
> to them. It got so that he couldn't do anything because
> the kids were always around and the head of this place

said that he couldn't have kids around all the time because he couldn't do his job but the kids used to hang
around and just be so proud that they knew this GI and
when they grew up they used to hope they'd be guards
too.

The political use to which Laurence puts his views of authority is
clear from his response to the picture-issue cards:

[*Demonstrators.*] Makes me feel that these are the
kind of people who aren't so patriotic and are just always going against our natural life just protesting and
it makes me feel bad that this is always going on.

[*Man in jail.*] This guy—well, the people who
protest, half the time they end up right there—right in
jail and it makes you feel not so great to think that just
about every jail cell is filled with people like this. [Like
what?] People who make a life of doing what's not right
—of doing everything wrong.

[*Nixon.*] Ah, here's somebody I know. Well, I
think that right now he's not talking about those people
because he's having fun and there's good people—luckily.
There's a majority of good people. They're not all that
kind. It makes me feel that if you don't do anything
wrong—just like him (I don't believe that he's done anything wrong)—you'll be happy and not behind bars half
the time.

[*Policeman.*] Makes me feel if everybody was as
good as that—as good as these police guys are—this
would be the best place in the universe to live but not
everybody's doing things like that.

[*Hands.*] I think that when you do something
wrong, you're put behind bars and they're not going to
let you see your family and say "Hi Ma, How you're doing?" . . . [pause] It's not very fun just to see your
family through wire—it's not a very good feeling.

[*Patton.*] Ah, Patton—the same thing—if everybody was like this, fighting for their country. No, let me
change that. If everybody *wasn't* like this—trying to keep
peace and not fight—like that policeman.

[*Youth.*] Makes you feel like people see these
kind of guys and say "God, that guy's weird—he ought

to be put behind bars." That's like judging a book by its cover. You can't do that; these guys might be the Presidents of the United States . . . They might be nominated, but they'd never make it because a lot of people would judge them and call them "Long-Haired Freaks."

[*Soldiers.*] Like I said before, these guys are fighting but they're never going to have any peace . . . No fighting like this can ever end in peace. You always lose something.

Finally, in the definitions he gives, Laurence again points to similar themes. He sees government's role as partially to "keep things settled down" and police as "people that try to keep everything in peace." To him, a good citizen is "a person that goes by all laws and never gets arrested and follows all the laws and the rules."

Laurence obviously has a value hierarchy which is radically different from Saul's. To Laurence, order (peace) and obedience are primary values. His vehement objections to lawbreakers suggest an intrapsychic foundation, yet his responses also suggest that intrapsychic needs are reinforced by a punitive moralism and political conservatism which are somewhat at odds with his personal values. Certainly, the integrity of his punitive, authoritarian views falters when he stops to empathize with the "hands" picture's subjects, when he contemplates war-associated pictures, and when he studies the "youth" picture (whose dress code he emulates—to be sure, in a more fashionable way). Laurence may later embrace a political ideology which is more consistently of the law-and-order genre because both his home values and the conservative bias of his school learning will likely confirm the rightness of this viewpoint. Yet his prepolitical ideology contains a basic degree of humanity, empathy, and identification with those branded as wrongdoers, so that—given a liberal college environment, for example—the incongruence of his personality needs and his stated values may lead him later to embrace a more humanistic set of values.

Significance of Prepolitical Ideologies

None of these data allow a definitive test of the proposed theses. Several conclusions seem warranted, however. First, it appears that children's support of political institutions is not uniformly positive and that support which is granted is done so tentatively, with the acquiescence which humans usually approach things established. This approval of political institutions is clearly tentative because children accept them only if they accomplish certain personally invested, politically relevant ends. Thus, while the grammar school child generally acknowledges the power and competence of the office of the President, the evidence suggests that any particular President (in Laurence's terms, for example) is granted approval only to the degree to which he maintains and supports order and can be viewed as moral. The view that children exhibit widespread, affectively based positive evaluations of political objects is becoming less credible as current studies employ more heterogeneous samples and less directive methodologies than had been used previously. But unless students are asked to evaluate particular leaders by name (Sears, forthcoming), paper-and-pencil tests continue to elicit a positivity effect which clashes with children's unstructured expressions about authority.

Thus it appears, second, that previous understanding of both the amount and the pattern of political socialization has been biased by the research instruments employed (Greenstein and Tarrow, 1970; Knutson, 1972b). When the child is not cued by written categories from which to choose, he is capable of meaningfully expressing the entire range of philosophical viewpoints upon which his elders' political ideologies are based. Our subjects' responses ranged widely in terms of their humanitarianism, authoritarianism, and ingroup orientation, as well as in their perspectives on political issues such as militarism, law and order, counterculture dress codes, and modes of political expression.

Third, the range and pattern of the responses support the thesis that children have organized and diverse prepolitical ideologies that cue individualized ways of relating to power, authority, and their fellow humans, that suggest the existence of different psychic needs, and that are a basis for later political beliefs and behavior. Thus it appears that while the child's knowledge of matters political is inexact and incomplete, the vessel into which this knowledge is being poured has already largely formed by the time the child begins the process of formal socialization.

The use of projective techniques highlights the idiosyncratic nature of the child's assimilation of formal learning. While discussing the utility of the original TAT, Murray (1943) suggested that it was not valuable for providing an independent assessment of conclusions gained from other methods, but rather for illuminating and deepening understandings that had been derived conjointly in other ways. Our data analysis above supports this view. To look only at the definitions of political concepts, one *necessarily* focuses on the incremental nature of factual learning and on the similarities and differences among age groups. By studying a wide range of the child's more and less structured responses, however, one understands that even the political definitions are quite personal and often provide clues to the child's intrapsychic needs and their dynamics. When one becomes privy to the child's own structuring of both prepolitical and political materials, his responses are thus seen to form a *Gestalt* through which additional socialization is assimilated. This *Gestalt* is grounded in his prepolitical ideology.

Finally, the data presented here have considerable import for the maintenance of a democratic polity. As the material shows young children (particularly third graders) show a great need for order. In dynamic terms, most of them have not yet internalized the many rules by which they are made to live. Their impulses are still (in a manner of speaking) on the side of the lawbreakers, yet they are forced to conform to the dictates of authorities which, for their self-protection, they generally view as distant, but facilitative. Thus, third-grade students are profoundly disturbed by evidences of lawbreaking and tell stories in which citizens initiate and support the punishment of wrongdoers. As the rules become internalized, it is no longer necessary for most children to see the world in manichean terms.

Hopefully, the educational system in a democracy will have the wisdom to employ this developmental potential so that growing children need not move from fear of authority to overidentification with its dictates. If the agents of formal learning encourage a sense of empathy and an understanding of the distinction between political goals and the variety of means which may be employed to attain these goals, children like Saul and Laurence can be helped to tolerate alternatives, in themselves as well as in others. In terms of the model I have used, such maximal psychic and political development can be accomplished only by an awareness of the intrapsychic as well as the experiential determinants of political learning.

III

The Multifarious Leader: Political Socialization of Amish, "Yanks," Blacks

DEAN JAROS, KENNETH L. KOLSON

In all likelihood, the discovery of highly positive youthful orientations toward the American Chief Executive remains to this day the most prominent and best-known accomplishment of political socialization research (Greenstein, 1960, 1965a; Hess and Easton, 1960; Easton and Dennis, 1969, chap. 8). At a minimum, inquiry into "presidential images" clearly demonstrates that children do indeed acquire political orientations at an early age, something often asserted but never before systematically demonstrated. In addition, such findings are noteworthy because they seem to have substantive significance for later adult behavior and attendant systems-level effects. Highly positive images of the President in childhood might presage generally regime-supportive outlooks in later life, and the United States has traditionally enjoyed a high level of regime support among the adult population. It is possible that these two phenomena represent different stages of a continuing socialization process. The inference of a connection and hence the attribution of great importance to childhood orientations toward the President make a great deal of sense.

Despite these findings, youthful orientations toward the Chief Executive have diminished in importance for several reasons. First, as children of diverse subcultures and minority backgrounds have come within expanding research perimeters, positive images of the President turn out not to be as universal as earlier investigation indicated (Jaros and others, 1968; Greenberg, 1970b, 1970c). (See also Chapters Four and Five.) Second, the age cohort on which much of the early positive-image research was conducted reached adolescence and early maturity during the late sixties. This age cohort demonstrated comparatively low levels of regime support (Westby and Braungart, 1970), but early research detected no sign of the high degree of political unrest and questioning of institutions by youth and young adults that characterized the late sixties; indeed, the positive image would have suggested the absence of any meaningful youth protest. Protest behavior may thus be disconnected from the presidential images of the very young. Third, research interest has broadened to include a host of other substantive areas. These later areas of interest have more nearly replaced rather than supplemented the earlier. Recent investigations have stressed childhood orientations directly parallel to commonly researched adult attitude and behavior. To name but a few, outlooks on party and policy, democratic attitudes (especially political efficacy), and questions of compliance to the directives of policemen or other proximate authorities began to occupy much research attention (Abramson, 1972; Dennis and McCrone, 1970; Lyons, 1970; Merelman, 1973; Rodgers and Taylor, 1971).

In spite of its present eclipse, the childhood presidential image may yet be a profitable avenue of inquiry. The President does seem to be an early object of political attention. Children see this figure relatively unambiguously; knowledge and affect about it are indeed among the first true political learnings. Thus, images of the President may reveal something about the agents of early political learning and the processes of that learning. Political learning processes are probably not entirely content specific; presidential-image learning may occur similarly to behaviorally relevant learning. Certainly the accumulated wisdom of the study of political socialization is not rich in knowledge of the processes by which that socialization occurs. Accordingly, by focusing on the process involved we can anticipate some benefits from the study of presidential images, temporarily leaving aside the substantive significance of such images. Indeed, in this light, testing hypotheses about the generation and maintenance of presidential images seems appropriate to current needs.

We examined the presidential-image learning of a group of fourth- through eighth-grade children. The group consists of children of the Old Order Amish faith, non-Amish white children, and black children. The inclusion of Amish youngsters makes this effort unique in political socialization research. The Amish, of course, are grossly atypical of American society and this atypicality might be expected to extend to political orientations such as presidential images. But we did not undertake this research with an eye toward describing the atypical, the bizarre, or the quaint. We chose the Amish because, in comparison with their non-Amish counterparts, they may differ not only in dependent, image variables, but also in a number of independent ones involved in the learning process. If these learning processes are not culture specific, this variance may offer an extremely clear set of research results and thus may highlight socialization processes of general interest. Just as we believe that study of presidential images can reveal something about generally applicable political socialization processes, so we believe that examination of so culturally unusual a group as the Amish can contribute to the same end.

So that some of our subsequent arguments may be readily understood, we must present a brief exposition of Amish culture in America. (A more complete discussion of Amish culture is available in Hostetler, 1963).

Old Order Amish

The Old Order Amish are one of several Germanic Anabaptist groups that live in cohesive agricultural communities. They reject most of modern culture for the style of seventeenth-century Europe. Their disinctiveness in dress and appearance, retention of old ways, aloofness from the rest of society, and extreme religious devotion are their best-known features. To maintain this culture with a significant population, the Amish depend on their ability to socialize their children. Unlike other related groups, such as the Hutterites, the Amish do not live communally, nor are they particularly hostile toward the dominant American culture. Coexistence with secular authorities has been for the most part peaceful, but the Amish maintain a way of life that is, in their eyes, singularly concerned with rendering unto God what is His.

The family is by far the most important institution in Amish societies. Families are quite large, owing to the inordinate amount of work that needs to be done on nonmechanized farms and to the fact that having many children helps to counter the affects of attrition. Although the biweekly religious meeting serves as an integrating institution, the transmission of cultural norms from generation to generation evidently occurs almost exclusively in the home. The family is primarily responsible for teaching the child a reading knowledge of German, for example, and for instilling discipline into the new members of the community. In addition to its function as a learning ground for substantive Amish values, the home is also the chief agent in communicating a proper understanding of the relationship of Amish people to the world around them. Both an aloofness from the surrounding society and an acknowledgement of its presence—at least in its principal aspects—must be instilled.

The Amish regard public schooling as the greatest threat to the preservation of their culture, and conflict with the larger society has occurred most often in relation to compulsory education. Given the educational goals of "practical knowledge and skills" and the suspicion of "that which is a useless accumulation of learning in worldly arts and sciences," any public education beyond the rural elementary school has been difficult for the Amish to accept. School consolidation and the closing of many small, rural public schools has presented a crisis to the Amish, as has increasing insistence on the enforcement of compulsory education laws (Hostetler, 1970, p. 199).

The Amish response has been to establish private schools in many communities. In other areas arrangements are worked out with public school officials to accommodate Amish needs. In such cases Amish children are typically required to attend elementary school, and then they are placed in the charge of their parents or employers. With a little fancy paperwork this arrangement becomes the "Amish vocational school," allowing the Amish child to leave the public school after the eighth grade and to acquire the skills necessary for such typically Amish occupations as farming, buggy-making, carpentry, or smithery. The Amish vocational school is a feasible alternative in most areas where the Amish are too sparsely settled to establish their own parochial schools, for although they can and do accept the small, rural public elementary school, and although they recognize the importance of learning English, they are steadfast in their opposition to schooling beyond the eighth grade (Hostetler, 1970; Rodgers, 1969). In a culture where childhood socialization occupies such a prominent place, one cannot help entertaining the possibility that some characteristic political learning takes place at tender ages.

Research Procedures

This chapter is based on survey data collected during May 1971 in a rural school district in northeastern Ohio. Observations on a complete enumeration ($N = 264$) of fourth- through eighth-grade students in two small community schools were obtained. Paper and pencil questionnaires were administered in the class during regular schooltime. All children read and completed the questionnaire at their own pace except fourth graders, to whom the instrument was read aloud. (The field work was supervised by Michael M. Kapral, whose assistance is gratefully acknowledged.)

The two communities are adjacent and similar socially and economically. Both contain considerable numbers of Amish, who must send their children to public school because of the remote location of Amish educational institutions. Both contain non-Amish whites (or *yanks,* as the Amish call them), who, like their Amish counterparts, have traditionally been a part of the agrarian population. Both contain blacks, comparatively recent migrants to this rural area. Although the communities are relatively homogeneous economically, rural poverty is the lot of some black families, while the Amish, owners of much of the best farmland, frequently achieve a modest prosperity.

This unusual context provided two exceptional research opportunities. First, access to Amish children is rare for the systematic researcher. Second, the opportunity to study three distinct cultural groups within the same context is unusual and confers distinct advantages. However, this situation is not without its limitations. Many types of inquiry—particularly relating to the nature of family life and peculiar cultural values and practices—had to be foregone in consideration of the sensitivities of the citizens of these communities. We were prevented from acquiring certain data which, as we shall see, would have been most useful.

Socialization Processes

Some of the most intriguing suggestions about how political socialization goes on involve the family or features of culture that are mediated by the family. Since the subjects of this study differ greatly on cultural and family-related variables, they constitute an ideal group in which to examine some of these processes.

Transfer of Father Image. It has often been suggested, though rarely shown empirically, that children's experiences with and emotional reactions to authority figures (typically parents) in their immediate environment are somehow transferred or generalized to more remote authority figures (including political ones). Later cognitions of the actual features of remote authorities may modify, but not entirely supplant, these earlier images. The idea is ancient. Confucius advised provincial rulers to promote filial piety in their realms in order to eventually become the objects of the positive affect thus generated. Early political socialization research, using this venerable hypothesis, showed that children who hold highly positive presidential images simultaneously report elevated views of their fathers, which suggests a relationship between the two views (Jaros, 1973, p. 90). Perhaps the father, perceived as providing and benevolent, is the prototypical authority figure; the President, when he enters the child's cognitive field, is conveniently fitted to the prototype, and indeed eventually the entire political regime becomes "the family writ large" (Easton and Hess, 1962). Though the amount of research supporting the existence of such a transfer process is small, the classic nature of the hypothesis plus occasional confirmatory evidence (Hess and Torney, 1967, p. 101) entitles it to continued testing.

If such a process operates in children, one would expect Amish youngsters to manifest extremely positive images of the President. The typical Amish father is granted much deference, congruent with Germanic tradition. There can be no doubt about the importance, strength, and providing nature of that figure in the Amish family. While a generalization of this prototype to the president would result in elevated impressions of the president, one would not expect it to persist throughout the life of the Amish youngster. Indeed, since the Amish eschew any significant interaction with political authority, as Amish children grow older they cannot help but realize that the paternal and the presidential are different worlds, with the president eventually receding to a peripheral position in their viewpoint.

Yank children, as we shall obligingly call non-Amish whites, would be expected to undergo a similar process, but a far less dramatic one. First, these youngsters probably do not in general have such strong, pervasive, all-providing fathers. Second, the President remains a more significant figure for yank children. Perhaps he can continue to be a father-like figure for a longer period, although previous research leads us to expect some decline in this image with age. But if the transference process operates, yanks, though exhibiting high initial presidential images that decline with age, will have lower initial images that decline less dramatically than those of their Amish counterparts.

If the more predominantly matriarchal features of the American black family extend to this rural population, image transference should have some characteristic features for the black youngsters as well. If black fathers are in eclipse, the relatively weak, negative image which this implies should be generalized to political authorities, resulting in less positive images of the President. The image, low to begin with, should change little with age. Given the relationships of blacks to the polity in this country, perhaps knowledge of the real world would do little to modify such a negative image.

In summary, if the image transference process does in fact operate, we anticipate that among the youngest children, the Amish would have the most positive presidential images, yanks somewhat positive ones, and blacks the least positive of all. Further, the images should decline with age among both Amish and yank children, with the process being most accelerated among the Amish.

Family Transmittal of Values. When we consider a different family-related socialization process, we come upon a rather different pattern of expectations for the children we are examining. Perhaps the most pervasive and obvious socialization process in any society is direct teaching of preferred values to children by parents. This occurs in many areas and it extends to at least a few areas of political relevance (Jennings and Niemi, 1968a). Though presidential images are often believed to be learned this way, the amount of hard evidence confirming this belief is modest (Jaros, 1973, pp. 82–84).

If direct learning, largely from parents, accounts for presidential images, Amish, yank, and black children should differ considerably. Unquestionably, there is little transmission of positive affect toward the President in the Amish family. The qualities of secular authority of any kind are simply not matters of central concern. Religious socialization is far more important than political socialization, and it is difficult to imagine any evaluative imperatives about the President being transmitted from parent to child. Accordingly, Amish children possess no positive presidential image learned at parents' knees. Probably no absolute negative teaching is done either, but one would suspect that the President, being clearly an outsider, might be rated low compared to most other adults which cross the Amish child's vision. One would further suspect that what would be an initially low image of the President would tend to remain so, for other socializing agents encountered in later childhood would also be fully a part of the Amish culture. For the particular individuals under investigation here, however, the non-Amish schooling undoubtedly portrays the President in a favorable light, and the children's images might thus be expected to show some change.

Suggestions of previous writings lead us to think that yank parents either deliberately or inadvertently present "the conventional ideals about political authority rather than about known or suspected grimmer realities" to their children (Easton and Dennis,

1969, p. 358). Since the President remains a key political authority, positive images of him will be transmitted. Of course, as these children grow older, the "grimmer realities" intrude upon the consciousness to the extent that the initially implanted positive image is somewhat tarnished.

Today's black parents may well be less positively inclined toward the political system—some of them may even be overtly negative toward it. If the President continues to be a key figure in youthful discussions of politics, this negative feeling should translate into the teaching of relatively negative presidential images to children. Increasing contact with grim realities—which for blacks are even grimmer than for whites—should serve to make the image of the President even less favorable as the child grows older.

Thus, if parents are directly transferring presidential image values to their children, we would expect Amish youngsters to manifest relatively negative images of the President, images which do not change appreciably with increasing age. Yanks, on the other hand, should exhibit the frequently reported pattern of high presidential images which erode with age, while blacks should display negative images which become increasingly negative as the child becomes older.

Cognitive Development. Finally, there is a third possible socialization process which may govern the character of children's presidential images—cognitive sophistication. This process centers around the notion that excessively positive regard for political authorities is essentially an unsophisticated response characteristically exhibited by the cognitively undeveloped; lack of exposure to the realities of a situation allows a "primitive" and unrealistic image to stand (Kolson and Green, 1970). In point of fact, more aware, more cognitively developed, older children do possess more negative images than their younger counterparts, so it does appear that the acquisition of worldliness diminishes a once unrealistically elevated impression of the President (Easton and Dennis, 1969, chap. 8). (See also Chapters Four and Five.)

Cognitive sophistication does not of itself completely interpret a socialization process, however. It says nothing about how unsophisticated young children initially acquire an unrealistically positive image. The cognitively undeveloped, very young child may indeed hold unrealistic views, but why would they be unrealistically positive views? Jaros (1967) and Greenberg (1970c) explain that the positive image of the President is supposedly the child's response to feeling vulnerable to that figure. The child is patently physically inferior, while the President is a superpower and thus capable of doing great harm. The child's helplessness and vulnerability creates an anxiety drive. In order to avoid the anxiety, the child responds by idealizing the President, for a benevolent President will not manifest his harmful potentiality. Anxiety is thus reduced, and psychic tranquility reigns. Then, as the child's cognitive field expands with increasing age, he typically becomes more clearly aware of the limitations of the President (or any authority figure). Anxiety potentials are thus reduced and so is the propensity to idealize; exaggerated presidential images are no longer "needed," and they recede.

If this process operates, we would expect very distinctive patterns among the children under examination in this study. Amish youngsters—like their yank and black counterparts—certainly become aware of the President at an early age. Amish culture makes no attempt to hide the existence of secular authority, and although not a great deal is said about it, certainly the key figures, including the President, are noticed. Cognizance of this figure is enhanced for these particular Amish children because of their public schooling. Very young Amish children will thus be likely to share in a nearly universal "unsophisticated" high image of the President. As they grow older, however, sheltered from most communications from the outside world, their cognitions about political figures cannot be expected to expand. Increasing sophistication which normally results in tarnishing the image is largely foreclosed, so it should change little and remain high throughout childhood.

Yanks and blacks have the same initial anxiety-related impetus to a very positive image. They should be indistinguishable from each other and from the Amish at the lowest age levels. But both may be expected to have relatively rapidly expanding political information horizons. It should become evident to them that the President is restricted, constrained figure with many human foibles, and their images should contract somewhat. This pattern should be more pronounced among the black children, however, since presidential failings may be more evident to a disadvantaged, minority population and since the blacks, in a sense, may be the most sophisticated and urbane of our three groups. In general, the blacks are the most recent arrivals in these communities and are the least integrated to its rural, relatively isolated, and removed character. They tend to retain ties with urban areas and expose themselves to more communications (especially television) and other stimuli from the world around them than do their relatively more provincial counterparts. Thus black children may well be the most cognitively developed.

Thus if the cognitive sophistication process accounts for the character of youthful presidential images, we would expect our three groups to be highly positive and invariant at the lower grades. The Amish should show relatively little diminution of that image with age, while the other two groups show decline, with that tendency particularly marked among blacks.

Obviously, many more socialization processes can be envisioned, but the three we are concerned with are important and worth considering.

Findings

Observational Validity. First we wanted to be sure the Amish children show a distinct cultural dissimilarity; compared with their yank and black counterparts. All distinct subcultures in America are suffering some dilution as continuous heavy external influences take their toll, so it is conceivable that the Amish under investigation no longer represent a clear cultural distinction, particularly since they are compromised on schooling.

We would expect the Amish to differ markedly from their counterparts on questions of career aspirations, military service, and competence with respect to the polity. Table 1 displays data on five relevant variables. Each was measured by a straightforward, single survey item. While yank and black children from these agricultural communities may well eventually desert the farm for more urban areas, the maturing Amishman cannot do so without dramatic rupture of tradition and expectation; accordingly, the great margin of preferences of the Amish for farm occupations is no surprise at all. Similarly, the pacifistic tradition of this religious group is reflected in the boys' eschewing of military service. The typical noninvolvement in the world of secular authority is shown in the disvaluation of political participation; it is neither adjudged as collectively efficacious nor regarded a likely future individual activity.

A few words are in order about differences between yanks and blacks who are treated together as non-Amish in Table 1. As we have already mentioned, blacks are less integrated with this rural

Table 1.

DIFFERENCE BETWEEN AMISH AND NON-AMISH CHILDREN ON SELECTED VARIABLES

Responses, in Percentages

	Amish (N = 70)	Non-Amish (N = 194)	*Difference*
Desirability of farming as future occupation	77.1%	36.6%	Z = 5.71, p < .0001
Desire to serve in Armed Forces (boys only)	9.1	68.8	Z = 6.25, p < .0001
Makes a difference which side wins an election	48.5	68.4	Z = 2.93, p < .002
Intention regarding voting at age 21			
Yes	13.0	47.9	
Don't know	65.2	44.7	
No	21.7	7.4	
	99.9%	100.0%	D = .349, p < .0001
Estimation of family say about what government does			
A great deal	18.8	37.0	
A little	43.5	41.3	
None	37.7	21.7	
	100.0%	100.0%	D = .182, p < .04

Note: Difference of proportions tests (Z) or Kolmogorov-Smirnov tests (D) as appropriate.

community, and they probably share fewer of its traditional values; black children are likely to be significantly less favorably inclined toward a farming career than yanks. Nonetheless, blacks and yanks in this community are of roughly the same social status and they possess some aspects of a common subculture, so there is no reason to expect differences between them on the other variables. Our expectations were met with one exception. Black children are significantly more confident than yanks that their families have influence over government decisions.

In any event, we did substantiate our basic assumptions about cultural dissimilarities and thus confidently proceed to examine the data bearing on socialization processes.

Images of President. The childrens' responses, displayed in Table 2, have some very prominent features. The data were elicited with three-category multiple-choice items identical to those used in much previous research (Hess and Easton, 1960; Jaros, and others, 1968). Certain parallels exist between the responses of these children and those middle-class white children researched years ago. Both groups are the least reserved in their positive evaluations of the Chief Executive on the item dealing with presidential knowledge, while they display the most restraint in evaluating the President as a person. But none of the three cultures represented in the present research manifests a presidential image as elevated as that reported for the same middle-class white children (Hess and Easton, 1960).

More to our immediate purposes, Table 2 shows clearly the great differences between the presidential images of youngsters of each culture. While the generally less favorable evaluations of the black children might be regarded as resulting from differential parental influence, it is impossible that the consistently positive evaluations of the Amish youngsters have their source in the views of apolitical, singularly religious mothers and fathers. Table 2 thus appears to rule out the possibility of a straightforward, parental teaching process in the political socialization of these children towards the Chief Executive. However, the data are consistent with the notions of both father-image transfer and cognitive sophistication. Amish children may have the most pervasive fathers and blacks may have the least; Amish children may be the least cognitively developed and blacks may be the most.

Table 2.

PRESIDENTIAL IMAGES OF AMISH, YANK, AND BLACK CHILDREN

Responses in Percentages

Image items	Amish (N = 70)	Yanks (N = 151)	Blacks (N = 43)	Difference
How hard does the President work?				
Harder than most men	48.6%	34.2%	32.6%	
As hard as most men	40.0	40.9	27.9	
Less hard than most	11.4	24.8	39.5	
	100.0	100.0	100.0	H* = 11.86, p < .002
How honest is the President?				
More honest than most	45.7	23.8	34.9	
As honest as most	51.4	59.6	48.8	
Less honest than most	2.9	16.6	16.3	
	100.0	100.0	100.0	H* = 8.50, p < .02
How many people does the President like?				
Likes most everybody	65.7	44.6	41.9	

Likes as many as most	32.9	48.0	41.9
Does not like as many	1.4	7.4	16.3
	100.0	100.0	100.0
			$H^* = 8.68, p < .02$
How much does the President know?			
Knows more than most	65.7	53.0	45.2
Knows as much as most	34.3	45.0	47.6
Knows less than most	0.0	2.0	7.1
	100.0	100.0	100.0
			$H^* = 6.06, p < .05$
How do you feel about the President?			
Best man in the world	11.4	4.0	7.0
A good person	84.3	77.3	62.8
Not a good person	4.3	18.7	30.2
	100.0	100.0	100.0
			$H^* = 13.76, p < .001$

Note: Kruskal-Wallis tests. **H*** results from a calculation procedure which corrects for a large number of ties inherent in an ordered frequency distribution. It typically differs little from the more frequently calculated H, which makes no allowance for ties in ranking.

Further analysis allows us to distinguish between these two explanations, however. While presidential images show a general marked decline with age, comparisons among Amish, yank, and black children reveal greatly differing patterns (Figure 1). The youngest children manifest comparatively favorable images, regardless of culture; they are virtually indistinguishable from each other. As we examine progressively older children, however, dissimilarities appear. Although there are not perfectly consistent, monotonic progressions from identities to significant differences on each item, the trend is unmistakable. Significant cultural differences are generally to be observed among the older, but not among the younger, as confirmed in Table 3. The nature of the differential change with age

Table 3.

DIFFERENCES BETWEEN PRESIDENTIAL IMAGES OF AMISH, YANK AND BLACK CHILDREN, FOURTH AND EIGHTH GRADES

Image item	Fourth grade ($N = 56$)	Eighth grade ($N = 54$)
How hard does the President work?	$H^* = 1.94$, $p < .39$	$H^* = 4.67$, $p < .10$
How honest is the President?	$\chi^2 = .33$ (2df), $p < .85$	$H^* = 1.60$, $p < .45$
How many people does the President like?	$H^* = 1.15$, $p < .57$	$H^* = 16.81$, $p < .0001$
How much does the President know?	$H^* = 2.35$, $p < .32$	$H^* = 10.19$, $p < .005$
How do you feel about the President?	$H^* = 2.35$, $p < .32$	$\chi^2 = 8.17$ (2df), $p < .02$

Note: Entries are Kruskal-Wallis tests (H^*) except where empty cells prevent their calculation, in which case the chi-square test is employed.

that operates to produce this effect is more precisely indicated in Table 4. The general high image of the President held by the Amish declines very little with age. Among yanks, only a modest general erosion occurs of the elevated impression of the chief executive. Only

Table 4.

RELATIONSHIP BETWEEN PRESIDENTIAL IMAGE SCORES
AND GRADE IN SCHOOL

Image items	Amish (N = 70)	Yanks (N = 151)	Blacks (N = 43)
How hard does the President work?	.10	.02	−.36
How honest is the President?	−.17	−.17	−.42
How many people does the President like?	.05	−.12	−.46
How much does the President know?	.06	−.13	−.16
How do you feel about the President?	−.14	−.12	−.54

Note: Entries are gamma ordinal correlation coefficients, based on the uncollapsed, grade-by-grade data.

among the black youngsters is there a substantial diminution of the image of the President.

The implications of these data seem clear and striking. The notion of the President as a father figure seems to be negated by the similarity of response from the youngest children, by the continuing positive image held by the Amish throughout their childhood, and by the severe erosion of presidential images among black children who supposedly have a relatively negative paternal prototype in the first place. The data do, however, support suggestions that images of the President may relate to cognitive development. The most isolated from contemporary life, possessing the least opportunity for acquiring knowledge about the nature of secular authority, are the Amish; they retain, therefore, an unrealistically elevated, "unsophisticated" view of the President throughout their childhood. Yank children are not shielded by a comprehensive web of religious tradition as are their Amish counterparts, but they are part of a relatively parochial, rural community which is in some ways isolated from the mainstream of American society. Accordingly, they have only a slightly better opportunity to encounter broadening stimuli, to become cognitively developed. Thus, though they do not retain the high fourth grade image

Mean
Score

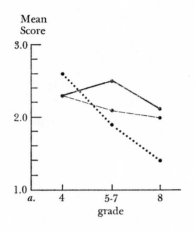

a.

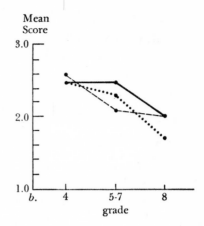

b.

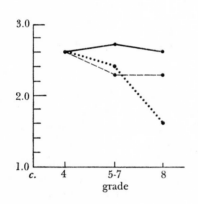

c.

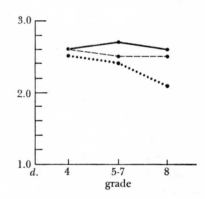

d.

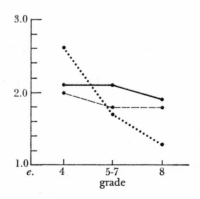

e.

of the President, neither do yanks exhibit a radical departure from it as they grow older. Black children, though they live in this rural community, are not really part of its particular traditions. As late arrivals, they retain contacts with city environments and experience patterns of stimuli characteristic of less peripheral communities. Opportunities for expansion of knowledge, awareness, and general cosmopolitan exposure are greater. Thus these youngsters are equipped to rapidly shed the elevated fourth grade image, and they do so in a much more pronounced fashion than either group of their counterparts.

Further Test of Cognitive Sophistication Thesis. While these data are clearly more consistent with the cognitive development thesis than with either the parental-teaching thesis or the father-image thesis, confirmatory evidence is needed. If our interpretation of these data is correct, the application of a control for a direct measure of cognitive sophistication should cause the cultural differences in response to disappear. In a sense, we have argued that culture is a surrogate for exposure to the outside world. Cultural differences by themselves are not a sufficient gauge of exposure, however. Within each cultural group, individuals vary in exposure—indeed such exposure is acknowledged as an erosive force in Amish communities.

Unfortunately, we have no direct measure of such exposure in our data. It is clearly not prudent to ask Amish youngsters about the extent of their familiarity with stimuli which are formally proscribed by their culture. We were able to make an oblique approach

FIGURE 1. Presidential image scores by grade in school. *a.* How hard does the President work? *b.* How honest is the President? *c.* How many people does the President like? *d.* How much does the President know? *e.* How do you feel about the President? Solid line indicates Amish. Dashed line indicates yanks. Dotted line indicates blacks. Mean scores are obtained by assigning a value of 3 to the most favorable evaluation of the President, 2 to the intermediate evaluation, and 1 to the least favorable, and calculating a simple arithmetic mean for each group. For grade 4, $N = 56$; for grades 5–7, $N = 153$; for grade 8, $N = 54$. The data for grades 5–7 are collapsed because the size of a given cultural group at a particular grade is small.

to this matter however. We asked the children to name a person that they want to be like. Arguing that a child's exemplars tell us something of the breadth of his cognitive field (Greenstein, 1965a, pp. 137–143), we arranged the responses into two groups. All responses indicating contemporary entertainment figures and contemporary political figures (excluding the President) were taken to indicate exposure or sophistication. All others, including the President, were considered to indicate a lesser degree of exposure. The reasoning behind this dichotomization is that children who choose contemporary figures *must* look well beyond their immediate environment in thinking about themselves. Children who do not—and their responses spanned the gamut from historical figures through religious leaders to members of the immediate family—*may* also be exposed and sophisticated, but it is less clear that they are. We opted for Type I error.

Our indicator of sophistication behaves much as we expect. It is strongly and significantly related to culture. Only 28 percent of the Amish are sophisticated by this definition, while the yanks number 48 percent in this category and the blacks—82 percent. Our earlier remarks about the differences between these groups in terms of their worldliness seem handsomely confirmed. Sophistication is also negatively related to presidential image—the more sophisticated have less positive images of the Chief Executive, significantly so on three of the five image items.

We then determine whether controlling for sophistication eliminates the cultural differences in the children's responses. By comparing the entries in Table 5 with those in Table 2, we see that the control does indeed produce some effect. While the differences do not completely disappear, the values of H* generally decline considerably.* It is tempting to speculate that if a less crude measure

---

* The contrast between the relationships in Table 5 and those in Table 2 is not entirely due to the fact that the former are calculated on the basis of smaller numbers of observations. The strengths of eight of the ten relationships displayed there are in fact less than the parallel relationships in Table 2. Strengths of relationships were determined by calculating gamma coefficients. To be sure, gamma is an ordinal measure, while differences in culture constitute no natural ordinal scale. However, an Amish-yank-black ordered dimension is suggested both by our theory and by our results. This order is employed in these calculations.

Table 5.

DIFFERENCES IN PRESIDENTIAL IMAGES OF AMISH, YANK, AND BLACK CHILDREN CONTROLLING FOR SOPHISTICATION

Image item	Sophisticated ($N = 106$)	Unsophisticated ($N = 111$)
How hard does the President work?	$H^* = 6.86$, p $< .04$	$H^* = 1.66$, p $< .45$
How honest is the President?	$H^* = 2.34$, p $< .32$	$H^* = 6.57$, p $< .04$
How many people does the President like?	$H^* = 6.72$, p $< .04$	$H^* = 1.99$, p $< .38$
How much does the President know?	$H^* = 2.03$, p $< .37$	$H^* = .78$, p $< .69$
How do you feel about the President?	$H^* = 3.70$, p $< .16$	$H^* = 5.93$, p $< .05$

Note: Entries are Kruskal-Wallis tests.

of sophistication had been available, more positive results would have been obtained. Nonetheless, one is justified in inferring that a considerable part of the presidential image measured by culture is a function of differential exposure to the outside world. Elevated images of the President, it appears, cannot endure the harsh glare of increasing cognitive development.

Conclusion

The implications of these findings are interesting for two distinct reasons. First, the data do suggest the importance of generalized awareness in political learning. The family does not appear to communicate specific political imperatives in these communities. Perhaps scholars of political socialization should focus attention away from specific agents with particular messages and towards the general information conditions in which people live.

Second, our findings raise a series of fascinating and significant questions. For example, "sophistication" appears to be an important variable in political learning processes. But what are the efficacious elements in sophistication? How does sophistication produce its effects? Does it imply that some substantive political learning takes place along with other input? Does sophistication mean, for example, exposure to television, and does television have political messages that are learned? Alternately, does sophistication merely imply declining credulity with a resultant reassessment of prior learning?

Similarly, one is confronted with the whole question of prior learning. Why do younger children share an elevated image of the President? The younger children of our sample exhibited such an image, but it remains an unexplained phenomenon. The most that can be said in this regard is that our findings are consistent with the anxiety notion, but they certainly do not prove it. Finally, why does the sophistication control fail to completely eliminate the cultural influences on responses? Are some important but presently unknown features of culture responsible for this variance? These questions may be as important as any answers that our findings have contributed.

IV

Language Environment and Political Socialization of Mexican-American Children

JAMES W. LAMARE

Although Mexican-Americans constitute the second largest non-European minority in the United States, systematic studies into the political socialization of Mexican-American children are quite recent and few in number (Garcia, 1973a, 1973b, 1973c; Gutierrez and Hirsch, 1973; Guzman, 1970; Hirsch, 1973). The literature about socialization has paid little attention to Mexican-Americans; for

Funds for this project came from two sources at the University of Texas at El Paso: The Cross-Cultural Southwest Ethnic Study Center and the University Research Institute. Ethel Galzerano, Z. Anthony Kruszewski, Sydney Dury Lamare, Jose Gabriel Loyola, and Salvador A. Sandoval were extremely helpful to me. Valuable comments on an earlier version of this manuscript were provided by John Carroll, Rudolph Gomez, M. Kent Jennings, Jose Gabriel Loyola, and Richard G. Niemi. While I appreciate the assistance of all of the above, none is responsible for the analysis and interpretation contained in this chapter.

63

instance, Goslin's compendium (1969) of writings in this field—even in the chapter entitled "The Socialization of American Minority Peoples" (Young, 1969)—virtually ignores this group.

Why social scientists have been remiss in analyzing the political socialization of Mexican-Americans is not crystal clear. Perhaps they have simply been ignorant of the existence and uniqueness of these people. While the vast majority of Mexican-Americans are concentrated in sections of five southwestern states (Arizona, California, Colorado, New Mexico, and Texas), most social scientists neither reside in these geographic locales nor are they Mexican-Americans. Scholarly indifference may have been further based upon the dubious assumption that members of ethnic groups, including Mexican-Americans, have blended into the "melting pot" of Americanism and thereby have become invisible as members of distinct cultural groups. Previous studies of the political socialization of children (Hess and Torney, 1967) did not focus on ethnicity as an important factor and possibly reinforced the impression that homogeneity in political socialization across ethnic groups is the rule. Recent discoveries about the political socialization of blacks seriously question this congruence perspective, since marked differences between the political orientations of blacks and whites are common, among both adults (Marvick, 1965) and children (Abramson, 1972; Greenberg, 1970b, 1970c, 1970d; Langton and Jennings, 1968; Laurence, 1970; Lyons, 1970). Furthermore, basic to understanding these racial differences is knowledge that the political socialization of children of minority groups is "best understood in terms of a concept of selective socialization: the socialization of each group is related to the position the group occupies in the American society" (Laurence, 1970, p. 192).

Supposing that the cultural characteristics of Mexican-Americans influence the political socialization of Chicano children, how would one identify accurately the cultural orientations peculiar to this group? Extant knowledge about Mexican-American culture is sparse, fragmentary, contradictory, frequently nothing more than a bundle of impressionistic stereotypes, and, in general, neither entirely valid nor fully reliable (Carter, 1970, chap. 2; Garcia, 1972b; Hirsch, 1973; Romano-V., 1971). Moreover, intracultural variation among Mexican-Americans is probably quite extensive. Romano-V.

(1971) has vigorously advised (especially Anglos) against viewing Mexican-Americans as a homogeneous entity, since this perspective "means that the historically pluralistic nature of these people is brusquely turned aside, and the pluralistic antecedents plus the pluralistic directions of change experienced by Chicanos never constitute either a theoretical or an analytical baseline for study or interpretation" (p. 21).

Use of the Spanish language makes Mexican-Americans unique in the United States, although language variations exist. Many scholars (Grebler, Moore, and Guzman, 1970, pp. 423–432; Moore, 1970, pp. 119–125; Sanchez, 1966) have commented upon the tenacity with which Mexican-Americans hold to the use of the Spanish language. Glazer (1966), in drawing out the implications of an extensive study of language loyalty in the United States among members of non-English-speaking ethnic groups, concludes that "it is the Spanish-speaking of the Southwest who . . . reveal less attrition in the use of their mother tongue than does any other group!" (p. 363).

A major reason for the persistence of the Spanish language among Mexican-Americans is isolation from Americans who speak English. Historically this separation was a product of Mexican-American settlement in geographic areas of the Southwest that were far removed from Anglo contact. Today this isolation is not only a product of rural living, which is steadily on the decline, but also a result of residing in predominantly Mexican-American urban enclaves. A continuous flow of migrants from Mexico into these areas reinforces Spanish usage. Among family and peers, many Mexican-Americans speak Spanish. In addition, language loyalty is maintained through the operation of an extensive Spanish-speaking public broadcasting system in the United States. Fishman (1966) estimates that as of 1960, Spanish broadcasts constituted two-thirds of the six thousand hours of non-English-language broadcasts aired over sixteen hundred radio stations in the United States (also Warshauer, 1966). Anglo institutions, especially the schools, have in general been unable to completely substitute English usage for Spanish usage. Indeed, Sanchez (1966) argues that "Spanish has been retained as a major language primarily by the default of the institutions of social incorporation" (p. 24). Finally, as Mexican-

American consciousness rises, Spanish-language retention will probably be intensely encouraged, for, in the words of Moore (1970), "the *Chicano* movement . . . with its emphasis on ethnic self-awareness, may contribute to a resurgence of the use of Spanish [especially] among young middle-class people" (p. 124).

Yet not all Mexican-Americans cling to Spanish as their primary language. Urban life, especially when coupled with middle-class socioeconomic status, diminishes Spanish usage. Moreover, recent efforts, particularly in some public schools, to instill English through bilingual techniques may increase the speaking of English. Grebler, Moore, and Guzman (1970, chap. 18) investigated the vernacular utilized in parent-child communications within Mexican-American families living in San Antonio and Los Angeles; 35 percent of the adult respondents stated they converse with their children in Spanish; one-fourth use English; and the remaining 40 percent communicate in both languages (p. 246). (See also Patella and Kuvlesky, 1973.)

In terms of political socialization, does variance in the language environment of Chicano children presage heterogeneity in their political orientations? Linguistic analysts concerned with the social and psychological consequences of language point to a strong relationship between language development and an individual's cognitive process (reviewed in Fishman, 1971; Greenfield and Bruner, 1969; Jenkins, 1969; Miller and McNeill, 1969). Stated briefly, by Tajfel (1969), some linguists have found "that language molds our experience of the outside world and determines accordingly the structure of thought and, perhaps, of perception" (p. 371). While this statement might appear obvious, serious students of language debate it. Controversy abounds in two areas: whether language determines or reinforces cognitive growth; and which aspect of language—for example lexicon, grammar, or syntax—has the greatest influence on cognitive development. It is beyond my scope (and expertise) to untangle all of the knotty problems involved in trying to understand the role of language skills in cognitive socialization; I will merely proceed upon the notion that these two variables are related.

Language skills, especially the recognition and internalization of words, are most instrumental in learning about environmental stimuli. Conceptual ordering of the external world appears to be greatly facilitated by the availability of appropriate linguistic symbols, codes, and guides. Reflecting upon the necessity of words for cognitive learning, social psychologist Roger Brown (1965) writes: "It is as if every linguistic community, parents at home, or nationals of another country or teachers of a science, adopts the same policy toward neophytes: 'Let us begin by defining our terms' " (p. 339). Without simple word definitions, much of the surrounding world is a maze of confusion and an object of ignorance. Moreover, a person without linguistic referents not only is unable to develop a complex, sophisticated, and interrelated set of beliefs about social matters but also has a feeble plank from which to spring to social action.

Those concerned with the assimilation and acculturation of ethnics in the United States either explicitly or implicitly recognize the importance of inculcating English as the predominate means of communication. Some possible political consequences of learning English are attachment to the American political system and participation—political interest and efficacy and voting. The United States Commission on Civil Rights, in a report dealing with Mexican-Americans, states: "Perhaps the most important carrier of a nation's culture is its language. Ability to communicate is essential to attain an education, to conduct affairs of state and commerce, and generally, to exercise the rights of citizenship" (1972, p. 13).

The increase in the use of English among immigrants— usually by the third generation—and their accretion in political participation might be more than mere coincidence. Furthermore, the continued low levels of political involvement among Mexican-Americans, even among some beyond the third generation, take on added meaning in light of the persistence of Spanish and its possible impact on cognitive socialization.

The existence of two language communities within a shared territory may also produce conflict. Tension occurs when members of each language population insist on the primacy of their language to the point of suppressing or excluding the utilization of the other's vernacular. Such a conflict is bound to influence the cognitive and emotional orientations of members of both linguistic groups. Dahl (1970) succinctly describes some reactions among those whose language is a minority but who still maintain its usage: "Wherever linguistic differences are rooted in tradition, as in Canada, Belgium, Switzerland, India, and literally dozens of other countries, linguistic minorities insist on the right to their own language. To deny this right would, and often does, produce violence: repression could easily lead to civil war. Language, after all, is deeply embedded in the inner recesses of one's personality: to say that the language of my people is inferior to yours is to say that my people are inferior to yours" (p. 16).

The English-speaking and the Spanish-speaking communities of the Southwest have known intense, often violent conflict (McWilliams, 1948). Within recent times much of the conflict has been conducted on the battlefields of the public schools. Most Anglo-dominated public schools have vigorously insisted that Mexican-Americans are going to learn and to speak English and *not* Spanish, even though a large number of Mexican-American school children are products of predominantly Spanish-speaking intimate environments. Many educators defend the "no-Spanish rule" on the grounds that: (1) acculturation and assimilation in "Americanism" are enhanced; (2) bilingualism stunts intellectual growth, because it is mentally confusing for a child; (3) the Spanish spoken in the Southwest is an inferior dialect and thus not worth perpetuating; and (4) communication between students and teachers and administrators, most of whom are monolingual in English, is hampered (Carter, 1970, p. 97; U. S. Commission on Civil Rights, 1972, p. 14). While the no-Spanish position seems to be softening, it appears to be still enforced in the Southwest, especially in Texas public schools. A recent survey of these schools estimates that one-third (two-thirds in Texas) discourages the use of Spanish in the classroom, and 15 percent (more than 33 percent in Texas) frown upon children speaking Spanish on the school grounds (U. S. Commission on Civil Rights, 1972, p. 15).

At present, the no-Spanish rule, where operative, is usually an informal policy of the schools that is enforced through a variety of means, some of which are coercive (Carter, 1970, pp. 97–98; U. S. Commission on Civil Rights, 1972, pp. 18–20). Mexican-American students have alleged that they have been beaten by school personnel for speaking Spanish in the public schools (U. S. Commission on Civil Rights, 1972, p. 19). Chronic offenders of the

no-Spanish rule say they have, on occasion, been suspended and ex-
pelled from school. "Spanish detention" for an hour after school
was the punishment, until 1968, for violators of the rule in
an El Paso high school (U. S. Commission on Civil Rights, 1968,
pp. 152–162). These more repressive sanctions for speaking Spanish
are reportedly declining in the public schools. Instead, schools now
discourage Spanish usage through (1) "suggesting that the staff
correct those who speak Spanish," (2) "requiring staff to correct
those who speak Spanish," (3) "encouraging English," (4) "ad-
vising students of the advantages of speaking English," and (5)
"encouraging other students to correct Spanish speakers" (U. S.
Commission on Civil Rights, 1972, p. 18).

Political orientations of members of both linguistic communities are probably affected by this conflict. English speakers are
likely to feel that Mexican-Americans who persist in the use of
Spanish are not to be accorded the privileges of American citizenship. A principal of a high school in San Antonio states that he
would "fight teaching Spanish past the third grade because it de-
stroys loyalty to America" (U. S. Commission on Civil Rights, 1972,
p. 20). Moreover, English speakers, including Mexican-Americans,
might be more disposed to feel positive about the practices and processes of the political system in the United States; acceptance and
use of English might be a sign of attachment to American politics.
Conversely, Spanish speakers, faced with the hostility of members of the English-speaking community, might respond by with-
drawing from, ridiculing, hating, or even attacking the political
world of the Anglo: in the words of a Chicano graduate of the San
Antonio public school system: "Schools try to brainwash Chicanos.
They try to make us forget our history, to be ashamed of being
Mexicans, of speaking Spanish. They succeed in making us feel
empty, and angry inside" (quoted in Steiner, 1970, pp. 212–213).

In sum, many instances suggest that the persistent use of
Spanish among some Mexican-Americans, and the negative reaction
to this practice on the part of some Anglos, have a bearing on the
political cognitions, political affect, and political involvement of
Mexican-American children. Chicano children who operate predominantly within the Spanish linguistic community are likely to be
less aware of stimuli pertinent to the American political system;

they are likely to express more sentiments of alienation, powerlessness, and indifference toward the system than are Anglos and Mexican-American children whose language environment is predominantly English.

To test these likelihoods, information was collected from all of the children in grades three through seven ($N = 785$) in an ethnically mixed, although imbalanced, public school located in urban El Paso, Texas. Structured questionnaires were distributed and administered to the children during a regularly scheduled class period, under the supervision of personnel associated with the project. All of the information was gathered during the second week of April, 1972.

While children in the higher grades (fifth through seventh) were able to fill in most of the questionnaire without assistance, the questions were read aloud to the younger ones. The items were worded and read in English, although bilingual test administrators were present during each data collection session. The English language was purposely chosen since the major focus of the research was to analyze reactions to the Anglo political process. Furthermore, a pretest among Mexican-American children in the Catholic schools in El Paso indicated that the vast majority of these children had little difficulty responding to a questionnaire written in English. Lastly, on the surface, as we shall see, the use of English did not prevent children of a predominantly Spanish-speaking environment from responding to items on the questionnaire, even though the response was often "don't know."

Three measures were designed to distinguish between Mexican-American and Anglo children. Put briefly, a Mexican-American, for the purpose of this study, is a child who *either* said his last name was Spanish *or* preferred to be called a "Mexican," a "Mexican-American," or a "Chicano," *or* reported that at least one of his parents was born in Mexico; conversely, an "Anglo" is a child who failed to meet any of these three criteria. In total, 38 percent of the sample is classified Mexican-American and the remainder is Anglo.

The environment of the school chosen for this study is primarily oriented to the English-speaking student. English is the prime means of communication among the Anglo students, the teachers, and the administrators. School officials have made no attempt to implement a bilingual or bicultural curriculum. While the no-Spanish rule is not formalized at this school, it appears to be present.

The intimate linguistic environment of the Mexican-American child was tapped through six questions: (1) "What language do your grandparents speak most?" (2) "What language do your parents speak most?" (3) "What language do you speak most with your friends?" (4) "Does your family watch Spanish or English television programs?" (5) "Does your family listen to Spanish or English radio stations?" (6) "Does your family listen to Mexican or American music?" (In El Paso, Spanish is the major means of communication and expression over many radio stations, in music, and on two television stations—both transmitting from Ciudad Juarez, Mexico.)

On each item, five answers with five different code numbers were provided. While the wording varied, the answers possible and their numerical weight were: "only Spanish" (1), "more Spanish than English" (2), "half Spanish, half English" (3), "more English than Spanish" (4), and "only English" (5). Respondents who had a summary score between twenty-two and thirty on these six items were classified as members of a predominantly English-oriented language environment. Children scoring between six and fourteen were called members of a predominantly Spanish-oriented linguistic community. Those between fourteen and twenty-two were included in the middle language group. Only the Mexican-American children are divided into three groups: 32 percent predominantly embedded in an English linguistic intimate community; 28 percent whose intimate language environment is mostly Spanish-oriented; and 40 percent in the middle group. Respondents not answering one or more of the six language questions were excluded from the analysis, lowering the number of cases from $N = 785$ to $N = 765$.

The variation in the language that permeates the close, personal surroundings of these children is likely to be associated with variance in their political perspectives. To test this assertion, an analysis is made of the effect of language on three general areas of political views: political awareness, political affect, and perceived personal role in the political system.

Political Awareness

A first step to personal involvement with the political system
and to movement beyond a parochial relationship with that system
is possessing the cognitive capacity to recognize political actors and
political institutions. While these cognitions might contain or come
to contain rich, sophisticated, and accurate perceptions about the
political process and those engaged in it, the beginning of political
awareness is usually marked by rather rudimentary and primitive
orientations. Hess and Torney (1967) note that a person's first encounter with his political system is simply the *"identification of political objects,* becoming aware of them and recognizing them as
part of the political realm" (p. 16). Previous research indicates that
political awareness commences among children at an early age and
grows, both in scope and depth, as a person ages. Usually the schools
stimulate the children to this awareness (Easton and Dennis, 1969;
Hess and Torney, 1967, chap. 5).

The children in this study were asked to respond to twenty-
two statements about practices, policies, and the process of the
American political system. The child marked "true," "false," or
"don't know." Although it is difficult to be exactly sure what "don't
know" means, at the minimum this reaction suggests a lack of familiarity with the item. A don't-know index was constructed by
summing the number of don't-know responses provided by Anglo
children and members of each of the three Mexican-American language groups and then dividing the score by the total number of
individuals in each group (Hess and Torney, 1967, Appendix C).

As the results in Figure 1 (p. 75) indicate, there is a clear
relationship between intimate language environment and political
awareness. While Anglos and Mexican-Americans who are English-
oriented have similar low scores on the don't-know index, Chicanos
whose personal environment is Spanish rank high in the number of
don't-know responses to the twenty-two statements. Considering the
strong possibility that the drop-out rate is high among children in
this linguistic environment, and since it is likely that age is inversely
related to political awareness, the high don't-know score of the
Spanish-oriented Chicanos might be nothing more than a reflection
of the overabundance of younger students in this group. To investi-

gate this possibility, the children were divided into lower (third through fifth) and upper (sixth and seventh) grades, and comparisons were made of each language group across these two grade levels. (Grade groupings were made to maintain a reasonable number of respondents at each level.) The results (not shown) point to the same pattern of scores on the don't-know index as that displayed in Figure 1 for each language sample.

A similar pattern emerges in the responses to questions asking the child "how much do you know about" the policeman, the President, the Mayor of El Paso, the Governor of Texas, the immigration official, Congress, the Supreme Court, and voting and elections. Possible answers are "a lot," "some," "little," or "nothing." Table 1 shows the percentage of respondents in each group who

Table 1.

POLITICAL AWARENESS OF ANGLOS AND MEXICAN-AMERICANS

		Percentage of MEXICAN-AMERICANS		
	Percentage of			
Know a lot or some about:	*ANGLOS* $N = 474$	*English-oriented* $N = 93$	*Middle group* $N = 116$	*Spanish-oriented* $N = 82$
Policemen	85%	79%	76%	57%
President	74	63	50	42
Mayor of El Paso	33	29	20	11
Governor of Texas	26	20	13	13
Immigration Official	22	22	33	37
Congress	35	31	19	16
Supreme Court	34	35	26	17
Voting and Elections	68	67	58	49

Note: Respondents who did not answer the question were excluded from the analysis. In no instance did this lower the number of respondents by more than 10.

answered "a lot" or "some." (Those who did not answer—never more than ten—were excluded from analysis.)

Again a congruence appears in the awareness of the Anglo child and his English-oriented Mexican-American peer. Chicanos

closely in the Spanish linguistic community show less political awareness. In only one instance, involving familiarity with the immigration official, does the Spanish-oriented child manifest more awareness than his schoolmates. This finding probably indicates the
greater contact that this child's family and friends have with the
immigration official (Grebler, Moore, and Guzman, 1970, chap.
21). Political objects outside of the personal environment of the
Spanish-oriented Chicano are not readily recognized.

Advancement in school years usually produces an increase
in the political awareness of children. Over the course of primary
school education, a pattern of cognitive growth is documented in
children, at least partially the result of the efforts of teachers and
the curriculum (Hess and Torney, 1967, p. 248).

Table 2 shows the percentage of increase in political aware-

Table 2.

PERCENTAGE OF INCREASE IN POLITICAL AWARENESS FROM
LOWER TO UPPER GRADES

		Percentage increase of MEXICAN-AMERICANS		
Know a lot or some about:	*Percentage increase of ANGLOS*	*English-oriented*	*Middle group*	*Spanish-oriented*
Policemen	− 3%	− 1%	− 3%	− 2%
President	+ 2	+15	− 3	+ 3
Mayor of El Paso	+12	+ 6	+ 8	no change
Governor of Texas	+10	+ 8	+ 8	+ 3
Immigration Official	+ 2	− 3	+23	+26
Congress	+ 7	+14	+11	+16
Supreme Court	no change	+ 3	− 5	− 8
Voting and Elections	+14	+ 5	− 4	+12

Note: Respondents who did not answer the question were excluded from
the analysis. In no instance did this lower the number of respondents by
more than 10.

ness from lower to upper grades, of each group. With the exception
of a growth in recognizing the immigration official, the gap in political awareness between Spanish-oriented Mexican-American children and their schoolmates is not closed over the school years. The

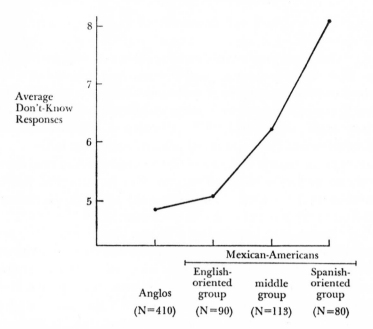

FIGURE 1. Average don't-know responses for Anglos and Mexican-Americans.

upper-grade Spanish-oriented Chicano's level of recognition remains a distance from the other upper-grade children, and the increase in his political awareness is slight, if not reversed.

The distribution of and growth patterns in political aware-ness among Mexican-American children immersed in an English-oriented intimate surrounding are very similar to those of the Anglo children. Although knowing about the President is lower among the young Mexican-American children of this linguistic group, their older counterparts manifest a recognition score (66 percent) close to that of the Anglos (74 percent).

While the information in this study precludes a conclusive judgment concerning the impact of the school on political aware-ness, there is some suggestion that the greater lack of political recog-nition among Chicanos who are Spanish-language-oriented is not offset by the school. Perhaps the overwhelming English language bias in this school serves as a hindrance and not an aid in stimulat-ing these children to learn about political objects pertinent to the Anglo-American political world.

Political Affect

One of the best-established observations in political socialization literature is the strong positive orientation that children have toward the American political community and the authorities operating in the political system (Easton and Dennis, 1969; Greenstein, 1965a; Hess and Torney, 1967). Children in certain locales may not be favorably disposed toward political authorities in the United States (Jaros, Hirsch, and Fleron, 1968), and children may experience a tempering in blind faith and trust in the American political process as they grow older, but most of the young people are quite attached to the political system in this country.

The political socialization literature has not examined, however, whether children whose intimates retain cultural traits of a non-Anglo origin are positively oriented to the American political process. Our sample was asked if they were "glad to live in the United States." Close to 90 percent of both the Anglos and the English-oriented Chicanos said yes, compared with 70 percent of the Mexican-Americans from a Spanish linguistic environment. These children cannot be said to be negative about living in the United States, but they do show uncertainty about the pleasure of residing in this country. A 17 percent increase in affirmative responses from lower to upper grades may show that the school is inculcating more national pride in these children, but even the older Spanish-oriented Chicanos are still 12 percent short of the positive orientations of their classmates.

Each child was further asked "how much do you like" the policeman, the President, the Mayor of El Paso, the Governor of Texas, the immigration official, Congress, the Supreme Court, and voting and elections. On each of these items, the alternative responses are "a lot," "some," "don't like very much," "don't like at all," and "don't know about it." While permitting the don't-know response lowers the number making a judgment, especially among Spanish-oriented Chicanos, this procedure avoids encouraging children to make appraisals while lacking familiarity with the item.

Only in the case of evaluating the President does language environment appear to have an impact. Children from the Spanish linguistic community are some 14 percent less positive in their feeling about the President than are their English-oriented peers. On every other item the responses are similar for all children and, for the most part, manifest a positive affect. In light of the previously reported findings about recognizing the immigration official it is interesting to note that the Mexican-Americans most familiar with this official rate him about the same as their schoolmates do.

The reasons for this overall positivism of the Chicano children, particularly those from the Spanish linguistic community, are not easy to pinpoint. Perhaps they may have marked "don't know" to items when they really wished to say "don't like." This explanation is weakened somewhat by data (not displayed) about the nature of the don't-know respondents. Many children noted ignorance about a political object on the awareness test and then passed over "don't know" on the affect test and rated the object positively. Other children who had earlier admitted no awareness were consistent in responding to the don't-know affective item. This pattern was found among children in all the language groups, hence there is little to suggest that ignorance of political objects is a guise for disdain. Perhaps if the Chicano children, especially the members of the Spanish-oriented community, knew or were taught more about the American political process, their affective scores would move in the negative direction.

The small number of cases makes risky an evaluation of the possible impact of the school on the affect toward these political items. The overall pattern that emerges in comparing children in the lower and upper grades points to little effect of the school system upon political evaluation. The one item of clear exception is the appraisal that the children at the two grade levels give the President. Over 85 percent of the young children express overwhelming positivism toward the President. In the upper grades this favorable response falls off some 10 percent for Anglos and English-oriented Mexican-Americans, but declines a full 30 percent for Spanish-oriented Chicanos. It is plausible (although not conclusive from this evidence) that Chicanos operating in Spanish-language intimate environment and an English-language school environment come to recognize this disjuncture and express general hostility toward one of the most visible symbols of Anglo power—the President.

In short, language does not appear to be as compelling a factor in evaluating political objects as in becoming aware of them. In only two instances does language environment relate to political affect—the comparatively low enthusiasm of Spanish-oriented Chicanos about the President and about living in the United States. The school appears to increase positivism toward living in the United States, but it does not produce increased liking of the President.

Personal Role

The impact of language background on the child's feeling about his influence on the world around him, especially the political world, is analyzed from two viewpoints: personal competence and political efficacy, as perceived by the child.

The psychological disposition that a person can manipulate his surroundings is multifaceted and probably multidimensional. This feeling is expressed in a variety of terms, including *personal competence, a sense of self, fate control, personal efficacy,* and *self-esteem,* among others (Greenberg, 1972). A common theme is the perceived ability to chart one's own course through life. In this study, two questionnaire items tap this attitude: (1) "Have you usually felt pretty sure your life would work out the way you want it to, or have there been times when you haven't been very sure about it?"; and (2) "When you make plans ahead do you usually get to carry out things the way you expected, or do things usually come up to make you change your plans?" The questions were combined to form a personal competence index. If respondents said they were "sometimes not very sure" how their lives would work out *and* noted that in making future plans they usually had to change them, they were classified as low in personal competence. From the lower grades, these children included 40 percent of the Anglos, 41 percent of the English-oriented Mexican-Americans, 65 percent of the middle group of Mexican-Americans, and 56 percent of the Spanish-oriented Mexican-Americans. From the upper grades were 35 percent of the Anglos, 35 percent of the English-oriented Mexican-Americans, 70 percent of the middle group of Mexican-Americans, and 73 percent of the Spanish-oriented Mexican-Americans.

Operating even partially in a Spanish linguistic community

and attending an English-oriented school appear to have a drastic effect on a child's sense of personal competence. The younger Mexican-American children caught in this conflict are less competent than their Anglo or English-oriented peers, and, more importantly, this disjuncture widens dramatically over the school years, while the perceived competence of Anglos and English oriented Chicanos slightly increases as they grow older. The growing lack of personal competence in Chicanos from a Spanish-language intimate environment may reflect the realization that the world they encounter daily —a school that has an informal no-Spanish rule—is hostile to their culture and thus to them as individuals.

In our survey of seven questions designed to tap the various shadings of political efficacy (Easton and Dennis, 1967, p. 29), interitem correlation indicated that only three measured a common attitude, especially among the Mexican-American children: (1) "There are some powerful men in the government who are running the whole thing and they do not care about us ordinary people," (2) "I don't think that people in the government care much what people like my family think," and (3) "Citizens don't have a chance to say what they think about running the government."

Each respondent marked "true," "false," or "don't know." On the resulting index of political efficacy, students tending to answer "false" were called high in political efficacy. From the lower grades, these children included 36 percent of the Anglos, 29 percent of the English-oriented Mexican-Americans, 19 percent of the middle group of Mexican-Americans, and 16 percent of the Spanish-oriented Mexican-Americans. From the upper grades were 37 percent of the Anglos, 37 percent of the English-oriented Mexican-Americans, 28 percent of the middle group of Mexican-Americans, and 33 percent of the Spanish-oriented Mexican-Americans.

For the younger children, language environment influences political efficacy. Young Chicanos from a Spanish-oriented environment are not as efficacious as their schoolmates. In the upper grades, however, this gap among language groups is bridged. Efficacy scores are similar for all students at this age. Why would the personal competence of Spanish-oriented children decrease over the years while their political efficacy improves?

Perhaps part of the answer is found in closely observing the wording of the questions used to measure these attitudes. Personal competence was tapped by asking the child to evaluate *his* relationship with *his* surrounding world, while the items in the political efficacy index refer to the governmental influence of relatively external factors, such as the "citizens," "ordinary people," and "family." Maybe the child embedded in a Spanish linguistic community accepts the idea that others can influence events, while not believing that he can control his own life. Unfortunately, items to measure the personal political competence of the children are not included in the questionnaire.

This study suggests that language environment has a major impact upon the political socialization of Mexican-American children, regarding orientations about the Anglo-American political world (see also Garcia, 1973a). Chicano students sharing the English language environment of Anglos manifest political views similar to those of the Anglos. But Mexican-Americans in the lower grades, whose intimate linguistic community is Spanish-oriented and whose school is geared to the child from an English-speaking background, differ from their schoolmates in many political orientations. They are less likely to be politically aware and politically efficacious, less disposed to be pleased about living in the United States, and more inclined to be low in their sense of personal and political competence. Over the school years, this chasm, in most instances, is not closed; rather the gap widens.

Amelioration of these differences between ethnic groups and within the Mexican-American sample would probably begin by teaching English effectively to Chicanos without at the same time damaging their self-esteem and cultural identity. Until recently, most social institutions, especially the public school system, approached the teaching of English to Mexican-Americans by attempting to eliminate the use of Spanish. While this strategy may have met with some success, it is also quite likely that for some Mexican-Americans this approach has created feelings of cultural denigration, embarrassment, harassment, and, in general, a retreat from the Anglo social and political world and its vernacular.

A start in devising new methods of instruction in English would be to recognize that Spanish is the primary means of communication within many Mexican-American intimate environments. To ignore or try to undermine the use of this language is an invitation for these people not to learn or to want to learn the English language. Since the public school is an important agent of language socialization, it is important to know how English might be transmitted effectively in the classroom to Mexican-Americans without damaging cultural and personal esteem.

Specific new methods of teaching English are varied. The school curriculum could include both English and Spanish as well as materials familiar to the Anglo, Mexican, and Mexican-American culture. Or schools could simply teach remedial English without eliminating Spanish as the primary language of the child. The bilingual-bicultural approach has been endorsed by the U. S. Office of Education, which recommends "the use of two languages, one of which is English, as mediums of instruction for the same pupil population in a well-organized program which encompasses part or all of the curriculum and includes the study of history and culture associated with the mother tongue (U. S. Commission on Civil Rights, 1972, p. 21).

Thus far, however, the federal government's attempt to stimulate a bilingual-bicultural curriculum has reached only an estimated 2.7 percent of the Mexican-American population (U. S. Commission on Civil Rights, 1972, p. 22). Other methods of teaching English without undermining Spanish as the Chicanos' primary means of communication are not much more widespread (Carter, 1970, chap. 5).

One consequence of these restricted efforts is that there is little evidence about the effects of the new ways of teaching English. The Office of Education speculates that a complete bilingual-bicultural program "develops and maintains the children's self-esteem and a legitimate pride in both cultures" (U. S. Commission on Civil Rights, 1972, p. 21). Carter (1970, chap. 5) presents some admittedly impressionistic evidence that substantiates this proposition. It is safe to conclude that more work is needed, both in devising and implementing new means of teaching English that further cultural and individual dignity among Mexican-Americans, and in measuring the effects of these approaches. In light of the evidence collected by this study, the attitudinal differences found among Chicano language groups might not emerge in schools where bilingualism is policy.

Finally, it should be noted that some Mexican-American children from a predominantly Spanish-speaking intimate environment do have the same orientations as their English-oriented peers. These findings suggest that socialization agents other than the schools have an impact on the beliefs and feelings of these Chicano children. More than likely parental influence is at work here. Even though their language is primarily Spanish, some Mexican-American parents seem able to teach their children political awareness, positive disposition toward the political system, and political and personal efficacy. Why these parents differ from others in the Spanish-speaking environment who are not effectively transmitting these orientations is perhaps a question worth investigating further.

V

Political Attitudes among Black Children

SARAH F. LIEBSCHUTZ, RICHARD G. NIEMI

The recent surge of interest in political socialization, resulting in a growing body of empirical research on urban schoolchildren, has concentrated mainly on mapping developmental attitudinal patterns of white children. Recent studies have reported interesting and suggestive contrasts in the developmental patterns of black and white schoolchildren (Abramson, 1973; Greenberg, 1969, 1970a, 1970b; Lyons, 1970; Rodgers and Taylor, 1971). Yet the studies done so far have been both fragmentary and contradictory, impelling further evidence and interpretation.

Unlike the major study of whites, no study of young blacks has questioned children as early as the second grade. Moreover, previous studies of blacks have typically skipped every other grade in gathering data (Greenberg's study, for example) or have combined two or more grades into one category at the analysis stage—Lyon's and Rodgers and Taylor's work, for example. These facts are more important than they might seem to be, since to determine the magnitude, scope, and timing of any possible divergencies, between black and white children complete data are needed. We have thus included second graders in our study and have analyzed data for each grade from second to eighth.

We also attempt to assess the impact of a curriculum in the lower grades which is designed explicitly to promote and strengthen the self-concept of culturally disadvantaged children. Evidence that blacks at the high school level are particularly affected by explicit teaching of civics (Langton and Jennings, 1968) suggests that blacks are also affected by teaching at the elementary level, particularly under a curriculum designed specifically for them.

In addition, we explore the suggestion that black teachers in positions of authority and as respected goal models heighten the self-respect and self-confidence of the developing young black child.

We obtained the data for this study in a June 1969 survey of 886 second through eighth grade children in selected classes of five schools in the Rochester City School System, New York. Three of the schools are inner-city, largely black, elementary schools; one is an elementary school bordering the inner city with about equal numbers of black and white children. An inner-city, largely black, high school provides the seventh and eighth grade respondents. During the regular social studies periods questionnaires were circulated. Lengths of questionnaires vary: the shortest for the second graders and the longest for children in grades five through eight. Each questionnaire took about twenty-five minutes to administer.

The test instruments were administered by black college students, who, we hoped, would cause the children less inhibition in expressing attitudes than if white administrators were used. The questionnaire was developed to allow for direct comparison of data with those obtained in earlier studies of white children (Hess and Torney, 1967). A pretest, however, showed that the questionnaire had to be considerably simplified and shortened for our sample. (For a further description of the survey and an analysis of peers as political socialization agents, see Liebschutz, 1971.)

To eliminate any cultural distinctiveness that might confuse the comparison of black and white children, we excluded Spanish surname (Puerto Rican) respondents, who comprised 4 percent of the sample. Black children are 76 percent of the sample; the rest are white. Judging by fourth through eighth graders' reports of their father's, stepfather's, or mother's occupation, 52 percent of the sample is of low socioeconomic status (unemployed or unskilled labor), 34 percent is of medium status (skilled labor, clerical, sales); and 14 percent is of high status (professional and managerial).

Attitude Development

White children's orientations toward political authority figures, especially the President and policemen, are relatively well documented (Hess and Torney, 1967; Tolley, 1973). (See also Chapter Six.) At least until recently (see Tolley, 1973; Chapter Six), youngsters regarded these political authority figures as benevolent, knowledgeable, powerful, competent, and responsive. The intensity of these idealistic attitudes is modified by the end of elementary school, but the disposition of children still remains highly favorable toward both the President and policemen.

Greenberg, examining levels of support for the President, the policeman, and "the government," suggests that children who have very similar orientations in the lower grades diverge as they grow older (1970b, pp. 343–344). Greenberg's divergence theory, however, is anything but conclusive, and other researchers show no real substantiation for a predictable divergence. While we make no pretense that present data are definitive, we claim a more accurate description of young blacks' nascent political attitudes, because our survey covers the elementary grades more completely than previous surveys and the items are presented separately, which avoids the problem of basing conclusions on one or two figures. While this procedure also opens up the possibility of conflicting, inconclusive patterns, some reasonable conclusions can be drawn. Finally, we draw on questions about the President, policemen, the fairness of laws, and political efficacy (and questions on "the government" to a lesser extent) in order to overcome possible biases due to the particular items chosen.

Our study examines children's evaluation of both personal and role performance attributes of the President and policemen as other studies have done. Ten statements on the questionnaire concern the coercive ability, knowledge, and magnitude of decisions—role performance—and the helpfulness and personal attractiveness—personal qualities—of the President and policemen. The items are as follows: Do you think the policeman (President) can make people do what he wants? Do you think the policeman (President) knows more than most people? Do you think the policeman (President) makes big decisions? Do you think the policeman (President) would want to help you if you needed it? Is the policeman (President) your favorite? The answers are: (1) YES, strongly agree; (2) yes, moderately agree; (3) don't know, no opinion; (4) no, moderately disagree; (5) NO, strongly disagree. Mean responses of the children by race and grade level are presented for each of the ten items in Figure 1, a through j. In calculating the means, don't-know responses were *not* excluded, so that possible scores range from one to five. (Figures la through 1j show only the mean range that applies.) Eliminating the don't-know responses obviously changes the mean scores, but not enough to make a significant difference in the overall patterns. Figure 1 shows that even in the early grades blacks often have more negative attitudes than whites do. In the second grade the differences between blacks' and whites' attitudes are about evenly split. Blacks have more slightly positive views of the President in four of the five comparisons, and whites have more positive views of the policeman in the same ratio. By the third grade, where Greenberg found no difference, blacks uniformly have more negative attitudes. This pattern of more negative attitudes by black children is maintained quite consistently throughout the remaining grades. In the next section we note that because of a special curriculum some of the black children had more realistic attitudes than might normally be found among second and third graders. However, the use of only the students not in this curriculum (Figure 4, p. 96) would leave our conclusion unchanged.

We do not wish to overexaggerate the differences found, especially at the second grade level. If our sample had contained more middle-class whites, whom Hess and Torney (1967, pp. 131–145) found to have more realistic views, blacks' and whites' attitudes may have been similar throughout all the grades. It is significant that black youngsters in second grade seem to view the President even more highly than whites and that their feelings about policemen are so similar to those of whites. But the important point here is that black children begin to develop more negative attitudes at an earlier age than whites do. Any efforts to build on youngsters' benevolent views must begin very early to be successful with black as well as white children. Conceivably this could be done in imaginative ways (for both blacks and whites) by using children's positive views as a basis for introducing them to notions of participation and governmental responsiveness (and unresponsiveness).

Our findings also indicate that the pattern of attitudes follow roughly parallel rather than divergent courses. There are some fluctuations, especially among whites where there are fewer cases; and there are some "reversals," where blacks have more positive views than whites. The predominant pattern, however, seems to show roughly parallel development. Blacks typically fall below whites on the curves, but not increasingly so. Even allowing for a generous infusion of error into the response curves, only *b, i,* and perhaps *j* of Figure 1 suggest divergent paths. Hence we conclude that the basic developmental pattern of black and white attitudes toward policemen and the President is parallel rather than divergent.

Additional corroborating evidence is found in black and white youngsters' views toward laws, the outputs of the political system. Analysis, by race and grade, of responses to the item "all laws are fair" again demonstrates differential, basically parallel, affect by black and white children (see Figure 2). Even as early as second grade, young children seem to be aware of the impact of laws on them, and attitudes erode at later grade levels, similarly in both racial groups.

Interestingly, Rochester students, both black and white, less often saw all laws as fair than did the white students in the "Chicago" study. On this question the format in both studies was the same (Hess and Torney, 1967, p. 233), so that a direct comparison is possible. Since Hess and Torney excluded don't-know responses before calculating mean scores, we did likewise to arrive at the comparison in Table 1.

In all grades except third, Rochester whites responded more negatively than did those in the "Chicago" study, and blacks' views were even more negative. The contrast is especially sharp at seventh and eighth grade levels.

The explanation for this contrast is not obvious. Comparison of our figures with those of Hess and Torney (1967, p. 141) indicates that the differences are not due to social class differences. The

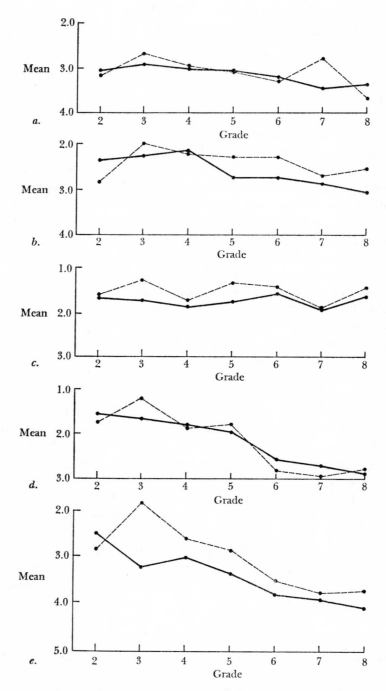

FIGURE 1. Responses to questions about the President and policemen. Solid line indicates blacks; dashed line indicates whites. *a*. President's coercive ability. *b*. President's knowledge. *c*. President makes big decisions. *d*. President's helpfulness. *e*. President your favorite. *f*. Policeman's coer-

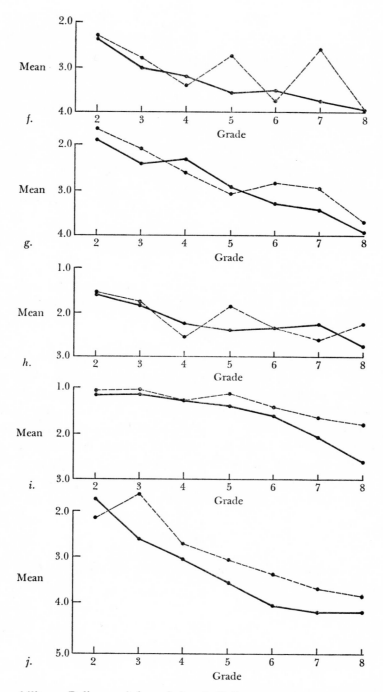

cive ability. *g*. Policeman's knowledge. *h*. Policeman makes big decisions.
i. Policeman's helpfulness. *j*. Policeman your favorite. Numbers of cases
(these vary slightly between graphs because of missing data): blacks—
110, 126, 93, 110, 105, 76, 41; whites—23, 21, 25, 23, 22, 13, 35.

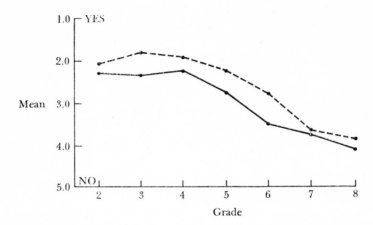

FIGURE 2. Responses to "all laws are fair." Solid line indicates blacks; dashed line indicates whites. Numbers of cases are the same as in Figure 1.

roughly eight years intervening between the two studies or the fact that the Rochester students are in largely black schools might account for the contrast. In either case, however, children appear to be more sensitive to the outside environment than we have given them credit for. Even in second grade, children's race affects their perceptions of laws. And the pattern of attitude development supports the concept of parallel rather than divergent development.

The development of political efficacy offers a stark contrast to the preceding results. Our measure of efficacy is a five-item index

Table 1.

COMPARISON OF "CHICAGO" AND ROCHESTER STUDIES

Grades:	2	3	4	5	6	7	8
"Chicago" study	1.40	1.50	1.54	1.76	1.92	2.14	2.38
Rochester whites	1.67	1.41	1.71	1.90	2.28	3.00	3.06
Rochester blacks	1.93	1.92	1.86	2.24	2.89	3.12	3.30

Source of "Chicago" study: Hess and Torney (1967, p. 53)

ranging from one to sixteen (Easton and Dennis, 1967, p. 30): (1) My family doesn't have any say about what the government does; (2) Citizens don't have a chance to say what they think about running the government; (3) What happens in the government will happen no matter what people do. It is like the weather, there is nothing people can do about it; (4) There are some big powerful men in the government who are running the whole thing and they do not care about us ordinary people; and (5) I don't think people in the government care much what people like my family think.

Figure 3 shows that the responses to the political efficacy statements offer an instance in which a divergent model seems appropriate. (Efficacy questions were not asked of second graders.)

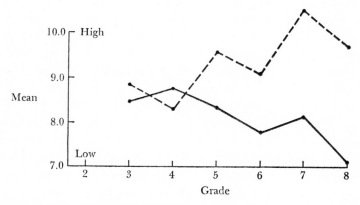

FIGURE 3. Political efficacy scale. Solid line indicates blacks; dashed line indicates whites. Numbers of cases are the same as in Figure 1.

In the third and fourth grades black and white children are not clearly different, but from fifth grade on, blacks become increasingly less efficacious than whites. Blacks, it would seem, become especially aware of the difficulties they will encounter in altering the political world, even though their views of the benevolence of political authority decline no faster than those of whites.

As one last comparison between blacks and whites we calculated mean responses on "the government's" knowledge, making of big decisions, helpfulness, and fallibility. (This was done only for fifth through eighth graders.) This set of items resulted in unstable results. If this were true only for whites, whose numbers are small, we could perhaps attribute it to sampling error, but the response instability is just as characteristic of the blacks' answers. We do not know why such fluctuations occurred so differently from the patterns found in the "Chicago" study. But we must conclude that these data lend little support to either a parallel or a divergent development model.

Overall, then, our data for the President, the policeman, and the fairness of laws support a model in which differences between blacks' and whites' attitudes appear early and develop in more or less parallel fashion. Political efficacy follows a divergent path, with whites becoming increasingly convinced that they can be influential in politics and blacks increasingly convinced of the opposite. Attitudes for the government seem to be in a state of flux for both races.

Thus, rather than supporting a single model of attitude development, our results suggest that models differ according to the types of clusters of ideas, with the parallel model being most appropriate for the trend toward realism in children's views of political authority figures. It is important that only in children's feelings of political efficacy does a divergent model adequately describe the results. The importance of this finding may be not that blacks view political authority as less benevolent than whites—for these views develop in concert with, if to a stronger degree, than those of whites —but that blacks increasingly see the government as unresponsive to them. Perhaps this trend can be reversed by increasing opportunities for political participation by blacks and, at a programatic level, perhaps by increasing efforts to show both black and white youths how to effectively take part in the political world.

Curriculum Effect

We now direct our attention to the possible effects on student attitudes of a specially designed curriculum for the early grades. Such an analysis seems appropriate to test whether blacks may be particularly affected by school material and whether a new curriculum designed for the very early grades might alter young children's views before they became firmly fixed. Our discovery of differences as early as the second grade cautions us that reality may already have been fully enough grasped that the curriculum could not completely erase the black childen's trend toward negative feelings.

The focus of our attention is a curriculum known as "Project Beacon," a program directed "toward the improvement of self-concept of the disadvantaged child within the classroom by the classroom teacher" (Franco, 1971, p. 2). While the ultimate goal of Project Beacon is to upgrade academic achievement in the primary grades of elementary school, its focus on improving the concept of self would seem to have implications for children's attitudes toward the political system. We compare the relative political efficacy scores and attitudes toward political authority figures and laws of those who have participated in Project Beacon and those who have not.

Project Beacon was developed by a team of guidance, curriculum, and teaching personnel of the Rochester City School District in response to a 1961 directive from the New York State Education Department to "demonstrate practical solutions to the problems of educating [culturally] disadvantaged pupils" (Rochester City School District, n.d., p. 4). Since 1964, Project Beacon has operated with pupils in kindergarten through grade three of five elementary schools that are located in low-income, low-middle-income, largely black, inner-city neighborhoods of Rochester. Project Beacon attempts to improve the self-concept of children from these areas by utilizing such techniques as photography, tape-recording, role-playing; by visiting parents and inviting them to volunteer to participate in the classroom, by emphasizing black historical and cultural materials; and by holding teacher orientation and sensitivity workshops.

While we did not directly measure levels of self-esteem among our respondents, an independent study confirmed the effectiveness of this curriculum in improving self-concept (Franco, 1971). That study, conducted during the same period as ours and including the same children from which our Beacon sample was drawn, reported that fourth graders who had been in Project Beacon from kindergarten through third grade scored higher on the California Test of Personality and exhibited more positive social and work habits than a matched sample of children who did not participate in Project Beacon (Franco, 1971, pp. 46–57). The

California Test of Personality consists of self-adjustment (feelings of personal security) and social adjustment (feeling of social security) components. For a description of the items and a discussion of the validity of the test, see Buros (1959).

Since the concept of the self (usually called *personal efficacy* or *effectiveness* in political science literature) has been shown to relate to political efficacy and some aspects of political participation (Milbrath, 1965, pp. 59–60), we have a unique opportunity to see whether a concerted effort to upgrade the black child's conception of the self also has effects on his developing political views. Although our initial concern is with second and third grade black students in Project Beacon and others in their schools who are not in Project Beacon, we also include students who were in Project Beacon classes during kindergarten through third grade but are now in a later year in school, comparing them with students in their grades who did not participate in Project Beacon. These students give us a chance to make an initial judgment on whether the effects of Project Beacon are temporary or more long lasting.

We begin by looking at the same personal and role performance attributes of the President and policemen that we considered earlier. Figure 4, *a* through *j*, graphically depict the mean responses for present and past Project Beacon blacks and those not in Project Beacon. Looking initially at the second graders, we find that mean responses of Project Beacon children are more negative for eight of the ten items than those of their counterparts who are or were not in Project Beacon. In several instances the differences are fairly large, indicating that Project Beacon children are considerably less idealistic about these two political authority figures. Their assessments of role performance characteristics are particularly noteworthy, as the Project Beacon second graders ascribe substantially less coercive ability and knowledge to the policeman than other second graders do. In addition both personal characteristics of the policeman are judged less favorably, suggesting that young Project Beacon students more accurately reflect the generally negative attitudes of black adults toward local law authorities (Marvick, 1965; National Advisory Commission on Civil Disorders, 1968).

For third graders, our analysis again suggests that the Project Beacon curriculum tempers idealism toward authority figures. For four of the five items regarding each the policeman and the President, Project Beacon children's mean responses are more reflective of adult attitudes than those of the other third graders. Again, the more realistic responses are concentrated on role performance characteristics. (Here we note as a more realistic attitude the attribution of greater decision-making prowess to the President, a trend also found in the "Chicago" study.) In addition, the third-grade Project Beacon child sees both the President and the policeman as having less coercive power and less knowledge.

The students' judgment of the fairness of laws is shown in Figure 5. The greater realism toward political authority figures among second and third grade Project Beacon students is also evident in their responses to this item. Among children at both grade levels, more negative perceptions are made by black Project Beacon youngsters, than by the others, about the fairness of laws.

Greater realism by Project Beacon students concerning political authority figures and laws may well derive from a more positive concept of the self. The political efficacy scores of Project Beacon children also seem to support this relationship. As seen in Figure 6, the mean efficacy scores for Project Beacon third graders are higher than for third graders without the special curriculum.

An examination of responses by third graders to the individual items on the efficacy scale indicates that those items which seem to tap a sense of internal self-confidence (whether family or citizens have a say in government) elicit higher mean scores from the Project Beacon children, while those which tap a sense of confidence in external response (what the government will do for people) elicit lower means scores, in comparison with third graders not in Project Beacon. Hence, political efficacy, especially in the dimension relating to internal control, does appear to be related to personal efficacy. Moreover these findings of lower levels of confidence in the responses of authority figures would seem to be consistent with our earlier findings of less idealism among Project Beacon children.

Overall then, our examination of political efficacy, as well as the analysis of attitudes, supports the proposition that curriculum can affect the socialization of minority group elementary schoolchildren's attitudes toward authority. In Project Beacon, an upgrading of the black child's self-concept appears to result in less idealism toward political figures and laws, coupled with a increased sense of

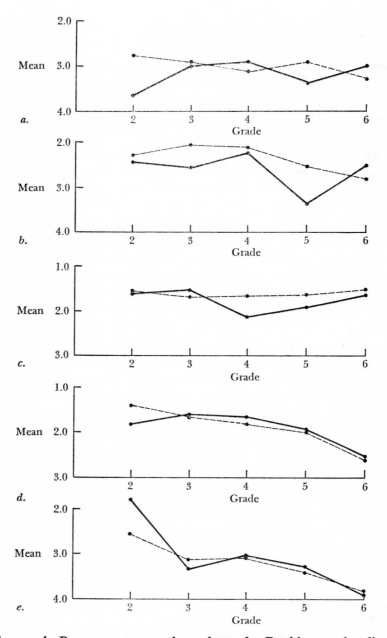

FIGURE 4. Responses to questions about the President and police-men. Solid line indicates those in Project Beacon; dashed line indi-cates those not in Project Beacon. *a.* President's coercive ability. *b.* President's knowledge. *c.* President makes big decisions. *d.* President's helpfulness. *e.* President your favorite. *f.* Policeman's coercive ability. *g.* Policeman's knowledge. *h.* Policeman makes big decisions. *i.* Policeman's helpfulness. *j.* Policeman your favorite. Numbers of

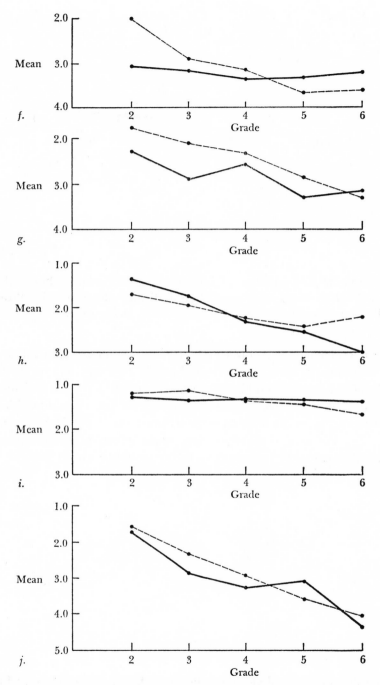

cases (these vary slightly between graphs because of missing data):
Project Beacon children—36, 50, 26, 26, 20; children not in Project
Beacon—74, 76, 67, 84, 85.

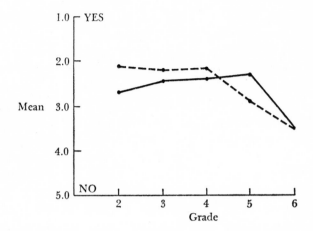

FIGURE 5. Responses to "all laws are fair." Solid line indicates those in Project Beacon; dashed line indicates those not in Project Beacon. Numbers of cases are the same as in Figure 4.

self-confidence as a citizen. In the broader context of relative socialization patterns of black and white children, it appears that Project Beacon intensifies the negative trend of the parallel model with respect to political authority figures but retards or diminishes it with regard to the internal control dimension of political efficacy.

We now consider whether these effects of Project Beacon last beyond direct exposure to the curriculum. To do this, we ex-

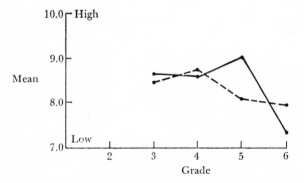

FIGURE 6. Political efficacy scale. Solid line indicates those in Project Beacon; dashed line indicates those not in Project Beacon. Numbers of cases are the same as in Figure 4.

amine the attitudes of black fourth, fifth, and sixth grade respondents who were in Project Beacon classes during kindergarten through third grade, in comparison with those who were not. Figure 4 shows that Project Beacon fourth graders express diminishing realism toward political authority figures. In only one instance (*h*) do former Project Beacon students become more realistic than other students, whereas they become less realistic in four cases (*a, c, e, i*). Where they remain more realistic than students who have not been in Project Beacon, the differences are reduced (*b, g, j.*) In the remaining cases, as well as in perceptions of laws (Figure 5), no change is observed in which group is more realistic.

The attitudes of former Project Beacon fifth and sixth graders, in comparison with their peers, seem to reinforce the trend in attitudes toward political authority and laws which we notice starting with fourth graders. Fourth grade appears to mark the beginning of a reversal in the trend toward realism by Project Beacon students. At the fourth grade level former Project Beacon students were more realistic on exactly half of the ten items about authority figures (*b, f, g, h, j*), as well as in their view of laws. Among fifth grade respondents we observe more realistic attitudes among former Project Beacon students on only four of the eleven items, counting the laws (*a, b, g, h*). By sixth grade this tendency is strengthened, as former Project Beacon students are more realistic on only three items (*e, h, j*).

The responses of sixth grade former Project Beacon children toward the policeman are particularly interesting, for they indicate that while the policeman is not regarded as a personal favorite of the child, his coercive ability and his knowledge are regarded with respect. These attitudes toward the policeman stand in sharp contrast to those of the other fifth and sixth graders and of black children in later grades. Since we do not have data to examine the effects of Project Beacon beyond the sixth grade, we cannot project with confidence whether positive attitudes would continue to grow toward political authority figures among former Project Beacon students.

Our data on political efficacy of fourth through sixth graders (Figure 6) makes us cautious about assuming that Project Beacon has long-term effects on political attitudes. The political efficacy levels of former Project Beacon students are lower at fourth and sixth grade than those of students not previously in the program. And although fifth grade former Project Beacon students show a high political efficacy score, both of the items that tap internal confidence are lower both for fifth and sixth graders who were in Project Beacon. Hence, the goal of improved self-concept of the disadvantaged child does not seem to have a consistent long-term effect of engendering improved political efficacy.

Direct exposure to the Project Beacon curriculum seems to induce realism about political authority figures and laws and a heightened sense of political efficacy among children. But almost immediately afterward, the realities of being a black citizen in a political system dominated by whites seem to impair the sense of political effectiveness found among children during their direct participation in the curriculum. On the other hand, as efficacy declines, idealism about authority figures increases. We return to these seemingly conflicting developments—that as idealism increases efficacy declines, and vice versa—in the conclusion.

Effect of Teacher's Race

The teacher's race might be expected to cause children to be more, or less, realistic and politically efficacious. Black teachers' attitudes might be more realistic or cynical than white teachers' attitudes. (Our sample of black teachers suggests this is so, although our data is not complete enough to be conclusive.) Thus to the extent that teachers' attitudes are expressed in class and influence students' views, it seems likely that children with black teachers would have more realistic attitudes than children in the same grade but with white teachers.

In addition to expressed attitudes, the race of the teacher may have an impact in terms of example. It may be important for young black children to have black teachers (as well as adults in other capacities) to serve as examples of goals to which they can aspire. The black child's self-esteem or ego strength may then increase, and spill over into political attitudes, increasing political efficacy in particular.

To test this hypothesis, we made comparisons between 122 black children with six black teachers versus 403 black students with twenty-one white teachers in the second, third, fourth, sixth, and seventh grades. The remaining grades have no black teachers. The results (not shown) indicate no consistent pattern throughout all the grades. In grades two through four, children with black teachers have, if anything, more naive or benevolent attitudes toward political authority figures and about laws than do students with white teachers. These attitudes shift somewhere between fourth and sixth grades, and by the sixth and seventh grades, children with black teachers are somewhat more realistic; but even then the difference is not very large. Thus, having a black teacher in the early grades does not in itself alter the typically benevolent views of young children. By sixth grade, the significance of the teacher's race may be beginning to make itself felt, but if so, it is only a weak tendency in our data.

Political efficacy levels differ from attitude development only to the extent that the teacher's race may have an impact slightly earlier. Third graders with black teachers were more efficacious—by a wide margin—than those with white teachers. But the decline of efficacy is particularly steep among subsequent grades with black teachers; fourth, sixth, and seventh graders with black teachers have consistently lower levels of efficacy than those with white teachers.

Overall, it seems as if the teacher's race is not an important factor in the development of political attitudes in the earliest grades. The instructor's race may be critical in other respects and may help determine political attitudes in later grades. But in the elementary school years, and especially the early grades, the race of the teacher seems not to detract from the relatively benign views of authority figures, of laws, and of the efficacy of political activity.

Conclusion

Perhaps the most important finding of our study is that the Project Beacon curriculum affects black students' feelings of political efficacy—but only while they are in these special classes. This suggests that specially designed long-term curricula, coupled with real changes in the political system allowing for and encouraging greater participation by blacks, might create more positive feelings of effectiveness on the part of minority group children. This suggestion supports the recommendation of long-term programs in an evaluation of the Head Start program (Westinghouse Learning Corporation, 1969) which concluded that short-term projects—especially summer programs—had no lasting effects on children.

But Project Beacon did not create artificially benign, naive views of authority in children—they saw authority more realistically and perceived more accurately the frequent unfairness of laws. Ironically, then, our results suggest that a curriculum can have a noteworthy effect on minority group children but that it does so by instilling in them a more realistic, and not necessarily more positive, appraisal of the American political system. We conclude that those who best understand the nature of the American political system can most effectively participate in altering it.

VI

Becoming Critical
About Politics

ROBERTA S. SIGEL, MARILYN BROOKES

As children mature they change their interpretations of the political world, its institutions, and its officials. They also become more adept at handling abstract political principles—such as liberty or justice— and understanding complex political processes. The precise nature of these changes is well-documented in the recent political socialization literature (Greenstein, 1965a; Hess and Torney, 1967; Easton and Dennis, 1969). Most of this literature, however, all but ignores the political events which the child witnesses as he passes from grade to grade and which might account for the observed changes in his opinions and attitudes. Such research focuses on changes associated with progression in school and attributes them to growing cognitive maturity as though the child grows and develops oblivious of the political world or as though the political world is static (Easton and Dennis, 1969, pp. 36–38). Information on the impact of historical events on youth's political thinking and on the interaction of the changing individual with the changing system thus is very sparse (but see Sears and McConahy, 1970; Sigel, 1965b).

In addition, most of the studies, especially the earlier ones, focus on the child's generalized affect for the system per se or for the system as represented by its prominent officials and institutions. They inquire into the depth and extensiveness of children's attachment to the system (what David Easton [1963], calls *diffuse support*), but they pay little attention to the child's evaluation and support of current policies, practices, and officials (Easton's *specific support*). Generalized affect is found to be high across all age groups and all youthful populations and to appear early in life, long before substantive information is acquired (but see Greenberg, 1970a, 1970b; Hirsch, 1971). (See also Chapters Three, Four, and Five.) Although naive idealization, so characteristic of the young child, drops with age and gives way to increased realism, confidence in the competence of government and its officials, as contrasted with the competence of ordinary people, increases (Hess and Torney, 1967; Easton and Dennis, 1969).

These findings for children are very similar to those for adults. Support for and pride in the system of the United States are high and widely distributed (Almond and Verba, 1963). But among adults this positive attitude toward the system coexists wth low levels of support for its officials and policies, as well as low esteem for politicians in general (Mitchell, 1959). It is as though the American system can draw from a large reservoir of goodwill maintained by the American public, whatever their immediate frustrations might be. This capacity for maintaining high affect for the system in spite of great disappointment in politics and politicians is attributed in part to the success of political socialization. Acquired early in life, affect for the system persists and constitutes a basic commitment to the system and the nation, which is not easily shaken by political events. Just how long diffuse support can remain high in the presence of low specific support is a question (recently raised in connection with the Watergate Affair) for which political science has as yet found no answer.

We think that children, like adults, are not insulated from historical changes and, in spite of their high system affect, their views of politics as well as their interest in it are affected by the events on the political scene. One of us made a tentative confirmation of this assumption in a previous study which showed that children were able to distinguish between the political system and the incumbent administration, between the President and the presidency. After the assassination of President Kennedy, for example, grief was significantly more intense among youngsters who thought of themselves as Democrats than among those who thought of themselves as Republicans (Sigel, 1965b). Grief, moreover, was related to specific policies associated with President Kennedy (Sigel, 1968). The assassination of a young and popular president is an event of a highly unusual and intensely traumatic nature (Greenstein, 1965b) and consequently might have accounted for students' great awareness of Kennedy's programs and policies. But we find it inconceivable that children would be impervious to the political events around them even in less dramatic times. Instead we venture a guess that children's political orientations are partially determined by events of the day and partially by changes in their cognitive development. If our guess is correct, then it is imperative that political attitudes and levels of support be examined within the context of the historical period in which they occur and not only on the basis of the chronological age of the child.

The Study

A study of children from our stated perspective cannot be done by a simple cross-sectional investigation nor by an exclusively longitudinal one. Cross-sectional analyses of the type customarily employed in political socialization research are one-shot affairs during which the investigator interviews children of different ages (usually different grades) and attributes the differences observed among grades to age-determined differences in cognitive and emotional development. A more direct way of observing development is the longitudinal study. There the investigator follows the same child over a period of years in order to observe his or her individual growth. This design would, therefore, be well-suited to our study if we were interested exclusively in studying the development of political cognition, for example, children's ability to handle abstract concepts such as justice or democracy, but it does not readily permit us to determine whether observed changes are due to maturation or to dramatic events and other changes in the political environment which the child has witnessed.

We add to the longitudinal analysis a way of assessing the impact of political events on children's thought processes and attitudes; we compare the same grade level at different points in time as well as the same individual child in different grade levels or different points of time. We thus combine the longitudinal design with a grade-across-time design. An example of such a combination study would be one which combined (1) a comparison of sixth graders at the time of America's entry into World War II with a similar group of youngsters who were in the sixth grade five years later, and (2) a comparison of the attitudes of each group of children with their own attitudes five years later. The standard longitudinal analysis is thus expanded to yield both maturational and historical information on children's political orientations.

While the advantages of a combination grade-across-time and longitudinal analysis are evident, it still is not easy to determine accurately the reasons for changes nor will it be easy to ascertain which contributes more to the magnitude of observed changes—maturation or historical events. Individual maturation and historical context probably interact with each other to affect change, so all we can do is to attempt to make some plausible inferences about the role played by historical events. These are distinctly *inferences,* however; no evidence can be gathered to offer proof positive about the differential contribution made by maturation and time events. Merelman (1971, p. 1045) well describes this dilemma: "men are social creatures, hence, environmental forces constantly interfere with and contaminate genetic maturation. It is, therefore, impossible to determine the true extent to which such maturation regulates . . . thought. Only if we could observe wholly uncontaminated subjects as they age would such an estimation become possible."

Our study was begun in the spring of 1966 in a middle-sized semisuburban, semiindustrial city near Detroit. In 1966 124 youths in grades four, six, and eight were personally interviewed: 54 percent came from middle-class and the rest from working-class homes; 23 percent were black. In the spring of 1968 we reinterviewed all but seventeen of the same young people—they all were now in grades six, eight, and ten. The seventeen we failed to reach were not school dropouts but had moved to other communities. Students were chosen randomly from the class lists, but the schools were selected adequately to represent the community's racial and economic groups. (We intended to return to the schools at repeated two-year intervals but had to abandon this plan when a sensitive political situation developed in the school district.)

In the two-year interval between our first and second visit, some dramatic and unhappy events had occurred in American history. This was clearly reflected in students' assessment. Pondering in 1968 on the "two most important events that have happened in the United States during the last two years," students thought almost exclusively of political events and of tragic ones at that. (All but 10 percent responded to the question; of the remaining 90 percent, only one student answered the question in nonpolitical terms.)' Moreover, they thought only of events which in their minds had affected the polity adversely, such as the war in Vietnam, the Detroit race riot, and the assassination of Martin Luther King, Jr. We thus begin our investigation confident in the knowledge that children have some awareness of current political events and that, in this case, they took a dim view of those events. For purposes of research, we had an ideal setting for testing our theoretical framework because our investigation spanned a period of important and dramatic political changes.

If, as we expected, children are sensitive to political events, they are likely to react to government in certain predictable ways. For example, since they seemed to think the times were bad in 1968, we would anticipate that they would be more critical of the adminstration, its policies, and performance—specific support should drop in 1968. Affect, on the other hand, is likely to be more stable and enduring and responsive to maturation rather than historical changes. We expect growth in knowledge and comprehension of the political process to relate to chronological age, because it is a function of cognitive development. We thus entertain the possibility of observing two types of change in political outlook: change largely due to age or genetic maturation (affect and cognition) and change largely due to ongoing political developments. We expect evaluations of governmental performance to be most affected by these changes. While we attempt to observe both types of change, we focus particularly on change due to political events.

Moreover, those who react to the political world are likely

to reflect the characteristics of their adult counterparts. Thus we anticipate that those who become more interested and critically oriented toward government will be more from middle-class than working-class backgrounds and more males than females.

Findings

Changes. To test for changes in diffuse support we asked students to evaluate government in terms of helpfulness and benevolence. The statements were drawn from the Hess and Torney schedule (1967). One statement dealt with the government's willingness to be helpful to the child, and the second statement asserted that "what goes on in government is all for the best." (A third statement—"all laws are fair"—was used, but is not included in our discussion, because the two possible answers seemed unsuitable for the upper grades. A similar trend occurs in response to this question, however.)

In general the findings conform to our predictions (see Table 1). Affect for government is positive; majorities of all the students, not just the youngest ones, think that government wants to help and generally performs well (what goes on in government is all for the best). Affect does drop somewhat with age, which supports the demonstrations of political socialization literature that affect is positive but does decrease with age. (We attribute the declining positiveness of affect to the simplistic wording also, which makes agreement difficult for older and more sophisticated youth.) This latter finding generally has been interpreted as pointing to the impact of maturation: greater maturity increases individual capacity for objectivity, which in turn decreases the tendency to idealize government.

The across-the-grade comparison for 1966 and 1968 shows no consistent tendency for more negative evaluations in 1968 than in 1966, but the proportion of don't-know responses increases slightly. Perhaps some students were not yet ready to condemn government but could no longer laud it and hence sought refuge in don't-know responses.

We posed an array of questions dealing with pupils' knowledge of United States institutions and comprehension of democracy

Table 1.

AFFECT FOR THE SYSTEM

"THINK OF THE GOVERNMENT AS IT REALLY IS."	Grade	1966	1968
Would usually want to help me.	4	69%	
(Collapses "always,"	6	57	69%
"almost always," and	8	58	51
"usually" responses)	10		51
Would not usually want to help.	4	31	
(Collapses "sometimes,"	6	44	32
"not usually," and	8	42	49
"seldom" responses)	10		48

"WHAT GOES ON IN GOVERNMENT IS ALL FOR THE BEST."			
Yes (Collapses "yes"	4	83%	
and "yes, but not sure"	6	72	77%
responses)	8	75	63
	10		40
No (Collapses "no"	4	14	
and "no, but not sure"	6	25	15
responses)	8	24	29
	10		45
Don't know	4	3	
	6	3	9
	8	0	9
	10		16
		$N = 124$[a]	$N = 107$

[a] By grade, 41, 41, 42 in 1966 for fourth, sixth, and eighth graders, respectively, and 35, 35, 37 in 1968.

and its processes. For illustrative purposes we show in Table 2 the answers to a question that is replicated from the "Chicago" study (Hess and Torney, 1967). Knowledge of democracy and of the practices or rights associated with it improved considerably with age, while don't-know responses dropped. The distributions of answers are similar for the two periods. Hess and Torney noted similar patterns and distributions, thus further corroborating that the acquisition of knowledge about the system is largely age-related—a function of cognitive development—and not much affected by the times. Other questions showed the same trend.

Table 2.

KNOWLEDGE

"IS A DEMOCRACY WHERE THE PEOPLE RULE?"	Grade	1966	1968
Yes	4	17%	
	6	44	37%
	8	67	69
	10		81
No	4	19	
	6	25	35
	8	30	17
	10		8
Don't know	4	64	
	6	31	27
	8	3	14
	10		11

Historical time does, however, play a part in students' willingness to evaluate government performance critically. It would be wrong to say that 1968 was the year when these students evaluated government negatively. It is more accurate to say they tend to be more critical, which, in turn, results in smaller margins of approval for government actions and greater willingness to pass negative judgments. In some cases the margin of change is striking, even if youth remained essentially approving. Equally significant is the steep rise in don't-know responses. As in the set of questions dealing with general affect, this pattern indicates that the group which was highly laudatory in 1966 found itself in considerable quandary about passing a positive judgment in 1968.

To reach this assessment, we used two different approaches. The first approach asks the young people to judge the responsiveness to the public of the government in general and the President in particular. (See Table 3.) The second approach asks them to judge the beneficial or harmful effect government has on them and their families and asks them to name the services or policies which have this effect. (See Table 4.) The last question is, therefore, more closely tied to the current historical context than any of the others are.

In the area of responsiveness, we expected that as the young people grew older they would doubt that the government or the President always responds to the requests and inquiries of all citizens or gives equal weight to all, regardless of kind and source. This indeed is the pattern both for 1966 and 1968 on most of the questions, except for the last one shown in Table 3. The drop from grade to grade in both periods is large; for example, in 1966, 63 percent of the fourth graders but only 47 percent of the eighth graders think the President pays much attention to letters. The same trend prevails in 1968. Older children are more equivocal about the government's likelihood of always being responsive to the public. But in 1968, more than just chronological age seems to be involved. Each age group in 1968 tends to be less sure of governmental responsiveness than the group of that grade was in 1966. For example, in 1966, 47 percent of the eighth graders were sure the President pays much attention to letters he receives; in 1968, 35 percent of the eighth graders thought so. In 1966, 68 percent of the sixth graders were sure the government did what the people asked it to do; 39 percent of them thought so in 1968. The willingness to entertain the idea that government is nonresponsive, therefore, seems to have been affected both by maturation and the tenor of the times. Finally, it must also be observed that uncertainty about government responsiveness (as expressed in the responses "don't know" and "sometimes") was larger in 1968, further suggesting that the times left their mark on student judgments.

Student evaluations of governmental performance also suggest that they were affected by current events. Students' criticism of government increased most noticeably in 1968. Since this willingness extends to all grades, we attribute it to changes in the events of the time. Students were far less likely in 1968 to reject outright the idea that the government is doing something which "is bad for you and your family." In 1966, 79 percent of the eighth graders

Table 3.

GOVERNMENTAL RESPONSIVENESS

"DOES THE PRESIDENT PAY MUCH ATTENTION TO LETTERS HE RECEIVES?"	Grade	1966	1968
Yes (collapses all affirmative responses)	4	63%	
	6	51	45%
	8	47	35
	10		24
Depends on the letter or letter writer	4	20	
	6	37	6
	8	17	3
	10		17
No (collapses all negative responses)	4	15	
	6	12	35
	8	35	44
	10		47
Don't know	4	2	
	6	0	14
	8	0	20
	10		14

Now LET'S MAKE BELIEVE AGAIN. *"One day the president has two letters on his desk— one from a worker on the assembly line of a big factory and another from the president of this factory. Would he pay the same amount of attention to both?"*	Grade	1966	1968
Yes (collapses all affirmative responses)	4	51%	
	6	54	42%
	8	38	28
	10		29
Depends on the letter	4	15	
	6	5	0
	8	5	0
	10		8
No (collapses all negative responses)	4	34	
	6	39	45
	8	52	47
	10		55
Don't know	4	0	
	6	2	14
	8	5	25
	10		8

Table 3. (Contd.)

GOVERNMENTAL RESPONSIVENESS

"DOES THE GOVERNMENT ALWAYS TRY TO DO WHAT THE PEOPLE ASK IT TO DO?"	*Grade*	*1966*	*1968*
Yes (collapses all affirmative responses)	4	59%	
	6	68	39%
	8	64	40
	10		34
Sometimes	4	0	
	6	0	47
	8	0	28
	10		37
No (collapses all negative responses)	4	39	
	6	29	8
	8	31	26
	10		26
Don't know	4	2	
	6	2	6
	8	5	5
	10		3

had rejected that notion; by 1968, eighth-grade rejection dropped to 41 percent. Fewer students thought the government was doing things helpful to them. (Several thought the government was remiss in maintaining law and order.) In 1968, far more students saw great need for the government to come to their aid than in 1966, when 58 percent of the sixth graders saw no need for government help for themselves or their families; by 1968 only 25 percent thought this help was not needed. Uncertainty about the quality of government performance increased. The proportion of don't-know responses rose quite sharply in almost every case. (See Table 4.) (It would be erroneous to attribute the increased critical tendency to the incumbency of President Johnson, as the community was heavily Democratic and interviews revealed little alienation from the President.)

What Tables 3 and 4 demonstrate is the extent to which time affects even relatively young people and exaggerates or distorts clear-cut developmental trends. Our observations leave little doubt that the events which occurred between 1966 and 1968 influenced many young people to be far more critical of government, its re-

Table 4.

GOVERNMENT PERFORMANCE

"DOES GOVERNMENT DO ANYTHING THAT IS HELPFUL TO YOU OR YOUR FAMILY?"	*Grade*	*1966*	*1968*
Yes (no specific reason)	4	20%	
	6	23	14%
	8	16	9
	10		11
Yes (miscellaneous political issues)	4	54	
	6	67	51
	8	54	37
	10		38
Yes, personal help only	4	3	
	6	0	3
	8	0	3
	10		0
No	4	9	
	6	3	6
	8	18	6
	10		11
Don't know	4	14	
	6	9	26
	8	12	44
	10		41

"IS THE GOVERNMENT DOING ANYTHING WHICH YOU FEEL IS BAD FOR YOU OR YOUR FAMILY?"	*Grade*	*1966*	*1968*
No	4	83%	
	6	77	54%
	8	79	41
	10		22
Yes (miscellaneous policies)	4	12	
	6	20	21
	8	16	24
	10		38
Don't know	4	6	
	6	3	23
	8	5	35
	10		38

Table 4. (*Contd.*)

GOVERNMENT PERFORMANCE

"WOULD YOU LIKE THE GOVERNMENT TO DO SOMETHING FOR YOU THAT IT ISN'T DOING NOW?"	*Grade*	*1966*	*1968*
No	4	56%	
	6	58	25%
	8	70	29
	10		29
Yes (miscellaneous)	4	33	
	6	30	68
	8	28	51
	10		34
Don't know	4	12	
	6	12	7
	8	3	20
	10		37

sponsiveness, and its performance than they had been in 1966. Even though general affect for the system remained high, support for its performance had begun to erode. While specific support remained substantial in many instances even in 1968, the tendency toward increased cynicism is clearly visible.

It is not surprising to find that as children become more critical of government actions, they also show greater interest in politics. To be critical of government and to specify what government should or should not do is in itself an indication of political interest. As a rule, Americans portray but scant concern for politics (although they think good citizens should be interested in it). Young people, especially the school-age population, show even lower levels of interest. Between 1966 and 1968, however, this changed dramatically. We had expected interest to go up with age. Though this expectation is only partly confirmed, the remarkable fact about 1968 is that interest is high for *all* age groups. At each grade level the 1968 youngsters profess more interest than the students in that grade did in 1966. In 1966 41 percent of the sixth graders talked politics with friends; 66 percent did so in 1968. In 1966 58 percent asked their families questions about politics; in 1968 83 percent did so. These are truly great differences; they amount to an increase of about 50 percent in political talk and curiosity. Nor was such talk restricted narrowly to the coming elections or the draft. Instead it ranged widely and focused on specific concerns about such topics as the war in Vietnam, racial disturbances, problems of law and order, and the like. Compared to 1966 this group had become politicized in a remarkably short time.

Further corroboration for our assertion that we were witnessing politicization can be drawn from Table 5, which shows that political leaders—in contrast to entertainers, athletes, and artists—have become the famous Americans these youngsters admire. Over three-quarters (77 percent) of the sixth graders chose political leaders as objects of admiration in 1968, in contrast with 46 percent in 1966. Given the generally low esteem in which politicians are held in the United States, this great admiration for political leaders seems almost an about-face and may be because of the popularity of certain leaders (the ones most frequently mentioned were John F. Kennedy, Robert Kennedy, Martin Luther King, Jr., and former President Eisenhower)'.

Among adults, talking politics did not increase during the two-year interval. Similar data are available for teachers and class instruction. And yet young people talked more politics with their peers. Clearly then the inspiration for such increased politicization does not come from family or school per se. We hold that it comes from changes in the political climate of the time.

Table 6 further corroborates this. Students in 1968 express far less willingness to accept bad times patiently and insist more that they must "get the government to do something" than students in 1966 did. Based on other information from our interviews, we know that "do something" only rarely involves protest activities; mainly it involves working through the system fairly forcefully, by joining organizations, broadening publicity, and applying other means of pressure. Support for the passive or uninterested citizen appears to have dropped markedly by 1968.

We conclude that some aspects of political thinking seem to be age-related (such as affect and knowledge) and others seem to be related to the nature of the political times (such as evaluations of governmental performance). Sensitivity to political change seems to have the effect of accelerating or intensifying normal maturational

Table 5.
POLITICAL INTEREST

"Do You and Your Friends Ever Talk About Politics, Voting, and Things Like That?"	Grade	1966	1968
Yes	4	34%	
	6	41	66%
	8	41	57
	10		73
No	4	66	
	6	59	34
	8	59	43
	10		27

"Do You Hear Anyone in Your Family Talk About Politics, Voting, and Things Like That?"	Grade	1966	1968
Yes	4	86%	
	6	85	89%
	8	86	89
	10		92
No	4	14	
	6	15	11
	8	14	11
	10		8

"Do You Ever Ask Them Questions About It?"	Grade	1966	1968
Yes	4	64%	
	6	58	83%
	8	54	83
	10		71
No	4	33	
	6	42	17
	8	45	17
	10		30

Please Name Two Famous Americans Whom You Admire a Lot."	Grade	1966	1968
Political leaders	4	23%	
	6	46	77%
	8	57	66
	10		70

Table 5. (Contd.)

POLITICAL INTEREST

Historical leaders	4	20	
	6	17	20
	8	5	20
	10		8
Nonpolitical leaders	4	34	
	6	14	3
	8	24	3
	10		14
Miscellaneous combinations	4	6	
	6	3	0
	8	3	3
	10		0
Don't know	4	17	
	6	20	0
	8	11	9
	10		8

changes in some instances (as in the case of political interest). Whatever the direction of the change, the data show that changes in youth's political orientations are not random but systematic and seem appropriate for the changes observed in the political environment. This lends support to our initial comment that historical time is an important socializer which should be incorporated into our conception of agents of political influence.

Changers. Given the documented trend toward decreased specific support, what about the students whose orientations are altered by the force of political events? Do the combined forces of maturation and historical events operate differently and with different results among different groups in our population? In short, we ask what *types* of students are likely to respond to current politics? To discover their characteristics, we isolated the young people in our sample who, in 1966, gave positive evaluations of government performance and responsiveness, but who, in 1968, had become critical or negative. (Since we are focusing on those who are reacting to political events, we isolate and analyze them instead of comparing variations between those who answered consistently and those who changed their viewpoints.)

We concentrate on evaluations of government performance

Table 6.

ROLE OF THE CITIZEN

"SUPPOSE *People were having a hard time finding places to live because the government tore down a lot of houses to build highways and schools. What should a good citizen do?"*	*Grade*	*1966*	*1968*
Be patient and take the good with the bad	4	12%	
	6	9	11%
	8	24	11
	10		5
Hope things will get better soon	4	20	
	6	18	17
	8	8	0
	10		5
Get the government to do something	4	68	
	6	73	71
	8	68	89
	10		89

and responsiveness and omit an analysis of general system affect, because general affect remains relatively stable over time. In addition, we analyze levels of interest in politics. We assume that increased interest and cynicism are likely to be concentrated in the same types of children.

The proportion of new critics and the newly interested varies somewhat from item to item but ranges from 18 to 40 percent—an uncommonly large group. Some of this switch is due to age, no doubt, because in 1966 and 1968 older children were more critical than the younger groups. But the proportion of switchers is well beyond the observed change between age groups, indicating that the source of increased cynicism and interest is more than the increased sophistication of maturation.

We are able to describe the composition of the group of newly estranged students along social background and sex lines, but we are not able to analyze it along racial lines because such a small number of blacks are classified as new critics. They had been critical in 1966 already, and by 1968 white orientations had become similar to those previously held by blacks; both were relatively low in specific support. About the only marked difference between evaluations of whites and blacks in 1968 concerns the content of demand input: blacks want the government to do something about civil rights; whites want the government to do something about the war, as well as about civil rights.

Table 7 shows the new critics' evaluations of governmental responsiveness and performance. On the first two items there are no class-evident differences; feelings of political efficacy are similar in both groups. On the third item, class-related differences begin to appear among the changers. More of the critics who think that government does *not* do what the people ask are middle class. The differences between the classes become clearer in relation to government performance. The changers are fairly evenly divided between middle- and working-class children, but the middle-class youngsters are more often able to designate just what they think the deficiencies in government are. The two groups also varied in the target of their discontent. Middle-class youths listed the type of complaints enumciated by the student movement of the period—the war, racial discrimination, and poverty; working-class students most frequently voiced complaints along more traditional lines, such as high taxes and unduly lax maintenance of law and order. In this respect they resemble their working-class parents more than they resemble their middle-class peers.

Students of middle-class backgrounds also constitute a larger proportion of those exhibiting increased interest in politics, and they exhibit it in a variety of ways. Of those talking politics with friends for the first time, 73 percent are from middle-class homes; barely a quarter of all new political discussants are of working-class background. Equal numbers from both classes report asking political questions of their families, but most of those who cite admiring political figures come from the middle class (62 percent of the new critics). This seems logical: American political leaders stem almost without fail from the middle class (Matthews, 1954). Middle-class youth, by exhibiting greater political awareness in response to political events, reflect the political mores of middle-class adults, who are also more politicized than working-class adults.

Greater middle-class response to the political world, even in youth, can be documented still further by the middle-class new

Table 7.

NEW CRITICS' EVALUATION OF GOVERNMENT,
BY FAMILY STATUS

Item Response	Family Occupational Status	
(1968 negative, from 1966 positive)	Working Class	Middle Class
GOVERNMENT RESPONSIVENESS		
1. The President does *not* pay attention to letters he receives. ($N = 33$)	49%	51%
2. The President would *not* pay equal attention to letters from the president of a corporation and from a factory worker. ($N = 27$)	54	46
3. Government does *not* try to do what the people ask. ($N = 39$)	41	59
GOVERNMENT PERFORMANCE		
4. (Decrease in) Government is doing something helpful to me or my family. ($N = 23$)	43	57
5. Government is doing *something bad* to me or my family.[a]		
Specific policy. ($N = 11$)	27	73
Don't know or unsure. ($N = 22$)	58	42
6. Government *should do* something it isn't.		
Named specific policy. ($N = 15$)	40	60
Don't know or unsure. ($N = 19$)	63	37

[a] Items 5 and 6 indicate the propensities of students who had not in 1966 named either things the government was doing which were bad or things the government should be doing to change their assessments by 1968. In other words, significant numbers in 1968 modified their previous acceptance of government as it existed to show either (1) specific areas they thought government was acting poorly in, or (2) a new uncertainty (evidenced in their 1968 "don't know" or "unsure" responses) about government performance.

critics being least willing to stand idly by when feeling politically aggrieved and most willing to make demands on government; they constitute 55 percent of the newly interested. This too is suggested by adult behavior; the voting literature has consistently shown that middle-class adults participate more than working-class adults in almost all aspects of politics (Campbell and others, 1960). Finding this pattern is particularly interesting to us because Litt (1963) demonstrates that middle-class schools encourage pupils to become participatory, while blue-collar schools encourage them to become conforming. In our population, however, two-thirds attended the same school in 1968, and yet the differences among the newly interested still show the middle-class students to be more participatory. What appeared to Litt to be differences caused by school context and instruction, therefore, might well be traced to differences in receptivity among children with different class backgrounds, middle-class children becoming more politicized in their homes.

In summary, growing dissatisfaction with governmental policies—or at least the ability or willingness to articulate it or both—and increased political interest seem to be much more characteristic of middle-class than of blue-collar youths. Middle-class youths seem especially better able to pinpoint just what caused them to become so critical in 1968. Their list of complaints closely resembles that of their middle-class elders rather than that of their working-class peers. Class distinctions also prevail behaviorally. The great political talkers, the potential participants, are more likely to be middle than working class. Some of the abiding cleavages in United States political life apparently extend down to youth as well.

Differences associated with sex are even more pronounced among the new critics than are differences between social classes. (See Table 8.) In some instances the differences are dramatic. Where as girls outnumber boys in the sample, boys constitute the bulk of the new critics. Girls are far more inclined than boys to maintain positive orientations toward both government in general and policy in particular, in spite of the fact that both have gone through the same school experience within the same political climate. It is probably not hyperbolic to suggest that girls are far more willing to let the political world—however turbulent and proximate it may be—swirl

Table 8.

NEW CRITICS' EVALUATION OF GOVERNMENT, BY SEX

Item Response

(1968 negative,
from 1966 positive)

GOVERNMENT RESPONSIVENESS	*Males*	*Females*
1. The President does *not* pay attention to letters he receives. (N = 33)	69%	31%
2. The President would *not* pay equal attention to letters from the president of a corporation and from a factory worker. (N = 27)	71	29
3. Government does *not* try to do what the people ask. (N = 39)	57	43
GOVERNMENT PERFORMANCE		
4. (Decrease in) Government is doing something helpful to me or my family. (N = 23)	69	31
5. Government is doing *something bad* to me or my family.		
Named specific policy. (N = 11)	54	46
Don't know or unsure. (N = 22)	45	55
6. Government *should do* something it isn't.		
Named specific policy. (N = 15)	67	33
Don't know or unsure. (N = 19)	42	58

around them without attempting to adjust their orientations accordingly.

Given the fact that girls are less numerous in the group of new critics, it comes as no surprise that they are also less numerous in the group of children whose political interest rose steeply in 1968. Of the youngsters reporting increases in political discussion 69 percent are male, and among those who would prod the government into action, 60 percent are male. Now that several years have passed and women's liberation is familiar, we wonder if girls would still profess as unhesitatingly and unblushingly to political lethargy as they did in 1968. Nothing is perhaps as dramatic as the apparent insulation of these girls from the tragic events which took place not only in the nation but right at their own doorsteps.

Conclusions

The evidence considered in this analysis leads us to conclude that the great political affect of youth seems to be able to withstand their considerable political frustration. Students' confidence in officials and their policies, on the other hand, seems to be heavily dependent on the quality of the government's performance. During the period of our study, political events provoked increasingly negative evaluations from students across all grades. The reactions observed among these young people, resembled those of adults and adolescents across the nation. In both groups, respect for governmental performance dropped from an early high to increasingly more negative evaluations (Bachman and Van Duinen, 1971; Jennings and Niemi, 1973; Sigel, 1974, chap. 5).

We hope to have demonstrated two noteworthy patterns. First, children are influenced by the political tenor of the time in that they reorient their levels of confidence in the governing administration according to how that administration appears to be coping with critical events. Similarly, their interest in politics is significantly affected by political events. A combined longitudinal and grade-across-time analysis shows that the impact of the political environment on young people's attitudes joins with normal maturation in the development of increased sophisticated political orientations in youth. Second, for children as well as adults, positive affect for the system can coexist with negative evaluations of government performance. Children at the age levels studied make meaningful distinctions between the ongoing system and its officials at a given point in time.

The analytical frame we use also allows us to assess the areas where political events exert influence most dramatically. Increasing disapproval in response to the events of the time was registered by male students and concentrated in the middle class. The groups which most consistently altered their orientations from positive to negative in the two-year period were also those most critical of and interested in the crucial issues of the day—the war in Vietnam, racial strife, and the political assassinations—leading us to suggest that these youths operate with more political constraints than we had heretofore suspected. Increases in political interest followed much the same pattern, being concentrated more in the middle class and among males. Whereas change in political attitudes has been observed to be random and amount to "nonattitudes" (Converse, 1970), our data do not permit such an interpretation. Change is systematic, quickly stabilizes, and is related to specific policies. In short, the characteristics of the group of "emergent critics" and "newly interested" support the proposition that events inspire negative reorientation more frequently in certain predictable groups—the middle class and male students—than in others.

Grade-across-time analyses were as useful for us in documenting changes due to political developments as longitudinal analyses were useful for observing maturational change. Neither type of analysis, in its present form, can answer the crucial question, however: What is the magnitude of the contribution that either maturation or political events alone make to change?

We did not ask if a time will come when dissatisfaction with governmental performance is so great that affect for the system no longer can remain positive, especially among the young. Steady exposure to government malperformance on a large scale may have a more deleterious effect on young people's system affect than on older people's. Young people's greater idealism causes higher expectations of their government, and they lack the historical perspective of having seen the system weather other crises. This is the question raised by thoughtful people in the era of Watergate and is one which can perhaps now be addressed by research.

VII

Children's
Party Choices

PAULINE MARIE VAILLANCOURT, RICHARD G. NIEMI

Of all the orientations studied by political scientists, party identification is thought to have outstanding stability—a stability that extends both across and within generations; children inherit a partisanship from their parents, and most of them retain this identification for the rest of their lives. Political scientists sometimes add qualifications to this assertion, admitting that party ties are temporarily loosened around late adolescence, or observing the occasional massive shifts that occur during realigning periods, but they nonetheless conclude that extreme stability in party identification generally characterizes the American electorate.

Moreover, a substantial amount of data is arrayed to prove this point. High correlations are cited between parents' and children's party preferences (Hyman, 1959, pp. 70–71; Jennings and Niemi, 1968a). Recall data in *The American Voter* (Campbell and others, 1960, p. 47) and in a number of smaller studies (Maccoby and others, 1954–1955; McClosky and Dahlgren, 1959) show that if

We would like to thank Theodore Anagnoson, Paul Allen Beck, and Roman Hedges for their comments on a draft of this chapter.

126

both parents identify with one party, their offspring usually do too. Within generations the aggregate stability of partisanship throughout the 1940s, 1950s, and into the 1960s suggests stability at the individual level. Recall data about individual changes also support this conclusion (Campbell and others, 1960, p. 148). Panel data from the 1950s show that for adults partisan stability is much higher than stability of other political orientations (Converse, 1964).

If we look only at switches between the two major parties, partisanship does show impressive stability both across and within generations. In 1965, for example, only 7 percent of the high school seniors with parents of one party deviated to the other (Jennings and Niemi, 1968a, p. 173). Similarly, within generations, available panel evidence shows a very small number of shifts from one party to the other over a four-year time span (Campbell and others, 1966, p. 225).

The level of partisan stability is far less impressive, however, if one includes movement into and out of the independent category. (We interpret *independents* to mean persons who say they are independent—independent, independent Democrat, and independent Republican—rather than weak or strong Republican or Democrat.) Across generations some 31 percent of the 1965 student sample deviated from their parents' independent, Democratic, or Republican partisanship, and we suspect this figure might be low for the total age cohort at that time. Similarly, within generations the level of stability is greatly reduced. Over the relatively calm period of 1956 to 1960, some 22 percent white adults and even more black adults changed their responses. Perhaps even more surprising, 21 percent of the population responding to both pre- and postelection interviews changed their responses over a three-month period before and after the 1960 elections (Dreyer, 1973, p. 716).

We might also note that life cycle changes in the proportion of independents (Campbell and others, 1960, p. 162; Jennings and Niemi, 1974, chap. 10) suggest that there has to be at least a moderate number of individual level changes. It is difficult to reason from the aggregate to individual levels and from a cross-section design to changes over time, but that 35 percent of the young people and about 15 percent of the older adults were independents during the 1950s and early 1960s belies extreme statements of stability.

Finally, a number of technical points of questionnaire design and analysis techniques have tended to exaggerate the amount of similarity within and across generations. Recall data typically heightens consistency. In addition, the recall questions used in the Michigan studies have never captured all of the possible changes in the tripartite partisan scale—change from an independent to a partisan was not tapped until the 1972 election study. Most intergenerational studies rely on respondents' perceptions of parents, which probably inflates stability across generations (Niemi, 1974, chap. 3). Moreover, intergenerational studies usually exclude or deemphasize families in which the mother and father disagree.

If there is more than token instability of partisanship among adults and between generations, one might especially wonder whether partisan feelings of children are prone to frequent change since most political ideas are less fully developed in childhood than later in life. And yet the idea persists that children "inherit" their parents' partisanship and maintain that identification with relatively little change. (Few have tried to specify exactly when partisanship develops, but our impression is that most people would put that development sometime in the middle years of elementary school.) And while evidence and theories about intergenerational change have increased, only fragmentary, indirect evidence has been presented so far on which to make a judgment about the stability of or instability of children's partisan responses.

But there are indications of at least moderate instability. For one thing, young people's partisanship is very much affected by parents' presidential voting behavior (Jennings and Niemi, 1974, chap. 2). Since votes do not always coincide with partisan loyalties, one would expect some shifting of children's attitudes. Judging from cross-sectional data, the growth in the proportion of independents at the elementary and high school levels (Hess and Torney, 1967, p. 90) is much faster than the comparable decline in the proportion of independents over the adult life cycle. This would suggest more instability among children. Lastly, children cannot have adhered to a party identification for very long. Among adults short-term identification with a party has been associated with weak partisan feelings (Campbell and others, 1960, p. 163; Converse, 1969), and one would expect, with more frequent partisan changes.

We examine here the partisan stability of elementary school children, using a three-wave panel study. We focus on establishing overall levels of stability and change, although variations in rates of change are noted where appropriate.

The importance of our results can best be seen by referring to Beck's theory of partisan realignments (see Chapter Ten). If partisanship is quite firmly fixed at an early age or even by the time individuals enter the electorate, it suggests little room for flexibility in the party system. If, on the other hand, partisanship remains weak and flexible throughout the preadult years, then there is room for maneuvering within and change of the party system. We argue that partisanship is not rigidly fixed, but then an additional complication emerges—why does every generation not witness large-scale changes in partisan identification? We believe that our data and Beck's theory are compatible, though the empirical evidence lends additional clarity and precision to Beck's generational concepts, as we make clear after examining the data.

Study Design

A three-wave panel survey of fourth, sixth, and eighth graders from three school districts in the San Francisco Bay area (Berkeley, Oakland, and the corresponding Catholic diocesan district) was begun in early December 1968. The second wave was administered in late January 1969, immediately after President Nixon took office. The final wave took place in late May 1969.

The seven schools and thirty-three classes participating in the study were chosen as an approximate representation of the racial and socioeconomic composition of the Oakland-Berkeley area. In the Berkeley schools, classes were already racially balanced, due to the two-way busing plan, which also balanced socioeconomic status. The two Catholic schools are in Oakland; one was about 20 percent black and the other about 40 percent black. Since the Oakland public schools are not as racially mixed as the other districts, one school with 92 percent white students, one school with 92 percent black students, and one relatively integrated school (47 percent white, 25 percent black, 28 percent Oriental and Mexican-American) were included.

While the sample is reasonably representative of the Oakland-Berkeley area, it contains considerably more black respondents than are in a cross-section sample of the whole United States. Consequently, the sample is considerably more Democratic (and more identified with black parties) than a national cross-section. Because of this, we control on race throughout our analysis. We do not present statistics for the entire sample, and we are cautious in making tentative generalizations to the whole population.

In any panel study, particularly one conducted over a relatively short period, respondents may simply remember their previous responses and opt for consistency or they may become more aware of the subject matter because repeated questioning stimulates interest. While we have no evidence that these factors influenced the responses, their presence, as well as the short intervals between questioning, would most likely increase stability in the children's partisanship. These possible panel effects would thus all work in favor of the traditional view of high partisan stability.

Panel mortality was not a serious problem. In only a six-month period relatively few students moved out of the district, and efforts were made to give the questionnaire to students who were absent from the general administration because of illness or for other reasons. The original sample included 940 children, of whom 737 (78 percent) were present at all three waves. There was only the slightest bias from lower drop-outs of students with higher ability and SES. For example, those rated high in school ability constituted 30 percent of the original sample and 31 percent of the panel group.

One other factor in the study setting affected the study design. The November 1968 elections in northern California witnessed more than the usual amount of third and fourth party activity. Rather than functioning as token, inactive opposition, the American Independent party and the Peace and Freedom party (the Community for New Politics and Black Panther party coalition) conducted energetic and well-publicized campaigns. While these parties made few inroads into the traditional two-party vote among adults (capturing a combined total of less than 8 percent of the presidential vote in Alameda County), we pay particular attention to minor-party identifiers, making sure that the minor parties alone do not account for most of the instability.

The presence of viable third and fourth parties also permits an investigation of question wording (Vaillancourt, 1972, chap. 7). The sample was thus divided into two groups—A and B. The A group was given the usual closed-ended party identification question at all three waves. The B group was asked identical questions in the first two waves of the panel, but in the third wave, the Peace and Freedom and American Independent parties were explicitly introduced into the question wording, which leads to an increase in the number of minor-party identifiers. It also makes panel analysis including the B group difficult, though not impossible.

Aggregate Results

The question used to tap party identification is patterned after that used by Hess and Torney (1967, p. 90). It differs from their wording by adding an "other" category, which was essential for this election in Northern California. The question is as follows: "If you could vote, what would you be? Republican; Democrat; Sometimes a Democrat and sometimes a Republican; I would be for some other party—please tell us what its name is———; I don't know; I don't know what Democrat and Republican means."

For the B group (third wave), "American Independent" and "Peace and Freedom" were substituted for "other." Also, the wording of two alternatives was changed to read "Sometimes I would be for one party, sometimes for another," and "I don't know what parties are."

The two categories "don't know" and "don't know parties" are necessary additions for young respondents. The proportion who don't know parties is quite substantial even at the fourth grade, but drops off quickly thereafter. The don't-know responses, on the other hand, remain quite high even at the eighth grade.

We interpret the response of "sometimes a Democrat and sometimes a Republican" as comparable to the independent category in adult questions. Though it might have been preferable to use the term *independent* in our answers, children may not be familiar enough with the term to give valid responses. Fortunately, two factors suggest the reasonableness of our interpretation. First, Hess and Torney observed a pattern of growth in the "sometimes" category which corresponds to the theoretical expectation of an increase in independents during adolescence. Second, there is a close correspondence between the proportion they found in this category among eighth graders in 1961 and the proportion of independents in a 1965 sample of high school seniors (Jennings and Niemi, 1968a). In any event, even if the correspondence is not perfect, it seems clear that the "sometimes" category indicates a form of independence from the parties.

The aggregate distributions of partisanship for the three waves of the panel are shown in Table 1 for blacks and whites separately. (Other minority group members are included with the whites. These are mostly middle-class Orientals, and separate analysis shows them to be similar to whites, except for a somewhat higher proportion of don't knows). The amount and pattern of change for the six-month period, by themselves, support the usual stereotype of partisan stability. Relatively little aggregate change occurs, and what change is observable follows previously noted patterns. For example, there is a moderate increase in the proportion of independents, which is in line with the one deviation from the perfect stability model that has often been noted. Add to this a small movement away from the winning party as one gets away from the election, and the changes do not seem large. Similarly, the decline in the proportion who do not know what parties are represents normal developmental change and does not violate the stability model. Moreover, this decline helps account for the increase in the number of independents.

The decline in minor-party identifiers is partly artifactual. The number of minor-party identifiers actually rose sharply in the third wave, largely due to the change in question format for group B. The respondents in group B who identified with the minor party were eliminated in calculating the distribution for the third wave of the panel (and from any analysis involving this wave). Undoubtedly some of these respondents would have opted for the minor party even without the question change—especially blacks, among

Table 1.

AGGREGATE DISTRIBUTION OF PARTISIANSHIP FOR
THREE WAVES OF THE PANEL

	December 1968	January 1969	May 1969
Whites			
Minor party	5%	3%	2%
Democratic	35	36	35
Republican	18	19	15
Independent	19	24	25
Don't know	16	13	20
Don't know parties	8	5	4
Total	101%	100%	101%
	(463)	(461)	(437)
Blacks			
Minor party	9%	8%	5%
Democratic	38	35	33
Republican	15	13	9
Independent	6	8	13
Don't know	18	22	29
Don't know parties	15	13	11
Total	101%	99%	100%
	(264)	(259)	(224)

whom 34 percent of the B group chose minor parties at wave three. Thus the proportion of minor party adherents is slightly under-estimated, by only a few percent among whites but by as much as 3 or 4 percent among blacks. Percentages for the A group only still indicate that the proportion of minor party identifiers declines slightly in the third wave but less sharply than appears in Table 1.

In short, from the aggregate distributions neither blacks nor whites seem susceptible to major partisan instability. The change that does occur is often developmental in nature; stability will presumably follow. The slight rise in the proportion of independents can easily be accommodated by the stability model.

Individual Stability and Change

As so often happens, when we move from the aggregate to the individual level the phenomenon we are describing seems to change drastically. Fairly large amounts of change become apparent. The degree of change is difficult to assess, however. Consider Tables 2 and 3, which show for each racial group the patterns of change between December and January and between January and May.

As a summary device one might like to use the correlation between reports at two time periods, as Converse (1964) did to compare the stability of partisan loyalties with stability on other attitudinal measures. Indeed we have argued elsewhere (Jennings and Niemi, 1968a) that correlations rather than percentage agreement should typically be used to measure intergenerational similarity. Here, however, the problem of ordering the categories precludes a sensible basis on which to calculate the usual turnover statistics. For example, shifting from "don't know" to being a Republican is not necessarily a greater change than shifting from "don't know" to being a Democrat. Moving in and out of the independent category is not quite the same when there are three or more parties as when there are only two parties. And certain of the changes do not represent partisan instability, in particular, any change from "don't know parties," and any from "don't know" (except back to "don't know parties").

In light of these problems, we calculate the stability of responses among those who were a Democrat, an independent, a Republican, or a minor party identifier in the first of the two time periods being compared. For example, 354 whites gave one of these four responses in December. Of these, 264 or almost exactly three-quarters gave an identical response in January. Or to put it the other way around, fully one-quarter of the white children who were able to place themselves in December had changed to some extent by January. Most of these changes were out of the independent category or into the independent or don't-know categories. A fairly substantial number of respondents who were seemingly sure of their positions in December were much less sure of themselves by January.

The same calculations for the second panel interval show

Table 2.

STABILITY AND CHANGE OF PARTISANSHIP FROM DECEMBER 1968 TO JANUARY 1969

December 1968	Minor party	Democrat	Independent	Republican	Don't know	Don't know parties	Total[b]
			January 1969				
Whites							
Minor party[a]	62%	14	10	5	10	0	101% (21)
Democrat	1	79	9	5	5	1	100 (164)
Independent	0	10	71	10	8	0	99 (87)
Republican	0	10	12	72	5	1	100 (82)
Don't know	0	14	20	9	49	7	99 (69)
Don't know parties	0	17	17	14	14	39	101 (36)

Percent stable of December 1968 partisans and independents: (264/354) = 75%

December 1968	Minor party	Democrat	Independent	Republican	Don't know	Don't know parties	Total[b]
Blacks							
Minor party[a]	64%	18	5	5	9	0	101% (22)
Democrat	3	65	6	6	13	6	99 (97)
Independent	7	21	57	7	0	7	99 (14)
Republican	8	25	2	35	22	8	100 (40)
Don't know	0	9	9	16	48	18	100 (44)
Don't know parties	0	15	5	8	31	41	100 (39)

Stable (99/173) = 57%

[a] Mostly Peace and Freedom party with a few American Independent party responses.
[b] Marginals calculated from Tables 2 and 3 differ slightly from distributions given in Table 1 because of a few blank question-naires at each wave.

Table 3.

STABILITY AND CHANGE OF PARTISANSHIP FROM JANUARY 1969 TO MAY 1969

January 1969	Minor party	Democrat	Independent	Republican	Don't know	Don't know parties	Total[b]
			May 1969				
Whites							
Minor party[a]	62%	38	0	0	0	0	100% (8)
Democrat	0	72	12	6	9	1	100 (155)
Independent	2	20	59	2	15	2	100 (106)
Republican	0	14	18	55	13	0	100 (87)
Don't know	0	9	14	4	68	5	100 (56)
Don't know parties	0	5	14	10	29	43	101 (21)
Stable (227/356) = 64%							
Blacks							
Minor party[a]	45%	20	15	5	10	5	100% (20)
Democrat	0	69	11	4	16	0	100 (74)
Independent	0	16	32	11	42	0	101 (19)
Republican	0	22	11	41	15	11	100 (27)
Don't know	2	14	14	6	46	18	100 (50)
Don't know parties	4	7	4	0	52	33	100 (27)
Stable (77/140) = 55%							

[a] Mostly Peace and Freedom party with a few American Independent party responses.
[b] Marginals calculated from Tables 2 and 3 differ slightly from distributions given in Table 1 because of a few blank questionnaires at each wave.

even greater change than that found in the first interval, especially for whites. Again, the changes are concentrated around the independent and don't-know categories. Of the partisans, Republican identifiers are most subject to change, no doubt due to the preponderance of Democrats in the school and in the surrounding adult environment.

As expected, the stability of partisanship among whites is higher than that among blacks (Campbell and others, 1966, pp. 233–235). Instability in the sample is not limited to one group, however, and is not due to the racial composition of the sample. Even among whites, first a quarter and then over a third shifted their responses between panel waves.

The stability model might still have to be revised only slightly if the youngest children were very unstable, with stability growing substantially in the later grades. But the data do not support such a conclusion. While stability is lower among the fourth graders—so much so that in some instances an absolute majority of the children changed between waves of panel—large proportions of students in the two higher grades changed also (see Table 4). Even by eighth grade, only four to five years or one presidential election away from voting age, partisan tendencies still appear to be rather flexible. (In these data stability actually declines from sixth to eighth grades. While we do not wish to overinterpret what could be random fluctuations, this does make some sense—the rising number of independents in adolescence may decrease their stability below the level of slightly younger children.)

We can narrow our focus even further, but we still find large percentages of changers. For example, we might expect greater stability among sixth and eighth grade whites from high socioeconomic backgrounds since they are presumably politicized earlier. But 21 percent of these children changed their responses between the first two waves of the panel, and 41 percent changed between the next waves. What may be happening in this case is that the greater politicization of these children pushes them away from a partisan position faster than other children. This appears to be the case since they go from 21 percent independent in December to 24 percent in January to 36 percent in May.

While there may be clusters of children who exhibit highly

Table 4.

Percentage of Stable Partisans and Independents, by Grade

	4th graders		6th graders		8th graders	
	December to January	January to May	December to January	January to May	December to January	January to May
Whites	66% (83)	58% (95)	79% (139)	68% (133)	71% (135)	66% (133)
Blacks	36% (47)	48% (29)	62% (66)	50% (64)	60% (60)	69% (48)

Note: Each entry is the percentage of December or January partisans and independents who gave the same response at the next wave.

stable partisan loyalties, instability is surely not limited to blacks or other minority groups, to the very young, or to those whose backgrounds suggest later politicization. And if the figures we have presented can be generalized at all to the entire population of elementary school children, they project an image quite different from that of the traditional stability model.

Change over Three Waves. There are limitations, however, in looking at only two waves at a time—we have no indication of the overlap in changers. If 10 percent of the population changed between December and January, and 10 percent changed between January and May, the total percentage who changed may be as low as 10 percent (complete overlap of changers) or as high as 20 percent (no overlap of changers). In addition, we have not been able to deal adequately with all of the changes. Moving from a don't-know response in December to being a Democrat in January may represent a normal developmental sequence where stability follows the initial partisanship, or it may represent something different, depending on the respondent's identification at the third (and later) waves. Hence it is necessary to look at change across three waves of the panel.

In order to make sense of change across all three waves, some categorization is necessary. With six response categories at each of three waves, 216 distinct response patterns across the three waves are possible. And even with the limited number of respondents in the present sample, over half of the patterns occurred at least once. No doubt there are numerous ways to classify and analyze these response patterns. For example, one might be interested in respondents who switch from one party to the other and then switch back again. Or one might be interested in respondents who switch from one party to an independent or a don't-know position and then switch either back to the original party or to another party.

For our purposes a fivefold classification seems to best capture the gross picture of change in which we are interested. The five categories are as follows:

I. *Perfectly Stable*—those who are stable across all three waves. This includes stable partisans and stable independents. It also includes don't-know or don't-know-parties responses at all three waves (thirty-five whites and fourteen blacks).

II. *Developmentally Stable*—those who begin with a don't-know or don't-know-parties response but move to a stable identification in May or in both January and May. The following examples illustrate response patterns falling into this category: Don't know (December)—Democrat (January)—Democrat (May); don't know—minor party—minor party; don't know—don't know—Independent; don't know parties—don't know—Democrat; don't-know parties—independent—independent; don't know parties—don't know parties—Republican. In addition to those who finally made a partisan or independent choice, this category includes a few children who answered "don't know parties"—"don't know parties"—"don't know" or "don't know parties"—"don't know"—"don't know" (five whites and eleven blacks). This category deserves to be distinguished from the top category because the respondents have had less time to indicate their stable affiliations. While they give no indication of instability once they attain some partisan or independent leaning, they report such a feeling at only one or two waves of the panel.

The remaining three categories represent change in some fashion other than a normal developmental sequence. It is easiest to begin with the fifth category and then move to the fourth and third categories:

V. *Confused Switchers*—those who switch to a response of don't-know parties from a previous choice of a party or independent response or from a don't-know response (they say first that they don't know which party they would vote for, but subsequently that they don't know what parties mean). (It would be possible to give a kind of "super sophisticated" interpretation of valid attitude change to these responses. That is, a student may initially say that he or she is a Republican but later decide that party labels are sufficiently vague, that party platforms are nonspecific, and so on, so that party labels themselves are rather meaningless. Consequently, a don't-know-parties response best represents his or her new understanding of the situation. Given what we know about children's lack of understanding of the political parties, we doubt very much that a single student in the sample answered in this fashion.)

IV. *Partisan Switchers*—those who switch from one party to

another (excluding those who fall into category V). These are respondents who are a Democrat and change to being a Republican or vice versa as well as those who change from a major party to a minor party or vice versa. The change could occur at any wave(s) of the panel. Examples include the following patterns: Democrat—Republican—Republican; Democrat—Democrat—Republican; Democrat—don't know—Republican; Republican—Democrat—Independent. Category V has precedence over category IV since a later response of don't-know-parties indicates to us that apparent partisan changes (as in a Democrat—Republican—don't-know-parties pattern) are rather meaningless.

III. *Independent and Don't-Know Switchers*—those who switch from a partisan response to a don't-know response or vice versa, and those who switch from a partisan response to an independent response or vice versa (excluding those who fall into categories IV or V). These respondents' partisanship appears to be somewhat unstable, but they do not actually shift from one party to another. This is a key category for our analysis. If the independent category is important (and the somewhat comparable don't-know category for children), then individuals who fall into this category represent a real switch (although not as severe a switch as for those who fall into category IV). Some examples of patterns included in category III are Democrat—don't-know—Democrat; Republican—Independent—Republican; Republican—Republican—Independent; Independent—Democrat—Independent; Independent—don't-know—Minor party. (Also included in this category are a few children—nineteen whites and five blacks—who answered Independent—don't-know—Independent; Independent—don't-know—don't-know; Independent—Independent—don't-know; don't-know—Independent—don't-know.) Respondents who could fall into both categories III and V (such as Democrat—Independent—don't-know-parties) are relegated to category V. Similarly, those who could fall into both categories III and IV (such as Democrat—Independent—Republican) are classified as category IV.

These five categories represent a kind of continuum, running from those who are perfectly stable (category I), to those who are stable after a developmental phase (category II), to those whose change involves the independent or don't-know categories (category III), to partisan changers (category IV), and finally to those who apparently do not understand the concepts involved (category V).

Table 5.

STABILITY AND CHANGE OF PARTISANSHIP
ACROSS THREE PANEL WAVES

Category	Whites		Blacks	
I. Perfectly stable	50%	52%	35%	40%
II. Developmentally stable	7	7	11	13
III. Independent and don't-know switchers	31	32	23	27
IV. Partisan switchers	9	9	17	20
V. Confused switchers	3	—	13	—
Total	100%	100%	99%	100%
	(431)		(222)	

Note: The second column gives the distribution for the first four categories alone. Persons in category v are deleted to give a clearer distribution of switchers and nonswitchers.

The distributions among these five categories are given in Table 5. The results substantiate and amplify the conclusion drawn from the two-wave data. Change is more than an occasional phenomenon and is quite widespread if we include change into and out of the independent and don't-know categories (category III).

Given the large number of children who changed their responses over just a six-month time period, the change over longer periods of time must be very substantial. This conclusion is bolstered if we compare the stability of responses over two waves with that over three waves. Similar amounts of stability showing over the two-wave and three-wave panels would indicate a nearly complete overlap of respondents who changed between December and January and January and May. If this were the case, further panel waves would increase the proportion of switchers very little, if at all. But see Table 6.

Table 6.

TWO-WAVE STABILITY AND CHANGE

Category	Whites	Blacks
I	68%	53%
II	11	15
III	14	14
IV	5	11
V	2	7
Total	100%	100%
	(459)	(256)

The addition of a third wave leads to drops of 18 percent in the proportion of category I respondents. Thus the total turnover in Table 5 is not the result of a small core of individuals who are unstable at all points in time. Rather, there is every indication that the proportion of changers would continue to rise, though perhaps by smaller and smaller increments, if additional waves of the panel were available.

Children in category V are an ambiguous group in regard to determining the stability or instability of partisanship. From one point of view, they clearly work against the "inheritance and then stability" model. All of these respondents gave a substantive response (other than a don't-know-parties answer) in one wave or another. Yet clearly they have not inherited a stable partisan identity, since they subsequently not only changed their response but indicate that they were really quite unsure of themselves. However, one could argue that these children are going through an initial, halting, developmental phase and that as soon as they develop some minimal level of understanding, they will assume a stable position.

Though we lean toward the first line of reasoning, there is no way of verifying either point of view. Because of this, one might ask: Among those who give a sensible set of responses (the first four categories), what is the distribution of switchers and non-switchers? This we provide in the second set of columns of Table 5 by deleting category V and repercentaging. All of the other percentages naturally increase slightly. In particular, the largest category—the perfectly stable—increases by as much as 5 percent. Still, the proportion of changers, which also rises, remains substantial enough to warrant rethinking of the notion that partisanship is very stable among children. (In an interpretation unfavorable to the stability argument, those in category I who are "don't know's" or "don't know parties" and those in category II who change to a stable "don't know" response could be eliminated on the grounds that they will eventually distribute themselves in categories I through IV in approximately the same way as those who already have some partisan or independent attachment.)

In Table 5, whites continue to show greater partisan stability, and any tentative projections of these results to the entire nation must weigh the distribution of white students much more heavily than that of black students. Nevertheless, even among the whites the proportion of changers is a substantial minority of the children, and our results cannot be ignored as simply indicative of instability in minority group populations. Nor, as we indicated earlier, can the results be judged indicative only of instability in the very early grades. The distribution for eighth-grade whites (here excluding Orientals and Mexican-Americans), by category, is as follows: (I) 52 percent, (II) 6 percent, (III) 34 percent, (IV) 8 percent, and (V) 2 percent. We must conclude that partisanship is far from uniformly inherited and internalized. At the very least there is a good deal of indecision, wavering, and reconsideration as partisan feelings develop.

Causes of Instability. Several factors help account for the large amounts of instability found in the Oakland-Berkeley school children, factors that are common to the experience of most children in the United States. First, there are really few major elections in the life of a child, and thus the child has little time to build up allegiances through repeated support for the same party. We think it unlikely that many elections other than presidential contests attract the attention of most elementary school children. No doubt there are exceptions, but given the level of adult interest in and turnout at local elections and in statewide off-year elections, we doubt that many students become emotionally involved in these contests. If we limit ourselves to presidential elections, at most, there are three presidential elections over the course of elementary and high school of which the student would have any awareness or interest. Even supposing a precocious youngster happens to be in first grade when there is a presidential election, and that he is interested in it and aware of it, only two more presidential elections would occur before he is out of high school. Supposing still further that a few other elections capture his interest, a still limited set of experiences are accumulated on which to build up allegiances to one party or the other. It is more likely that a student is largely unaware of a presidential election until he or she is in fifth or sixth grade, so that only one more presidential election takes place while he or she is still in high school.

A second factor is that elections are considered less important for children than for parents. While they sometimes wear campaign buttons, vote in mock elections, and so on, young children clearly do not have the same level of personal involvement in elections as adults. That children's attitudes change on something which is not of direct, sustained relevance to them should not be too surprising.

A third factor contributing to instability of young people's partisan feelings is that children seem to be especially sensitive to conflicting personal directives. When parents' votes contradict their partisanship, the extent to which children inherit their partisan feelings drops off considerably (Jennings and Niemi, 1974, chap. 2). In recent presidential elections, a significant minority have voted contrary to their partisanship, and the number of individuals who switched votes (but not necessarily partisanship) between elections has been substantial. If young children are attuned at least in part to their parent's voting behavior rather than to their partisanship, fluctuation in children's feelings is likely.

More significant in terms of the number of children involved is the effect of the voting behavior of parents who consider themselves independents. Young people's partisanship appears to be heavily colored by the voting behavior of these parents. For one thing this contributes to intergenerational instability (independent parents and partisan children). More important here, if the parents indeed act independently by switching their voting preferences from time to time, this is likely to contribute to instability of children's partisanship.

Though it is clear that in the area of partisanship the influence of parents is greatest, peers and teachers do exert some marginal influence (Jennings and Niemi, 1974, chaps. 8–9). In particular, the increase in the proportion of independents observed in late adolescence is often attributed to the influence of teachers.

A fourth potential explanation for the observed instability is simply measurement error. Models have been developed which permit a simple calculation of the reliability of a question, given measurement at three points in time (Heise, 1969; Achen, 1974). Application of these models is difficult because of the same ordering problem that prevented us from using correlations to summarize the panel change. Nevertheless, in order to obtain some estimate of the reliability of the partisanship question, we calculated the reliability coefficient of the children who were Democrats, independents, or Republicans at all three waves (using Heise's model); it is .71. As Achen points out, however, this unreliability may be traced either to the respondents or to the questions. To help sort this out we calculated the reliability coefficient for eighth-grade whites (excluding Orientals and Mexican-Americans); the coefficient is .88. The two reliability coefficients suggest that the question itself is quite reliable, and that the unreliability for the whole sample (.71) is in large part due to what Converse (1970) called "nonattitudes" rather than to measurement error. Thus the observed changes in the children's partisanship are not likely due to measurement problems. (Estimates of reliability should, of course, be taken only as suggestive since they depend on the specific assumptions of the model.)

Theory of Realignments

The results of our investigation tie in nicely with the theory developed by Beck (see Chapter Ten). Beck argues that the weakest link in the transgenerational partisan chain within any family lies in the preadult years. Although we cannot substantiate this point fully without further data, our analysis indicates that the preadult phase is a weak—if not the weakest—link in the intergenerational partisan chain.

We go further than Beck, however, by suggesting that individual change of partisanship—especially if one includes movement into and out of the independent categories—is not limited to preadults or to periods of partisan realignment of the electorate. Indeed, the children in our sample are probably not part of a realignment phase, assuming that a realignment or at least a period of electoral instability occurred sometime in the late 1960s and continued into the early 1970s. Ordinarily these young people would not have entered the electorate until 1977 for the eighth graders and 1981 for the fourth graders. Even with the reduction in the voting age, they will not enter the adult electorate before 1974 and after. Moreover, adult data from the 1950s substantiates our view that individual fluctuations continue into adulthood at a higher rate than has usually been acknowledged.

If one accepts our view, then the question perhaps changes from why do realignments occur to why they do not occur with much greater frequency? The answer would seem to lie in Beck's contention that realignments cannot be sustained for long and in the coming of age of those he calls the children of realignment. Realignments burn themselves out, but we add that they burn themselves out slowly. The continuing presence of the realignment generation itself, which is probably less susceptible to partisan change, and the slowness with which the realignment burns out (for example, the extent to which new voters in the 1940s and 1950s were still influenced by the Depression) keeps a new realignment from occurring even though there is individual change and wavering of partisanship. Moreover, the children of realignment enter the electorate at a time when the previous realignment might otherwise burn itself out completely. These people, who are the children of the previous realignment generation, are unlikely to be subject to mass changes because they are raised across the dinner table, as Beck says, on the last realignment. Were it not for this particular set of new voters, realignments might be expected years earlier than they have historically appeared.

After the children of realignment enter the electorate, there comes a time when both the previous realignment is of little direct significance for new adults, and voters whose parents came of age after the previous realignment are entering the electorate. These two conditions set the stage for a new realignment period. Thus we suggest that realignments are facilitated by the relative weakness of preadult partisanship. This weakness is exaggerated during actual periods of realignment, because of the presence of individuals twice removed from the previous realignment. But changeability of partisanship is not limited to this time period nor necessarily even to preadults.

In conclusion, we emphasize that partisanship is not comparable to the "nonattitudes" found by Converse (1970) for many adults' opinions about public issues during the late 1950s. Partisanship, even among children, is too stable and too meaningful for this interpretation. One can, for example, point to the greater stability of partisanship than of other attitudes in Converse's (1964) study of adult respondents. Or one can refer to the relative stability of partisanship intergenerationally, compared with other political orientations (Jennings and Niemi, 1968a). Or one can draw on data from the present study. Evidence of the "sensibleness" of partisanship among these children is available. Although we do not have data from these children's parents, the greater frequency of Democratic identifications, even among the whites, suggests the transmission of parental identifications in this predominantly Democratic area. The extent to which Peace and Freedom Party identifiers are blacks suggests that partianship even among children is not entirely divorced from policy matters. Partisanship was also found to be children's most stable political orientation (Vaillancourt, 1973). Finally, the fact that change across the party spectrum is less frequent than changes in and out of the independent category suggests again that partisan wavering is often limited in its extent.

Thus partisanship is sufficiently stable to be an important component of theories of socialization and electoral behavior and is perhaps very stable in relation to certain other kinds of political orientations. But this does not mean that partisanship is anywhere near as stable as is frequently argued. Our point has been, first of all, to recognize this malleability of partisanship, particularly at the preadult level, a malleability which extends across as well as within generations. At the same time, we have attempted to incorporate this view of a less rigidly fixed partisanship into a theoretical explanation of the role of socialization in determining stability and change of the partisan division of the electorate.

VIII

Environmental Influence on Political Learning

GUNNEL GUSTAFSSON

An intensive decade of research and theorizing has resulted in contradictory evidence regarding the relative influence that parents, schools, peers, and other socialization agents have on children. Some studies of partisanship, for example, emphasize the crucial role played by the family, while other studies (such as Jennings and Niemi, 1968a) find the family much less influential in regard to a wide array of topics. Sometimes the school is shown to have an important impact (as in Litt, 1963), sometimes it is shown to have no such effect (Langton and Jennings, 1968). At least some popular writers (such as Mead, 1970) assert the pre-eminence of playmates or the mass media.

One possible explanation for these contradictory results is that political learning is situation specific. The nature of political learning—specifically, the influence of socialization agents—may vary considerably, depending on macro-level factors of the political and social system which surrounds the learner. Macro-level influences are frequently acknowledged in comparisons between societies of widely differing types, but within single societies, interaction between the socialization agents and the environment is recognized much less often (for an exception, see Litt, 1963).

A related explanation is that the general environment in which people are socialized is typically underrated, while the importance of specific people in the child's environment is overrated. The views and behavior of children as well as adults are likely influenced, for example, by whether their society has high employment or unemployment, housing availability or shortages, good or bad communications, and an expanding or contracting population. Similarly, the economic situation likely has indirect effects on the transmission of values from agents to children.

The economic situation in a society or part of a society indirectly affects the transmission of values from agents to children; it directly affects the orientations of both adults and children within its milieu. I have studied the transmission of political values to Swedish children from their parents, playmates, and teachers, focusing on political interest and activity and on a number of salient issues in Swedish politics. I have analysized macro-level economic factors along with data about particular socialization agents.

Both indirect and direct environment influences can be observed by comparing the values of children from three distinctly different communes (subnational governmental units) in Sweden with the values of their parents, peers, and teachers, as well as with those of other adults in each area.

In Sweden, as in most countries, some areas are characterized by rapid growth and economic expansion while other areas are characterized by stable or even declining populations and a faltering economy. Increased mass production, extended international trade, increased demands for social services, and changed regional planning have led to population emigration from areas where economic life is based on raw products, usually dominated by agriculture and forestry, to areas characterized by a differentiated and industrialized economic life. The areas that people are moving from have high rates of unemployment, an aging population (as young people move to expanding areas), low educational levels (for the same reason) and unsatisfactory social services because of the character of the remaining population and of problems (such as transportation) of the area in general. In contrast, the expanding areas have plentiful jobs, accelerating urbanization, high income and education levels, and high geographic mobility. The expansion brings problems that are not found in the declining areas, such as a shortage of housing and of facilities for leisure-time activities. In the areas which fall between these extremes of expansion and retardation, the population is relatively stable, and development occurs as a transition from agriculture and forestry to industrial occupations; problems associated with both declining and rapidly expanding areas are typically avoided.

I hypothesized that the expanding or contracting nature of a commune would have a considerable impact on the socialization of its young people. Accordingly, samples were taken in each of three communes, which were picked to represent the two extremes and the "in-between" of expansion and retardation (within certain limitations).

No communes were selected where merger was imminent. Mergers of communes were taking place in Sweden when the investigation was carried out in 1970; these strongly affected the degree of optimism, as well as the degree of uncertainty, which the inhabitants of these regions felt about the future. (From 1963 to 1973 the number of communes was reduced from 816 to about 280.) The frequency of emigration and immigration, for example, is affected by prospects of new divisions in the administrative units. Hence, communes which were soon to undergo mergers were avoided in this study.

Second, we concentrated the investigation on one level of urbanization and one measure of population distribution. Selected communes had five thousand to ten thousand inhabitants; 51 to 70 percent of their population lived in densely populated areas. (This was considered since we hypothesized that the nature of the children's environment affects their socialization.)

Of the twenty-six communes meeting these criteria, we selected Upplands-Bro, where the population increased on an average of 6 percent each year from 1962 to 1968; Ovanåker, where the average migration was virtually zero; and Jokkmokk, where the population decreased on an average of 5 percent per year from 1962 to 1968. The retarding commune, Jokkmokk, is situated in the far north, in the part of Sweden that is least industrialized and most subject to emigration. Ovanåker lies in the border district between this area in the north and the rest of the country. The expanding unit, Upplands-Bro, is in the region around the capital. While all three communes have similar numbers of people, their geographic sizes and consequently their population densities differ substantially. Jokkmokk covers 4,481,568 square acres and has an average of one inhabitant per five hundred square acres. The area of Ovanåker is 233,622 square acres, with an average density of one person per thirty square acres. Upplands-Bro is the smallest of the three, with 58,786 acres and an average density of one person per ten acres (Årsbok för Sveriges Kommuner, 1969). Some additional data on the three communes is presented in Table 1.

In each of these three communes, 20 percent of the children in every first, sixth, and ninth grade class were randomly selected (N = 190). Children in Sweden enter school later than children in the United States; these respondents were eight, thirteen, and sixteen years old. They were interviewed in their homes. During this interview each of their parents (N = 365) answered a questionnaire. Interviews were also conducted with the childrens' teachers (N = 75) —the principal teacher for the first and sixth grades; for the ninth grade, teachers of geography, history, religion, civics, and Swedish (who could be expected to deal with social problems in their teaching). Finally, interviews were conducted with the chairman and vice-chairman of local government councils, boards, and committees (N = 49); political party representatives (N = 92); local trade union officials (N = 42); administrators within the communal government (N = 38); and communal office workers (N = 46). (Dan Brändström and Harry Forsell directed the last-mentioned interviews; these are mainly for a larger project, part of which includes what I report in this chapter. For more details, see Gustafsson, 1972.)

These data allow a study of the relationship between socialization and the economic character of the surrounding society. Effects will be sought along two dimensions. On the one hand, both Jokkmokk and Upplands-Bro represent communes which are characterized by a high rate of change, whereas Ovanåker is a static commune. At times, the presence or absence of change may be the important characteristic dividing the communes. On the other hand,

Table 1.

SELECTED DATA ON THE THREE COMMUNES

	Retarding (Jokkmokk)	*Static* (Ovanåker)	*Expanding* (Upplands-Bro)
Medium income in Swedish crowns in 1970	12,536	13,862	20,950
Percentage economically active population; ages 20 to 66	54	60	68
Percentage (of economically active) employed in agriculture and forestry in 1970	16	24	15
Percentage employed in water (hydraulic) power construction in 1970	30	—	—
Percentage of adults having only primary school education in 1970	67	76	44
Social-Democratic votes (as a percentage of total votes) in 1968	61	53	53

Note: Unemployment data are not available by commune, but the percentages economically active—working at least twenty hours a week—as well as other data make it clear that unemployment is especially high in Jokkmokk.

Jokkmokk and Upplands-Bro are at opposite extremes in terms of the type of change taking place, with Ovanåker in the middle. At times we can expect the nature of the change to be the determining factor.

Political Interest

A society wrestling with important political problems is likely to generate greater citizen interest and participation in politics than a society where such problems are absent or less intense. With regard to political interest, then, we expect differences in our study results between communal situations with changes and those with lack of change. Concern will naturally be expressed with different types of problems in a retarding commune than in an expanding one, but individuals in both of these types of commune should express greater interest and willingness to participate in politics than people in a static commune.

This hypothesis is strongly substantiated by the data in Table 2. On both measures, children, parents, and teachers in the changing communes express a moderate to high degree of political interest and willingness to participate in politics. Percentages tend to be highest in the expanding commune, but clearly the most consistent pattern is the lower rates of interest in the static commune. (The apparently greater political interest and willingness to participate among children than among parents is probably due to internalization of norms and expectations outstripping actions.)

Another manifestation of the difference between changing and static communes appears in the young people's development of partisan tendencies. In Sweden practically all fundamental political work has long been done within the political parties. Earlier investigations have shown that children acquire a party preference at an early age ("Svenska institutet för opinionsundersökningar," 1959). This situation now seems to be changing, judging by the fact that only about 30 percent of the youths in our sample expressed a party preference.

From our point of view, however, the important point is that party preferences vary from one commune to another. In Jokkmokk, 40 percent of the young people have a party preference; this falls off to 30 percent in Upplands-Bro and reaches a low of 20 percent in Ovanåker. In some respects this result is contrary to expectations; one might expect satisfaction with and hence identification with the party to be lowest in areas beset with problems. This seems true among the party leaders. Party representatives in the changing units are most inclined to grant that nonparliamentary groups have an important role in society today (85 percent in Jokkmokk and 63 percent in Upplands-Bro), while fewer in the static commune see such a role (57 percent in Ovanåker). Among the young people, however, the result seems to manifest varying levels of political interest. Identification with a party, as was the case

Table 2.

POLITICAL INTEREST AND WILLINGNESS TO PARTICIPATE IN POLITICS

Commune	Percentage rather or very much interested in politics			Percentage willing to participate in politics		
	Children	Parents	Teachers	Children	Parents	Teachers
Retarding (Jokkmokk)	40 (68)	30 (121)	64 (25)	33 (43)	15 (121)	36 (25)
Static (Ovanåker)	29 (62)	26 (117)	43 (28)	17 (41)	14 (117)	14 (28)
Expanding (Upplands-Bro)	33 (61)	39 (112)	82 (22)	39 (35)	21 (112)	32 (22)
Total	34% (191)	30% (350)	61% (75)	30% (119)	16% (350)	27% (75)

Note: Eight-year-olds were not asked about their willingness to take an active part in politics. They were asked, "Do you think it is fun to talk about how much money fathers and mothers are paid for their work, about how to help people living in poor countries, and other things that I have asked you about?" The question for older children and parents was: "Are you interested in politics? [If yes] Would you say that you take a great interest, a rather great interest, or relatively little interest in politics?"

with other expressions of interest and potential participation, was lowest in the relatively unchanging area. We interpret this, therefore, not to mean less satisfaction with the political parties in Ovanåker, but rather another indication of less attention to political and social problems in an unchanging environment than in a changing one.

Given the uniformly greater political interest of parents and teachers in the expanding and contracting communes, compared to the static commune, what can one say about the sources of children's feelings? An initial part of the answer can be observed in Table 3. Instruction on different social problems is clearly affected by the communal situation. Problems associated with expanding and declining populations and economies are apparently of little interest in the classrooms of Ovanåker. But in both the expanding and retarding communes, questions of wages and migration are emphasized.

Table 3.

PERCENTAGE OF CHILDREN RECEIVING A GREAT DEAL OF
INSTRUCTION ON SELECTED ISSUES

Issues	*Retarding* (Jokkmokk) (*N* = 68)	*Static* (Ovanåker) (*N* = 53)	*Expanding* (Upplands-Bro) (*N* = 61)
Wages and wage differences in current Swedish society	42	0	46
Migration from sparsely populated areas to small densely populated places and to big towns	52	9	49
Advantages and disadvantages of mothers working outside the home	45	38	43
Swedish aid to developing countries	37	43	78
US and the Soviet Union expenditures on space exploration	5	11	53

Note: Figures are based on data provided by the teachers.

Issues in the international and foreign domains are of little interest in the retarding community, which must be chiefly concerned with its internal problems; they are also of relatively little interest in the static commune. But in the rapidly expanding commune, these problems are dealt with much more frequently. While this may be explained to some degree by the proximity of Upplands-Bro to the capital, it is also consistent with the forward-and-outward-looking position enjoyed by an expanding community.

The probable effects of teachers can be inferred from the greater political interest of young people than of parents. While children's responses may be expressions of norms and expectations, these responses may be inflated partly because of the teachers' considerable interest and willingness to participate in politics.

While these data indicate some influence of teachers on children's feelings, Table 4 shows that children's political interest is by no means independent of parental viewpoints. Agreement with parents is considerably higher than agreement with teachers in every commune. Teachers and parents frequently disagree, and teachers pull students toward their own feelings, which are typically feelings of great political interest. At the same time, large numbers of children still reflect their family background. (For all pairs of individuals, the similarity of willingness to participate in politics is less than that for political interest. However, the rank order of communes and pairs of individuals is the same for both variables.)

In regard to the influence of the surrounding environment, agreement follows a consistent pattern, with the static commune showing the highest levels of similarity in each comparison. This may not be due to any conscious effort on the part of socialization agents in any of the communes, but rather a function of a greater degree of homogeneity in Ovanåker than in the other areas. Homogeneity is suggested especially by the high percentage of agreement between parents and teachers in that commune. The greater political interest observed in the changing communities does not affect everyone uniformly. Hence children diverge frequently from their parents and teachers in expressed levels of interest.

In general, then, the economic and social situation in the surrounding area does have an influence on the extent of children's political interest and willingness to participate politically. This may

Table 4.

PERCENTAGES SIMILAR IN POLITICAL INTEREST

Commune	Parent-Child	Child-Playmate	Child-Teacher	Parent-Teacher
Retarding (Jokkmokk) ($N = 68$)	72	65	31	10
Static (Ovanåker) ($N = 62$ for first two, 53 for last two)	96	79	66	56
Expanding (Upplands-Bro) ($N = 61$)	78	77	52	9
Total ($N = 191$ for first two, 182 for last two)	82	73	48	23

Note: A pair is regarded as similar in political interest if both individuals take some or a great deal of interest in politics or if both individuals are slightly or not at all interested. In the child-parent situation, similarity means agreement with either or both parents. This naturally inflates the amount of agreement observed, but it does so consistently across communes. In the child-teacher situation, if the student had more than one teacher, similarity indicates agreement with at least half of the teachers. Child-peer agreement was based on perceptions of friend's attitudes. These measures also affect the rate of agreement, but, again, consistently so for all the communes.

be partly a direct consequence of children's perceptions of the environment in their local area, but more likely it results from the parents' and teachers' reactions to the social situation. Political involvement was particularly high among more educated respondents —the teachers. Direct influence of teachers' viewpoints along with the related differences in instructional emphasis may account for much of the greater interest of children in the two changing communes, compared to the static commune. Nevertheless, children still agreed in large measure with their parents.

The emphasis on domestic versus foreign and international issues in the classrooms of the three communes indicates that the type of change as well as the rate of change may be important in some aspects of political socialization. This appears clearly in the children's views on pressing political issues.

Attitudes on Political Issues

Table 5 shows the responses of children and parents to six policy issues. The statements were designed to tap three different dimensions of political attitudes—morality, economics, and depopulation. Two of the issues—attitudes toward working mothers and toward Swedish aid to developing countries—are moral issues. Though both of these issues involve economic considerations as well, in Sweden they are typically discussed privately and publicly as moral concerns. Responses to these issues differ only slightly among the three communes. The matter of working mothers seems to evoke a similar degree of concern in all three communes, as we indicated earlier. The matter of Swedish aid to developing countries, however, is a greater concern in the expanding commune than in the others. The lack of differences in expressed attitudes about this issue in part substantiates the viewpoint that it is considered primarily as a moral rather than economic question.

Wage and space exploration issues are primarily economic matters. As one would expect, individuals in the retarding unit most often think that wage differentials are too great and that money is wasted on space exploration. Least concern is shown with wage differences and with expenditures on space in the expanding unit, which is relatively well off economically. Attitudes on these economic issues vary, then, according to the character of the change in the commune, with the retarding commune at one extreme and the expanding commune at the other.

Attitudes on depopulation are mixed, though it is likely that people in the retarding commune have the strongest feelings about population movements. People in all communes agree that a declining population is undesirable. They do not agree that depopulation could be stopped if politicians really faced up to the problem. People in Jokkmokk, where the population is declining, are most convinced that the problem can be solved if it is faced. Children in the other two areas are much less certain of this. Presumably these differences

Table 5.

ATTITUDES OF CHILDREN AND PARENTS ON SIX POLITICAL ISSUES, IN PERCENTAGES

Issues	Retarding (Jokkmokk)		Static (Ovanåker)		Expanding (Upplands-Bro)	
	Children (N = 68)	Parents (N = 121)	Children (N = 62)	Parents (N = 117)	Children (N = 61)	Parents (N = 112)
It is not proper for mothers with little children to work outside the home	54	56	55	57	46	52
Sweden does not do enough for developing countries	57	20	63	24	56	18
Wage differences in Sweden are too great	75	87	71	87	57	79
The Great Powers spend too much on space exploration	82	81	68	82	64	72
Depopulation is not good for a commune	90	97	88	92	94	89
Depopulation could be stopped if the political will to do so existed	62	70	39	67	43	58

Note: Eight-year olds were not asked whether depopulation could be stopped; for this issue $N = 43$ for Jokkmokk, $N = 41$ for Ovanåker, and $N = 35$ for Upplands-Bro.

arise out of the concern in Jokkmokk that the population must somehow be stabilized for the area to survive, and that it therefore can be stabilized. In other areas, where there is understandably less immediate concern with the issue, people can more easily face up to what they regard as economic inevitability.

Attitudes on political issues thus offer a contrasting picture with that seen earlier for political interest. Here, the character of societal change (the tendency toward expansion or retardation) helps determine children's (and parents') views. The communal situation seems to be particularly important on issues of immediate or special relevance to the commune.

The parent and child generations differ dramatically and consistently on only one issue, that of Sweden's aid to developing countries. Children in all three communes are convinced that Sweden should increase its aid to developing areas. Even though many of these children will very likely change their opinions as they get older and become more directly concerned with economic problems, the differences are sufficiently large to suggest that the upcoming generation will probably take a different viewpoint than its predecessor on at least this aspect of Sweden's participation and role in the international system.

On economic and depopulation matters the parents seem generally more concerned about wage differentials and about expenditures on space exploration. Parents are also more convinced that the negative effects of depopulation can be averted if politicians chose to do so. In part this may again be a reflection of direct involvement with economic problems. The parental generation may also be more concerned with these matters because it feels less mobile than the younger people feel. Children always consider the possibility that they will emigrate to an expanding area as they get older. With parents this is less likely. Perhaps this explains as well why young people are more likely to be resigned to the opinion that depopulation is inevitable.

Significantly, the differences on economic and depopulation matters are least in the retarding commune. Children in Jokkmokk are just as likely to oppose excess expenditures on space exploration as their parents. On wage differentials and whether depopulation can be stopped, children differ from parents in the same direction as in the other areas, but to a lesser extent. These relatively small generational differences are no doubt due to the significance of the problems faced by Jokkmokk.

Agreement between children and their parents, friends, and teachers varies somewhat from issue to issue. Table 6 shows an overall picture of these similarities, the average percentage agreement between child and parent, child and playmate, and child and teacher. The comparisons between communes remain highly con-

Table 6.

AVERAGE PERCENTAGE AGREEMENT ON POLITICAL ISSUES

Commune	*Child-Parent*	*Child-Playmate*	*Child-Teacher*
Retarding (Jokkmokk)	71	61	58
Static (Ovanåker)	65	52	57
Expanding (Upplands-Bro)	65	46	50

Note: Each entry is the average percentage agreement on the six issues listed in Table 5.

sistent with our other data. Children's agreement with parents, playmates, and teachers is highest in the retarding commune; their agreement with playmates and teachers is lowest in the expanding area. This supports the conclusion that attitudes on political issues, as opposed to interest in politics, seem to relate to the character of societal change and not simply to the existence of change. The commune with a faltering economy and a declining population contains an inflated attitudinal agreement among socialization agents. The commune with an expanding economy and a growing population, even though faced with growing pains, generates dissimilarity between attitudes of individual socialization agents.

How can we explain these differences among the communes? The answer may partly lie in homogenization of attitudes among all groups in the retarding communes and diversity of attitudes in the expanding one. To the extent that this is true, communal differences might be said to have a direct effect on young people's attitudes as well the indirect effect of influencing most or all socialization agents with which the young person comes in contact. (Concordance of views between children and socialization agents need not imply that the agent has influenced the children.) The evidence from parents and teachers as well as from the other groups of commune workers and leaders that were interviewed, suggests that this might be a partial, though by no means total, explanation. Upplands-Bro, the expanding commune, clearly shows the greatest diversity of opinion, even on the issues on which the other communes show a high degree of consensus. In contrast, the declining commune of Jokkmokk shows considerable homogeneity of opinion. Significantly, the exceptions to homogeneity in Jokkmokk are on the issues of working mothers and Swedish assistence to developing nations. On these issues there were no differences of opinion among communes, and on the issue of foreign aid the diversity of adult opinion may help account for the large generational difference.

Homogeneity of opinion, however, does not fully explain the differences we have observed. Ovanåker is clearly more homogeneous than Upplands-Bro, and quite similar in this respect to Jokkmokk. Yet the static and retarding communes differed in some attitudes and in the extent of agent-child similarity. It would seem, then, that the communal situation does to a degree have an indirect as well as a direct effect on socialization of children in the area, but that there are also additional factors that must be included to fully explain the socialization process. To the degree that communal differences are important in the formation of political attitudes, it seems that the direction of political and economic changes rather than simply the existence of change must be considered.

Conclusion

It is indeed fruitful to relate socialization data to macro-level features of the political system, and in particular, to subnational characteristics of young people's environment. The clearest results relate to political interest and willingness to participate in politics. In this case, the existence of change and not the direction of change seems critical. In both the expanding and declining communes, poli-

Table 7.

INFLUENCE OF POLICY EXPECTATIONS ON PREDICTIONS FOR THE FUTURE

	CASE 1	CASE 2	CASE 3
POLICY:	Swedish cooperation with the European Economic Community (EEC) is not intensified. The nation continues to be the fundamental economic, social, and cultural unit, the present regional policy implying continued concentration of population and houses is maintained.	Swedish cooperation with the EEC is not intensified. The nation continues to be the fundamental economic, social, and cultural unit. A new regional policy is introduced so that expansion as well as retardation of certain regions ceases.	Swedish cooperation with the EEC is strongly intensified, particularly in regard to trade and economic matters. The present regional policy, implying continued concentration of population and houses, is maintained.
CONSEQUENCES FOR POPULATION AND ECONOMIC CHANGE:	The majority of the population lives in expanding communities.	The majority of the population lives in communities that are static in the sense that neither immigration nor emigration is great.	Population movement is toward Central Europe. The whole of Sweden retards (in spite of the migration within the nation, the expansion is smaller in the Stockholm region than in the rest of Europe).
PREDICTION: *Participation*	Great interest in politics and great activity in groups that aim at influencing public opinion, perhaps with low activity in parties and established organizations of various kinds.	Relatively small interest in politics and little political activity.	Great interest in politics and great activity in groups that aim at influencing public opinion, perhaps with low activity in parties and established organizations of various kinds.

	Attitudes		
Attitudes	Fewer demands than at present to lessen the economic inequalities within the country.	Much the same demands as at present to lessen the economic inequalities within the country.	More demands than at present to lessen economic inequalities within the country.
	Increased demands for help to developing countries.	Increased demands for help to developing countries.	Increased demands for help to developing countries.
	No demands to change the prevailing sexual role pattern.	No demands to change the prevailing sexual role pattern.	No demands to change the prevailing sexual role pattern.
Sense of efficacy	The chances of a change in the situation are considered small. Even if politicians want to bring about a change, economic forces make it impossible.	(The question is relatively meaningless since the policy assumption of itself implies no change.)	The chances of a change in the situation are considered small. But economic forces could be checked if political willingness to do so existed.
Generation gap	Particularly great on economic questions and on a sense of efficacy.	Particularly great on economic questions.	Small generation gaps.

tical interest as well as classroom discussions of social and political problems were heightened, while interest and discussions in the static commune were lower. The direction of political opinions, on the other hand, is more complicated to analyze. For one thing, the communal situation does not have a uniform effect on all political issues. In some instances, opinions are quite uniform throughout the nation. But to the degree that communal characteristics influence political opinions, the character or direction of change seems significant. This may be partly explained by the homogeneity of opinion in retarding and static areas and the considerable diversity of opinion in an expanding area.

Additional factors must be considered to fully understand the transmission of political values across generations. That this should be the case is not unexpected, for it would be surprising if subnational differences accounted for all of the variations in the socialization process. But it is nonetheless significant that part of the explanation should rely on important macro-level features of the subnational political system and not simply on the major socialization agents of the young person.

Relating socialization processes to macro-level factors has another value. It is notoriously difficult to project children's attitudes to adult attitudes and behavior. Situational factors in communities, in nations, and in the entire world can change drastically between childhood and adulthood, especially middle and late adulthood. If, however, situational factors are used to understand the socialization process (of children and of adults), the connections between childhood socialization and its individual and systemic consequences can be better understood.

We conclude with an example (Table 7) of how our expectations about policy decisions help determine our predictions about some aspects of the future of the Swedish political system. Depending upon the policy adopted and the resulting consequences for population movement and economic growth or decline, our predictions about the future of participation, political attitudes, and generational differences vary. (In my opinion, Case 1 is the most probable and Case 2 the least probable future alternative.)

IX

Political Education for Minority Groups

CHRISTINE BENNETT BUTTON

Political education in American secondary schools in under vigorous attack. Most of the criticism focuses upon the "unrealistic" and ethnocentric interpretation of government with its emphasis on the study of government structure and institutions, while the study of political behavior, processes, and conflict are largely ignored (Hess and other, 1968; "Political Education in the Public Schools," 1971). According to Massialas, "what is presently offered in the school is basically obsolete, irrelvant, and has no social or political significance" (1972, p. xii). Hess (1969) writes that the emphasis the school puts on stability and consensus contributes to the very fragmentation which political socialization is meant to prevent. Most American school children develop a highly idealized view of government and remain ignorant of legitimate channels of political influence other than voting. Such patterns of political socialization apparently are leading "more toward compliance and complacency on

This chapter is based upon the results of a research study performed pursuant to a contract with the Office of Education, U.S. Department of Health, Education, and Welfare (OEG-6-71-0531 [509]).

167

the one hand, and toward disillusionment, helplessness, anger, and perhaps even rejection of the system on the other" (p. 25).

While the criticism is clearly justified, it also implies that the schools can make a difference—an assumption not consistently supported by research (Langton and Jennings, 1968). Research is desperately needed, to illustrate the possible impact of alternative curricula on the political attitudes and behaviors of American youth.

A current review of the most outstanding social-studies curriculum projects (Krug, Poster, and Gillies, 1970) indicates that most programs establish learning objectives which are consistent with those recently set up by the Committee on Pre-Collegiate Education, American Political Science Association ("Political Education in the Public Schools," 1971). The Committee's objectives include knowledge of political "realities" as well as ideals; knowledge of political behavior and process as well as institutions and structures; knowledge of international political systems; understanding of political socialization processes; thinking, inquiry, and judgment skills; understanding of participatory skills and capacities; and the development of such political orientations as interest, feelings of efficacy, and so on. Attitudes are the focus of many of these objectives. While educators often expect to influence student attitudes, however, there is little evidence that they do (Ehman, 1970; Fisher, 1968; Langton and Jennings, 1968; Leslie and others, 1972; Litt, 1963; Patrick, 1971; Seasholes, 1965; Somit and others, 1970; Zellman and Sears, 1971). Perhaps they fail because they make little or no attempt to modify and measure changes in student behavior in either the classroom or more importantly, in the community. Despite growing evidence that behavior modification may be crucial in promoting attitudinal change, innovation in social studies education has been largely limited to canned inquiry episodes, problem "solving," and value-clarification models contrived for the classroom.

Even the most vigorous and thoughtful proposals for pre-collegiate political education do not suggest effecting change in student behavior as a means of promoting attitudinal goals. The Indiana Curriculum Project in Government (Mehlinger and Patrick, 1968)' represents one of the few such curriculum proposals which has been intensively researched. This program draws upon current political science emphases and research and offers a "realistic" view of the American political scene; it is found to be successful in enchancing high school students' knowledge of selected concepts and in promoting students' inquiry skills. Yet, researchers do not find in this curriculum the effect on political attitudes that they are looking for (Patrick, 1971). This lack may be due to a neglect of student political action—simply "studying about" is not the same as being "involved in."

It is difficult to validate yet if student attitude change is best promoted by modifying student behavior, since few curriculum programs that use this approach have been tested. Few such programs even exist, because a common social misconception asserts that "attitudes cause behavior" (Bem, 1970, p. 54). Hence, even though student behavior may be the ultimate target (for example, cross-cultural friendships, political participation), most educators focus directly upon attitudes with little success in changing either attitudes or behavior. While educators appear to assume that a change in attitudes brings about a change in behavior, several researchers assert the reverse—that behavior changes cause attitude changes (Bem, 1970; Triandis, 1971; Zimbardo and Ebbesen, 1970). Although a simple cause-effect relationship between behavioral and attitudinal change is unlikely, sufficient evidence suggests that changing attitudes by changing behavior may be more effective than vice versa.

Many people argue that educators do not have the right to attempt to change student attitudes—that students have a right to their own biases, prejudices, and apathy. These people forget that society, including the school, does mold and socialize. The question is, what values, attitudes, and behaviors should be promoted? I take the position here that educators must promote belief in the basic democratic values (such as political participation, majority rule with minority rights, human brotherhood and concern for community, and the right of dissent) and behavior that is consistent with these beliefs.

Thus, I developed experimental units in government and tested the extent to which these units influenced the political orientations of Anglo, Black, and Mexican-American twelfth graders. My curriculum focused on modifying student behavior, but I discovered that behavior modification, although necessary, is not a sufficient ingredient. Equally important are students' self-analysis of their own political socialization and their study of avenues of political involvement and change.

Experimental Curriculum

The overriding goal of the experimental units was to "teach for political efficacy" (C. Button, 1971). This goal was based on research which indicates that among important segments of American youth, feelings of political effectiveness and trust decrease as children reach adolesence (J. Button, 1971; Fox, 1970; Greenberg, 1970d; Keniston, 1968). This decrease is especially visible among Black and Mexican-American youth (Billings, 1970, 1971; Greenberg, 1969; Gutierrez and Hirsch, 1972, 1973; Hirsch and Gutierrez, 1972; Kenyon, 1969; Lyons, 1970). (See also Chapters Three, Four, and Five.) To teach young people to be more effective political actors, we educators must increase their feelings of political effectiveness. Assuming that we can do this, how should we do it?

In my experimental units, I concentrated on getting students to think about the development and use of political strategy to bring about social and political change and to become involved in community action related to their study. I developed the lessons and materials for these units during the six months preceding the experimental period. Herbert Hirsch, Associate Professor of Government (University of Texas at Austin), and Frances Nesmith, Superviser of Social Studies in the Austin Independent School District reviewed and critiqued the units.

Unit One emphasized each student's analysis of his own political socialization, particularly the key agents which have shaped his present political attitudes. The most meaningful and motivating place for the student to begin an exploration of the political system is within himself. Furthermore, individuals who are apathetic, politically angry, or racist can liberate themselves by discovering how these orientations develop and change and how they influence and are influenced by behavior and experience. In addition to introspection, students explored the meaning of political socialization by observing the process among small children, Appalachian Americans, and non-Anglo minorities. They then analyzed the "vicious cycle of political alienation" and how it might be broken.

In Unit Two the students are introduced to elitest theories of the American political system. Key questions for the student to ask and explore included: Who rules America? What political linkages exist between those who hold power and those who do not? How does institutional racism operate in the political system? (Dahl, 1967; Dolbeare, 1969; Domhoff, 1967; Dye and Ziegler, 1970; Knowles and Prewitt, 1969; Kolko, 1962). Students formed small groups to explore "realistic" political problems that occur in a power structure of both a single ruling elite and plural elites. Working in groups of five or six, nearly all students became involved in attempting to resolve hypothetical political problems. This activity is based upon the theory that student participation in an open-class atmosphere increases feelings of efficacy (Almond and Verba, 1963; Ehman, 1970). Students are expected to pick up ideas in the classroom for solving actual political or social problems that confront them outside the classroom; the sense of efficacy gained in the classroom should "spill over" into the actual political sphere. This is especially true in this case since students were involved in social or political fieldwork in the other units.

Unit Three posed the question: How have some dissatisfied groups attempted to change America? Students analyzed channels for exercising political influence and promoting change. Much of the material focused upon racial or poverty-ridden minorities, but each individual student was remined that he might at some time find himself in a political-minority position. Students used historical and current case studies to examine recurring techniques (such as parties, coalitions, elections, and interest groups) and time-specific techniques (such as sit-ins, boycotts, freedom rides) for bringing about political and social change. To counterbalance two possible myths about American history—that progress has been mainly peaceful, with little violent protest and that community violence is a phenomenon unique to Black Americans (Skolnick, 1969)— "mainstream" protest and political violence throughout American history were surveyed, using an evolution-to-revolution continuum. Patterns of political protest and influence employed by Black and Chicano groups were then examined in perspective.

Students also explored the goals and effectiveness of political violence in America. An in-depth analysis of the 1965 Watts riot was used to probe the validity of the "riff-raff" theory that characterizes people who riot (Sears and Tomlinson, 1970) and to begin examining the causes and meaning of riots in general. The goals, techniques, and effectiveness of nonviolent civil disobedience were examined. Speeches and letters of Martin Luther King and Cesar Chavez were used as expressions of the basic philosophy; examples such as the Montgromery bus boycott and the California grape-picker strikes were examined as instances of the philosophy in action. The historical development and current meanings of both the Brown Power and Black Power movements were also analyzed.

Unit Four involved student action research in the community. Early in the experimental period each student selected a community problem of interest to him, explored it, and worked on it by himself or in a small group for about four months. Thus the student could apply the concepts and skills learned in the classroom by extending the learning environment into the actual political structure.

The experimental period lasted four months during the fall semester, 1971. During this time, students in the contrast groups were taught according to the government-curriculum guide of the Austin Independent School District (1966). The guide emphasized the study of government structures and institutions. Teacher-directed discussion was the main teaching strategy used in all contrast classrooms. In both the contrast and experimental groups, students had similar perceptions of teacher knowledge, preparation, and enthusiasm and of the "freedom for student expression" and the "openness" of the classroom climate (C. Button, 1972).

Study Procedure

The study population originally consisted of 262 Anglo, Black and Mexican-American twelfth graders in two high schools in Austin, Texas. Attrition due to student transfers, dropping out of school, and early graduation reduced the final study size to 235 (114 at School A and 121 at School B). With the advice and decision of school district administrators and the consent of teachers, four twelfth-grade government classes were selected at each school;

of these, two were designated experimental and two as contrast groups. Classes were selected by school district officials so that one-third of the sample was Anglo, one-third was Black, and one-third was Mexican-American. This triethnic population made possible a comparison of the effects of the experimental curriculum on each of the predominant ethnic groups in the school district. Since the ethnic composition of individual classes did not approach the desired ratio, an ethnic balance was achieved by choosing four classes from School A, where Anglos and Blacks predominated, and four classes from School B, where Blacks and Mexican-Americans predominated. No measures of social class were obtained for individual students. School A drew students largely from middle-class and lower-class residential areas; the majority of students in School B came from lower middle-class and lower-class communities.

In both schools, students were assigned to their government classes according to the computerized scheduling procedures regularly used by the school district. Although these procedures did not group students by ability, they did not yield truly random groups. Nevertheless, students enrolled in the selected classes are assumed to be representative of twelfth graders in their respective schools, since no known biasing factors in scheduling indicate otherwise.

A political attitude and political knowledge questionnaire was administered to all students immediately before and after the experimental treatment. Embedded in the questionnaire were items to measure political cynicism, political efficacy, and political knowledge.

Political cynicism has been defined as distrust of government, disbelief that government leaders are usually honest and competent, and will usually act in the interest of the people. The items I used to test cynicism are almost identical to scales used in research by Jennings and Niemi (1968a) and Agger and others (1961):

> Do you think that most of the people running the government are honest, not very many are, or do you think hardly any of them are?
>
> Do you think that people in the government waste a lot of money paid in taxes, waste some of it, or don't waste very much of it?

How much of the time do you think you can trust the government in Washington to do what is right—just about always, most of the time, or only some of the time?

Do you feel that almost all of the people running the government are smart people who usually know what they are doing, or do you think that quite a few of them don't seem to know what they are doing?

Would you say that the government is run for the benefit of all the people or that it is usually run by a few big officials looking out for themselves?

Cynicism (CYN) scores can range from five to fifteen, using a range of three points for each question (a score of fifteen represents high cynicism). A Pearson's test-retest reliability check was computed on each attitudinal scale. One additional government class in each of the target high schools was selected for testing; identical forms of the questionnaire were administered twice in each class, two weeks apart. Test-retest reliability of this scale was computed to be $r = .52$.

Political efficacy is defined by Easton and Dennis (1967) as an individual's sense of direct political potency, a belief that government is responsive to the desires of individuals. I tested this concept with an eight-item scale (EFF8) and a five-item scale (EFF5), with the latter embedded in the former (Easton and Dennis, 1967). (Items three through seven constitute EFF5.)

Voting is the only way that people like my mother and father can help run things.

Sometimes I can't understand what goes on in government.

What happens in the government will happen no matter what people do. It is like the weather, there is nothing people can do about it.

There are some big powerful men in the government who are running the whole thing and they do not care about us ordinary people.

My family doesn't have any say about what the government does.

I don't think people in the government care much what people like my family think.

Citizens don't have a chance to say what they think about running the government.

How much does the average person help decide which laws are made for our country? (Just about always, most of the time, some of the time.)

Five responses can be given to each item (on a Likert scale): strongly agree, agree, disagree, strongly disagree, and don't know or no opinion. Scores on EFF8 can range from eight to thirty-two and on EFF5 from five to twenty.

I developed a third political efficacy scale (EFF2) to probe students' perceptions of their abilities to deal with the local and national problems they considered most pressing: What do you think are (Austin's) (America's) two biggest problems? Do you feel that you personally can do anything to help solve these problems? (Yes, no, don't know), if so, what? if not, why?

Four points are awarded if a student checks "yes" and gives an example of action he can take, three points if he checks only "yes", two points if he checks only "no"; and one point if he checks "no" and gives an example. The highest possible score on the scale of EFF2 is eight—four for the question concerning Austin and four for the one concerning America.

Test-restest reliabilities for the three measures of politicial efficacy were as follows: EFF8, $r = .85$; EFF5, $r = .78$; and EFF2, $r = .64$.

Political knowledge (KNOW) was measured by an objective test of twenty-eight items related to objectives of the experimental units and general civic knowledge. The total number of correctly answered questions is the student's score.

In addition to the tests, a stratified sample of sixty individuals from the original study population was chosen at random to be interviewed. Male and female students and the three ethnic groups were equally represented in the interview sample; twice as many students from the experimental as from the contrast group were selected for interviewing.

The interview was intended for probing in depth the student's sense of political efficacy and political cynicism, as well as his participation in political action and his interest in politics. An attempt was made to ascertain the extent to which the student's government course had affected these orientations. Beyond this, the student's perception of his government teacher's interest, enthusiasm, knowledge, and preparation in the subject matter were probed, as well as the degree to which the student felt free to express his opinions and actually did participate. Uniform questions were asked each interviewee according to a schedule I developed (C. Button, 1972), but probing was necessarily individualized.

Interviews were conducted two to three months after the experimental period had ended and the questionnaire posttest had been administered. Each interview was taped, took place in either an empty classroom or in a small private office, and lasted approximately an hour.

Another aspect measured by the study was student-initiated interaction. *Student-initiated interaction* was defined as a question initiated by a student and directed at the teacher or another student, or as an unelicited statement made by a student (C. Button, 1972). Each of the eight classes was coded for student-initiated interaction by three trained observers for two full class periods each week, during seven weeks of the experimental period.

Data on student-initiated interaction were gathered to study the impact of the experimental curriculum on behavior. Increases and decreases in verbal interaction initiated by a student were assumed to show changes in efficacious student behavior. These changes were related to changes in student scores on the scales of political efficacy and cynicism.

Analysis of Data. Analysis of variance of the pretest scores revealed no significant differences on any of the criterion measures between the experimental classes at either school and no significant differences on these measures between the contrast classes at either school. Thus in both schools the experimental classes could be studied as one group and the contrast classes as another group.

The anlysis of variance of the pretest scores also revealed that even before the experimental period began there were significant differences on the dependent variables between the experimental and contrast group of School A (not of School B, however). To take these differences into account, analysis of covariance of pretest scores on posttest scores was utilized as the major statistical treatment of obtained data.

The analysis of covariance may be conceptualized as follows: As in an analysis of variance, posttest scores of students in the experimental and contrast groups were compared to see if the obtained differences were significant. But, before these comparisons were made, the posttest scores were adjusted to take into account variance in scores on the pretest. Thus significant differences between the experimental and contrast groups on any of the dependent variables in the pretest would "disappear" in the posttest comparison unless these differences were promoted during the period between the pretest and postest. Since students comprising the study's experimental and contrast groups were believed to be comparable, once any initial differences on the dependent variables were "subtracted out," any remaining significant differences obtained on the posttest comparisons were assumed to be caused by differences in their government courses.

Limitations. Four teachers were used to teach the four groups at School A and B. I taught the experimental group at School A. This teaching arrangement causes real limitations in this study. But if only one teacher had been used in each school, it would have been impossible to prevent "contamination" from the experimental curriculum in the contrast groups.

In addition, the decision to analyze the data separately by school has disadvantages. Given the small number of Blacks in each school, it could be argued that data analysis should be conducted on the entire sample of students. But most of the Black students at School A had attended all-Black schools until the fall of 1972, when busing of Black students was begun. School B was a well-established school with close ties with the Black and Mexican-American communities in the eastern portion of the city. Very few Anglos attended School B and few Mexican-Americans attended School A. Thus I believed it best to control for school effect by analyzing the data separately for each school.

While these limitations mean it is difficult to separate out teacher and curriculum effects and the interaction of the two, the study findings were nonetheless highly consistent for both schools, using all the different techniques to gather data.

Study Results

Results from the analysis of covariance and the in-depth interviews suggest that the experimental units increased students'

feelings of political efficacy and knowledge.* Results for cynicism
are mixed, although for an important reason.

Table 1 summarizes mean scores on political cynicism, efficacy, and knowledge at School A, by ethnic group and treatment
group (experimental and contrast). ANCOVA results are reported in

Table 1.

MEANS AND ADJUSTED MEANS OF CRITERION SCORES
OF SCHOOL A SUBJECTS

ETHNIC GROUP

	Blacks		Anglos	
Treatment	*Pretest*	*Adjusted Posttest*	*Pretest*	*Adjusted Posttest*
Experimental (Blacks, $N = 10$; Anglos, $N = 43$)				
Scale				
CYN	10.20	9.87	8.84	8.75
EFF8	20.10	21.52	20.70	20.90
EFF5	13.80	15.31	14.28	14.09
EFF2	4.90	4.78	5.30	6.01
KNOW	14.80	16.08	13.37	19.84
Contrast (Blacks, $N = 7$; Anglos, $N = 54$)				
Scale				
CYN	11.86	11.08	10.63	11.27
EFF8	16.14	19.98	20.65	19.71
EFF5	10.00	13.05	13.78	13.16
EFF2	3.57	4.95	5.11	5.21
KNOW	12.43	14.81	13.22	13.41

Table 2. The analysis of covariance at School A revealed a significant main effect for treatment on three dependent variables: CYN,
EFF8, and KNOW. In the contrast group, CYN mean scores increased
from the pretest to the posttest, while EFF8 and EFF5 mean scores
decreased. In the experimental group, however, mean scores on all
three EFF measures increased. Although the main effect for ethnicity
was significant on EFF2 and on KNOW, no significant main effects

* The reader not interested in the statistical details of the study
results is encouraged to skip to the discussion of the in-depth interviews below.

Table 2.

ANALYSIS OF COVARIANCE OF SCHOOL A SUBJECTS'
PRETEST SCORES ON POSTTEST SCORES

Scale	Source	DF	Adjusted MS	F	P
CYN					
	Treatment	1	66.29	17.05	.00
	Ethnicity	1	5.11	1.31	.25
	Sex	1	10.31	2.65	.10
EFF8					
	Treatment	1	24.10	3.70	.05
	Ethnicity	1	2.91	.45	.51
	Sex	1	.68	.10	.75
EFF5					
	Treatment	1	7.94	2.20	.14
	Ethnicity	1	7.44	2.06	.15
	Sex	1	.86	.24	.63
EFF2					
	Treatment	1	6.68	2.29	.13
	Ethnicity	1	9.40	3.22	.07
	Sex	1	.05	.02	.90
KNOW					
	Treatment	1	805.14	78.21	.00
	Ethnicity	1	39.60	3.85	.05
	Sex	1	3.39	.33	.56

Note: $N = 53$ in experimental group; $N = 61$ in contrast group.

for sex and no interactions were discovered on any of the dependent variables at School A.

To probe the nature of these data from the analysis of covariance, four planned comparisons were performed between the adjusted means of the four ethnicity/treatment groups (C. Button, 1972). Differences obtained between blacks and Anglos in the experimental group were significant on the following dependent variables: EFF5 (p = .03), EFF2 (p = .05), and KNOW (p = .00). Blacks manifested higher EFF5 scores than did Anglos in the experimental group, while Anglos' scores on EFF2 and KNOW were higher than blacks'. No significant differences were found between the adjusted means of blacks and Anglos in the contrast group on any of the dependent variables, or between blacks in the experimental group and blacks in the contrast group. However, differences between Anglos in the two treatment groups were found to be significant on CYN (p = .00), EFF8 (p = .07), EFF2 (p = .07), and KNOW (p = .00). The adjusted means of Anglos in the contrast groups were significantly higher on CYN, and lower on EFF8, EFF2, and KNOW than were those of their counterparts in the experimental group.

To further interpret the results of the analysis of covariance, analysis of variance of pretest and posttest scores for each ethnic/treatment group were performed to determine whether changes on the posttest were significant. The following significant differences were obtained (C. Button, 1972): (1) Anglos in the contrast group gained on CYN (p = .06) and decreased on EFF8 (p = .10); (2) experimental group Anglos gained on EFF2 (p = .01) and KNOW (p = .00); and (3) experimental group blacks gained on EFF8 (p = .11) and on EFF5 (p = .00).

It appears that while feelings of political efficacy may have increased among both Black and Anglo students in the experimental group, different facets of political efficacy are involved. The Anglo student, as measured by EFF2, may have developed increased confidence and knowledge of how to take concrete action to help solve the local and national problems he perceives to be most important. Among Black students, on the other hand, a more generalized sense of political efficacy seems to have increased. Or perhaps the experimental group Black students revealed slight decreases on EFF2 (compared with significant increases on EFF8 and EFF5) simply because EFF8 and EFF5 involve checking a response, while EFF2 is more open-ended and requires the respondent to fill in blanks as well.

Finally, an assessment of the differential impact of the experimental units on the two ethnic groups should include that prior to the experimental period Anglos scored significantly higher on the EFF scales and lower on CYN than did Blacks (C. Button, 1972, p. 45). It is obviously more difficult to increase a high sense of efficacy than it is to increase a low one. In the words of one student (who was representative of Anglo males in the experimental group): "Before I took government I already felt that I could have a say in what the government does, but I didn't know exactly how to go about it. Now I know what I can do."

The main point about School A, then, is that experimental group students seemed to develop an increased sense of political effectiveness and interest. Students who possessed relatively high feelings of political efficacy before the experimental period appeared to have these feelings reinforced by becoming better informed about avenues of political participation.

Results of the analysis of covariance at School B, where blacks and Mexican-Americans predominated, differ from those obtained at School A. Mean political cynicism, political efficacy, and political knowledge scores are summarized by treatment, sex, and ethnic group in Table 3. ANCOVA results are reported in Table 4. Examination of Table 4 reveals that the sex main effect was statistically significant on three criterion measures: CYN, EFF8, and EFF5. Only one significant main effect, for KNOW, was obtained and neither significant main effects for ethnicity nor interactions were noted.

A series of planned comparisons between the adjusted means of males and females (with treatment/within ethnic group) were performed on all five dependent variables to explore the nature of the significant sex effect (C. Button, 1972). A discernible pattern emerged. In every comparison, except Mexican-Americans in the contrast group, females' CYN mean scores increased, whereas their EFF8 and EFF5 scores decreased. For males, the findings were exactly reversed. With regard to EFF2, the results are less clear.

While black females in both the experimental and contrast group scored higher on CYN and lower on the EFF measures than did their male counterparts, these differences were found to be significant only in the contrast group (C. Button, 1972, p. 58). The reverse pattern emerged among the Mexican-Americans. Here, significant differences between the sexes were found in the experimental group rather than in the contrast group. Mexican-American experimental group females' adjusted posttest means were higher on CYN and lower on EFF8 and on EFF5 than were the adjusted posttest means of Mexican-American males. These findings suggest that the experimental units probably had a "positive" impact on blacks

Table 3.

MEANS AND ADJUSTED MEANS OF CRITERION SCORES OF SCHOOL B SUBJECTS

BLACKS

	Males		Females	
Treatment	Pretest	Adjusted Posttest	Pretest	Adjusted Posttest
Experimental (Males, $N = 8$; Females, $N = 21$)				
Scale				
CYN	10.63	9.21	9.57	10.30
EFF8	17.89	19.89	18.76	18.28
EFF5	11.50	13.11	12.81	11.82
EFF2	4.38	5.35	4.24	5.06
KNOW	9.50	15.34	10.38	15.11
Contrast (Males, $N = 15$; Females, $N = 4$)				
Scale				
CYN	10.47	9.23	11.00	11.38
EFF8	19.47	19.47	17.50	17.50
EFF5	12.87	13.16	11.50	11.65
EFF2	4.47	4.85	5.75	4.56
KNOW	11.67	13.25	12.25	12.08

MEXICAN-AMERICANS

	Males		Females	
Treatment	Pretest	Adjusted Posttest	Pretest	Adjusted Posttest
Experimental (Males, $N = 14$; Females, $N = 23$)				
Scale				
CYN	10.21	9.26	9.78	10.28
EFF8	18.64	19.76	18.47	18.76
EFF5	12.64	13.30	12.17	12.08
EFF2	4.43	4.30	4.48	4.86
KNOW	14.07	16.73	9.04	15.86
Contrast (Males, $N = 17$; Females, $N = 19$)				
Scale				
CYN	10.24	9.34	9.84	9.59
EFF8	18.77	18.83	17.68	18.62
EFF5	12.35	12.76	11.68	12.22
EFF2	4.47	4.43	4.11	4.57
KNOW	11.82	10.54	9.53	11.67

Table 4.

ANALYSIS OF COVARIANCE OF SCHOOL B SUBJECTS'
PRETEST SCORES ON POSTTEST SCORES

Scale	Source	DF	Adjusted MS	F	P
CYN					
	Treatment	1	3.35	.70	.40
	Ethnicity	1	.32	.07	.79
	Sex	1	21.59	4.53	.03
EFF8					
	Treatment	1	.58	.08	.78
	Ethnicity	1	.63	.09	.77
	Sex	1	31.82	4.32	.03
EFF5					
	Treatment	1	4.24	.03	.86
	Ethnicity	1	2.31	.55	.46
	Sex	1	29.09	6.86	.01
EFF2					
	Treatment	1	2.65	.59	.44
	Ethnicity	1	3.87	1.46	.22
	Sex	1	.159	.06	.80
KNOW					
	Treatment	1	519.38	53.79	.00
	Ethnicity	1	9.66	.10	.75
	Sex	1	.50	.05	.82

Note: $N = 66$ in experimental group; $N = 55$ in contrast group.

and Mexican-American males and that Mexican-American females may have been "negatively" affected by the experimental curriculum.

Results of the covariance analyses were probed by an analysis of variance of individuals' pretest and posttest scores for each sex/ethnicity group to see whether the posttest scores of any of these groups were significantly different from the pretest scores on any of the dependent variables. In the contrast group, no changes on the posttest scores were significant except among black males, where CYN decreased ($p = .09$). Within the experimental group, all sex/ethnic groups increased their scores on KNOW ($p = .00$), and black females increased on EFF2 ($p = .04$). In addition, a pattern emerged which may be interpreted to mean that the experimental units were more salient than the contrast units in promoting increased feelings of political efficacy—at least for blacks and Mexican-American males (that is, gains on the EFF posttests were close to the .10 level of significance in the experimental group but not in the contrast group) (C. Button, 1972).

Making practical sense out of this type of statistical analysis is always a problem. It is difficult to equate a mean score on CYN or any of the EFF scales with an expected attitude or behavior. It is difficult to judge the degree of score increase or decrease that indicates attitudinal or behavioral change. Data from the student interviews provided valuable insight into this problem of interpretation. Indeed, the interview technique, especially through the use of semi-projective items, appeared to have been more valuable than the pencil-paper questionnaire for tapping various added dimensions of political attitudes.

At both schools, results from the student interviews reinforced and amplified the statistical findings of the analyses of variance and covariance. While the statistical findings were less than conclusive at School B, the student interviews revealed marked differences between the experimental and contrast groups at School B. Evidence from the student interviews was highly consistent in both schools and suggested that the experimental units may have increased feelings of political efficacy among all the groups studied, with the exception of the Mexican-American females.

Tables 5 and 6 show interview data summarizing the extent and direction of influence the government course had on each interviewed student's feelings of political efficacy, trust, and interest and general feelings of political effectiveness. (See also C. Button, 1972.)

Differences indicated between the treatment groups are striking. At School A, 75 percent of the interviewed students from the experimental group indicated efficacy increases at the local level and strong influence from their government course; in the contrast group, 100 percent of the interviewees indicated no attitudinal change and no course influence. This pattern is found at School B as well, with 75 percent from the experimental group indicating increased efficacy and 90 percent of the contrast group indicating no

Table 5.

GOVERNMENT COURSE INFLUENCE AT SCHOOL **A**

	Experimental (N = 20)			Contrast (N = 10)		
	Strong	Weak	None	Strong	Weak	None
Efficacy at Local Level						
Increased	75%	20%				
Decreased						
Same			5%			100%
Efficacy at National Level						
Increased	35%	50%		10%		
Decreased						
Same		5%	10%	10%	80%	
Political Trust at Local Level						
Increased	30%					
Decreased	20%	10%		40%		
Same		5%	35%			60%
Political Trust at National Level						
Increased				10%	10%	
Decreased	30%	5%		40%		
Same		5%	60%			40%
Political Interest						
Increased	75%	10%		30%		
Decreased						
Same			15%			70%
Political Effectiveness						
Increased	60%	25%		30%		
Decreased				20%		
Same		5%	10%	10%		40%

attitude change and no course influence. The findings are generally similar for political efficacy at the national government level, except that influence from the experimental units appears weaker at School A.

Table 6.

GOVERNMENT COURSE INFLUENCE AT SCHOOL B

	Experimental (N = 20)			Contrast (N = 10)		
	Strong	Weak	None	Strong	Weak	None
Efficacy at Local Level						
Increased	75%	5%		10%		
Decreased	10%					
Same			10%			90%
Efficacy at National Level						
Increased	55%	15%		10%		
Decreased	5%					
Same			25%			90%
Political Trust at Local Level						
Increased	20%					
Decreased	35%					
Same			45%			100%
Political Trust at National Level						
Increased	10%					
Decreased	25%	5%				
Same			60%			100%
Political Interest						
Increased	70%	5%	5%	10%		
Decreased					10%	
Same		20%				80%
Political Effectiveness						
Increased	70%	20%		10%	10%	
Decreased						
Same			10%		10%	70%

Furthermore, the data from the interviewees reveals a clear trend of sex differences in the experimental groups at both schools (C. Button, 1972). Anglo and Black females, who appeared to have developed increased feelings of political efficacy, indicated stronger course influence than did their male counterparts; Mexican-

American males show efficacy increases and stronger course influence than do their female counterparts.

An interest in politics is believed to be integral to a high sense of political efficacy. Political interest was not tested in the EFF scales but was probed in the in-depth interviews. Impact from the experimental units on students' interest in politics (as well as in the government course) appears to be marked. Most of the experimental group at School A (85 percent) and at School B (75 percent) indicated increased political interest. Most students from the contrast group at both schools did not appear to have increased interest in politics, and influence from the government course seemed weak or nonexistent. The data show a similar trend by sex as that indicated in the findings on political efficacy: Anglo and Black females in the experimental group appeared to have increased interest in politics, while the Mexican-American girls tended to remain unaffected.

In-depth interviews probed a further dimension of political efficacy that was not measured by the EFF scales. Near the end of the interview, each student was asked directly whether or not he felt politically effective, and whether or not he had always felt this way. Findings on the students' stated political effectiveness are similar to those obtained for political interest and efficacy: 85 percent of the experimental group students at School A and 90 percent at School B expressed increased feelings of political effectiveness, as compared with 30 percent in the contrast group at School A and 20 percent at School B.

Influence from the experimental curriculum on students' feelings of political trust varied more than influence on students' feelings of political efficacy. In the experimental groups, political trust of the national government tended to decrease or remain the same, while at the local level some increases in political trust were indicated. Among Black students and female Anglo students, trust of both the national and local government tended to decrease. A comparison between the experimental and contrast groups, however, suggests that the experimental units had more impact on political trust (or distrust) than did the contrast units: 60 percent of the contrast group students at School A and 100 percent at School B indicated unchanged political trust at the local level and weak or no course influence. Concerning political trust at the national level, 40 percent of the contrast group at School A and 100 percent at School B indicated no increase or decrease in trust and weak or no course influence. Noteworthy is the finding that 40 percent of the interviewees from the contrast group at School A indicated decreased political trust at both the national and local levels. Apparently the curriculum used in the contrast group at School A did have a "negative" impact on students' political trust.

One of the most interesting findings of the study concerns the relationship between political cynicism and political efficacy. The political efficacy of Blacks in the experimental group (and also perhaps that of Anglo females) was apparently raised not by giving them a false sense of high trust or confidence in the government, but by actually increasing their cynicism about the government. Mexican-American males showed the same reaction in the interviews, although statistical analyses of their responses did not make it evident.

One Mexican-American male expressed the relationship between political cynicism and efficacy in the following typical comment: "We saw how if you don't feel something is right, get involved! I've learned that I don't have to be afraid to stand up and try. Before I thought someone would just call me a dumb Mexican. Now I see I have a chance. . . . I also learned what a crooked politician is; I used to think they were holy. From the first grade, I was taught ours was the best government in the world. Brainwashed! Like the Pledge of Allegiance—it's just a routine."

Results from the student interviews suggest that influence from the experimental units was even more clear-cut at School B than at School A. These results are puzzling because the statistical findings of the analysis of covariance were much less conclusive at School B than at School A. But there are several possible explanations for the inconsistency. First, it might be possible that too many "leading" questions were asked during the interviews except that most interviewees were eager to talk and literally "gushed forth" with information before it could be elicited by the interviewer, and the same interviewing schedule was used with both groups of students.

A more probable explanation is that the written question-

naire did little probing, and a student could easily respond super-
ficially. The extensive probing used in the interview technique, plus
the use of several semiprojective items, may have tapped more
dimensions of political attitudes than the questionnaire could have
tapped. This may have been especially true at School B, since Blacks
and Mexican-Americans may have a disadvantage among middle-
class Anglos with possible cultural biases in the questionnaire method
or wording (Labov, 1969; Labov and Robins, 1969).

Finally, it is possible that the experimental curriculum had a
delayed impact, and hence greater attitude changes were expressed
during the interviews, which were conducted some two to three
months after the questionnaire posttest had been administered. This
is what happened with Anglos at School A in regards to racism; so
perhaps it applies to other areas also.

Many of the students reacted with hostility or indifference
when racism was discussed in class. Hence, their favorable and
spontaneous comments several months later during the interviews
came as a surprise. It appeared that, by studying the process of
political socialization, most students gained insight into how their
feelings about other racial groups had evolved. The following statements made by two Anglo males are illustrative: "My ideas about
discrimination and racism against your minority groups have
changed from saying they have quite a bit of say to believing they
don't have much say. We read about Chavez and Martin Luther
King and how discrimination has affected minority groups—and
it kind of made me change my opinion to feel that minority groups
are discriminated against more than I thought before I went into
the government class. . . . Sometimes my friends are really racist
and I kind of feel towards them that all Blacks are bad and no
good. But government class had a great influence on me as far as
not agreeing with my friends on discrimination and minority
groups." "This kind of went against a basic fact that I got from my
own political socialization—that people choose their own class, and
if you ever want to get ahead you can. I never really believed institutional racism existed before; since government class, I've done
research on this. . . . It adds to my idea about inefficiency of
government."

Curriculum Impact. The nature of the influence from the

respective government courses was also probed during the student interviews. Each student was asked to pick out one or two things about his government course which had had the greatest impact on his thinking. Student choices of the most influential aspects of the government course are summarized in Table 7. The categories used in these tables were derived from comments made by the students and are therefore different for each school. From the contrast group in School A, half of the students who were interviewed could cite no specifics or think of any influence their government class had on them, in contrast to only one-tenth of the interviewed students from the experimental group at School A. The most salient aspects of the experimental curriculum appeared to be the study of racism and minority group culture, political socialization, and among Anglos, the action research.

At School B the evidence of curricular impact is similar. Seven of the ten students interviewed from the contrast group were unable to cite anything influential about their government course, in contrast to only one of the twenty interviewees from the experimental group. Beyond this, however, the pattern at School B was different from that of School A. Among both Black and Mexican-American students, the categories which appeared to be most salient were changing the government and the Blue Book of readings. (This pamphlet replaced the regular government textbook and contained the written materials developed for the experimental units.) While it is impossible to isolate the Blue Book from other aspects of the course, and many students at School A did refer to it at some point during the interview, students at School B were remarkably more impressed by it. As two of them put it:

> The Blue Book told it like it really was and not how the white newscasters say it. In the textbooks we're doin' everything wrong and the whites are doing it right. This book talked about the bus boycott, Watts, and Chavez. It showed you the different approaches and which ones work and what doesn't. In other words, if you ever have the urge to change something you will know what to do.

> There's a lot of my black friends in organizations

Table 7.

STUDENT CHOICES OF INFLUENTIAL ASPECTS
OF THE GOVERNMENT COURSE

SCHOOL A

	Experimental (N = 20)		*Contrast* (N = 10)	
	Anglos	*Blacks*	*Anglos*	*Blacks*
Teacher on Cynicism			2	1
Teacher on Writing Congress			1	
Racism, Minority Cultures	8	5		
Political Socialization	4	2		
Readings	1	1		
Action Research	6	1		
Courts		1		
Congressional Simulation				2
Problem Solving		1		
No Specifics Mentioned	1	1	2	3

SCHOOL B

	Experimental (N = 20)		*Contrast* (N = 10)	
	Blacks	*Mexican-Americans*	*Blacks*	*Mexican-Americans*
"Changing the Government"	4	3		
Reading Booklet	5	2		
"Raps"	2	2		
Action Research	1	1		
Racism, Minority Histories	2	4	1	
Newspaper				1
Court Field Trip				1
No Specifics Mentioned		1	4	3

to help black people, and this in a way coordinates with the book we were studying, and also our fieldwork. And suddenly, I wanted to be part of an organization, that's how much the course influenced me. . . . And a lot of it was just that book. I really liked it.

At School B students seem to have taken case studies as models for "changing the government," while at School A students frequently perceived them as providing insight into interracial relations, perhaps because at School A many students were experiencing school desegregation by busing for the first time.

Finally, while many of the experimental group students at both schools spontaneously referred to the action research as having had some impact on their thinking, many more students at School A chose this experience as having been most influential. This may possibly be because more students became actively involved in the fieldwork at School A (90 percent) than at School B (50 percent), where most students held after-school jobs and had more difficulty than the students at School A in obtaining released time from school to carry out their research.

In an attempt to assess possible course impact on actual political behavior, the interviewer asked each student whether or not he had registered to vote, whether or not he was currently involved in any new political or social action, and whether or not he intended to become involved. Table 8 summarizes this data.

Whether or not the government class influenced students to register to vote was often impossible to ascertain. No pattern emerged to indicate that treatment and registration were correlated. Proportionately, approximately as many students in the contrast group as in the experimental group in both schools registered to vote.

A slight trend emerged at each school indicating that more students from the experimental group than from the contrast group were currently involved in some new political or social action. Among the students from the experimental group, the government class appeared at least to a degree to have influenced students to become involved in some new activity. Students from the contrast group appeared to have been stimulated by sources outside the school, such as Upward Bound. Furthermore, a number of students from the experimental groups at both schools expressed the clear intention of becoming involved in such action in the near future (eight at School A and seven at School B); no students from the contrast group at School A and only two at School B expressed this intent.

Table 8.
POLITICAL BEHAVIORS OF INTERVIEWED STUDENTS

SCHOOL A

	Experimental Group		Contrast Group	
	Anglos (N = 11)	Blacks (N = 7)	Anglos (N = 5)	Blacks (N = 5)
Registered to vote	64%	43%	60%	40%
Not registered to vote	36	57	40	60
New political action	45%	14%		20%
No political action	55	86	100%	80

SCHOOL B

	Experimental Group		Contrast Group	
	Mexican-Americans (N = 10)	Blacks (N = 10)	Mexican-Americans (N = 5)	Blacks (N = 5)
Registered to vote	70%	60%	80%	60%
Not registered to vote	30	40	20	40
New political action	40%	20%	20%	
No political action	60	80	80	100%

These findings may well reflect influence from the government classes. While all students were targets of a "register eighteen-year-olds to vote" campaign, only those students in the experimental groups emphasized political action alternatives to voting. If anything, the experimental curriculum deemphasized the vote and stressed other channels of political participation, such as political parties, interest groups, protest, and direct action.

Student-Initiated Classroom Interaction. The results of the analyses of the student-initiated interaction data tend to corroborate the findings from the attitude measures and in-depth interview phases of this study. Student initiations increased in the experimental group at School A, and though initiation increases were less pronounced at School B, a wide range of students initiated in the experimental groups at both schools. Furthermore, in the experimental group at School A, Blacks initiated proportionately more than their Anglo classmates, with the largest differences occurring at the end of the experimental period. No differences were discovered between Anglo and Black students in the contrast group. Finally, the results of attitude-behavior correlations at School A suggest an association between student initiations and their scores on the scales of CYN and EFF—student initiation was negatively correlated with scores on CYN and positively correlated with scores on EFF. These correlations were most pronounced among Anglo females in the experimental group. (For more details, refer to C. Button, 1972, and Ponder and Button, 1973.)

Implications for Political Education

While this study is clearly exploratory, its findings support the critics of the traditional approach to political education who advocate emphasis upon political behavior, processes, and conflict, rather than the usual emphasis upon government structure and institutions. Since all three methods of data analysis corroborate each other (except possibly the analysis of covariance results in School B), the experimental units did have impact on the political orientations explored in this study. The tested curriculum seemed to increase feelings of political efficacy, interest, and knowledge among the Anglo, Black, and Mexican-American students studied. Results from the student interviews reinforced the statistical findings and suggest also that the experimental curriculum enhanced political interest and selected political behaviors. The analyses of student-initiated interaction suggest that the experimental curriculum may also have had impact on students' behavior in the classroom and that increased scores on the EFF scales often link with increases in student-initiated discussion, especially among Blacks and Anglo females.

Political cynicism among Anglos using the experimental materials did not appear to increase. Hence, as is noted by Patrick (1971), the study of conflict and the "sordid realities" of the American political system seems not necessarily to diminish feelings of political trust. Blacks in the School A experimental group, however, demonstrated increased feelings of both political cynicism and political efficacy. These findings are consistent with Ehman's (1970) conclusions that the discussion of controversial social issues does not erode the political trust of Anglos, while it does increase feelings of political cynicism among Blacks; it increases feelings of political efficacy among both Black and Anglo students, however. Ehman also suggests that "Increased opportunity for participation in class appears to be the relevant linkage for white adolescents; for Blacks, exposure to successful models of political participation is the explanatory factor" (p. 119). Data from the student interviews support this conclusion. Blacks and Mexican-Americans were strongly influenced by the case studies of political change in the experimental curriculum and viewed them as models of political action for change; the actual political fieldwork, along with the study of minority groups, appeared to be most salient for Anglos.

Findings from the contrast units may be related to the findings of Langton and Jennings (1968). The contrast classes seemed to reduce cynicism and increase efficacy among black students, but had the reverse effect for Anglos. Langton and Jennings conclude that the traditional twelfth-grade curriculum has more "positive" impact on Blacks than on Anglos and that it is largely redundant for Anglos. Perhaps redundancy also explains the lack of impact these units had on Mexican-Americans. Other possible explanations include the basic political orientations among Mexican-Americans which differ from those of Black and Anglo-Americans (Garcia, 1972a) or the nature of the instrumentation itself.

In contrast to the Langton and Jennings findings of no change at all among Anglos, the government course experienced by students in the contrast group appeared to have increased Anglo students' feelings of political cynicism and decreased their feelings of political efficacy. These findings must be cautiously interpreted, since a traditional government course in other settings might have a different impact than that of the contrast group studied here. But at the very least, the data indicate that twelfth-grade government curricula which emphasize structure and institutions and deemphasize political conflict and change may sometimes operate to increase feelings of political alienation in the student.

The apparent impact of the experimental curriculum on Anglo, Black, and Mexican-American females suggests the most "positive" effect on Anglos, with blacks also positively affected. The increased interest and efficacy of these two groups may be because their political attitudes were initially less well developed than those of their male counterparts or possibly because the experimental units influenced their perceptions of the current women's liberation movement, making that movement more comprehensible and salient. Mexican-American females show the opposite effect, however. Several of the girls who were interviewed stated that studying about conflict—nonviolent or violent—was unpleasant and even frightening. The personal involvement and group action sanctioned in the experimental curriculum may also have conflicted with the way some of these girls were socialized at home. Several of the girls also disliked the political socialization self-analysis, possibly because this introspection pointed out the conflict.

The results from these and other data should give hope to educators who accept the assumption that "teaching for political efficacy" and interest in politics should be major goals of political education. While the relative impact of the school was not assessed in comparison with other key agents of political socialization, curricular changes did appear to increase the salience of the school.

I do not suggest that the experimental units which I developed are the "only," the "best," or necessarily even "one of the best" means of teaching government. I assert, however, that the type of approach underlying these units ought to be used. Behavior modification is an important ingredient, but other parts of the curriculum are important too, especially the student's self-analysis of his own socialization process.

The content focus of the experimental course was on political change, including behavioral and attitudinal aspects of political participation, as well as models of political change. This content should become part of political education curricula. Educators should promote the belief that political and social change is necessary and good; that American society has problems (a "reality" students are well aware of); that there are means by which citizens can work to resolve these problems; and that when the channels of political change within the system are closed to certain groups, conflict (not necessarily violent) may emerge. Conflict should be treated as creative rather than necessarily destructive, because eventually it may open up avenues of participation to those who have been excluded. Conflict is thus a vital and constructive aspect of the American political system.

Since the goal of the experimental curriculum was to effect political attitudes which would help students to be more effective political participants, several teaching strategies were designed to take students beyond merely studying, reading, and talking about the course content. In addition to open-class discussion, a technique used extensively in the contrast groups as well as in the experimental groups, three techniques were used to modify student behavior and thought: depthful introspection by each student; small-group "problem resolving" before and after analysis of political change and system models; and fieldwork within the political structure of the student's community. I proposed that these strategies also be incorporated into political education curricula.

Each strategy directly modifies the student's thinking or behavior within a politically relevant context, but more is involved. The self-analysis of political socialization encourages students to expand inward and to analyze the psychological and social processes which shape their own perceptions of political reality. As one black girl from the experimental group at School B put it: "For a while I've been feeling kind of down on the establishment, and when I found out how you can be influenced this way—how some groups can make you feel effective and others make you feel alienated, I had to stop and think. You begin to realize all the influences around you, and it made me feel a little bit less down on the establishment, because like the Black Panthers can have this influence."

And educators must also encourage students to expand outward—to go beyond the classroom and the school, into the political structure of their community and beyond. Fieldwork, or action research, helps the student become a self-directed learner and makes political education a part of his life, rather than a preparation for life in the future. The same girl quoted above described her fieldwork experience in these terms, revealing an enhanced self-direction and a direct link beween what she was learning in government class and experiencing in her community: "Speeding is a real problem over here [East Austin] . . . People get hurt . . . We chose the speeding problem for our research. We had to contact officials and police . . . , and we were successful. That made us feel a lot better. If it worked once you can do it again."

Finally, this study has clear implications for the political education of minority groups, who especially benefited from the study of models of political change, combined with political socialization self-analysis. The apparent impact from the experimental units on the Black and Mexican-American students who experienced them is typified by the following statement made by a Black male student, in describing his government course: "It was a very relevant part of my education . . . *Now*, if I want to change something I know how to do it. Knowing keeps me from being as pessimistic and apathetic as I was, and I don't feel as if I'm as pessimistic as I was, and this is one of the things which brings tension and violence. If you don't know how to participate in your government, you're going to be very frustrated because the government is going to kick you around 'til you know how to use it."

X

A Socialization Theory of Partisan Realignment

PAUL ALLEN BECK

Students of politics since the time of Plato have posited the existence of strong linkages between preadult political learning and the operation of political systems. For all their concern, however, there was little systematic research on preadult political learning prior to the late 1950s. Students of socialization outside the field of political science largely ignored socialization into explicitly political roles, while those few students of politics who were interested in political socialization focused narrowly and often impressionistically on civic education in the schools.

In slightly over a decade, all of that has changed. As Herbert Hyman (1969) observed in the preface to a new edition of his inventory of political socialization research:

> Now—by 1969—the study of political socialization
> has become a large-scale enterprise. It has become the

My thinking has been stimulated greatly by the work of Walter Dean Burnham and Philip E. Converse, and I would like to take this opportunity to acknowledge my intellectual debts to them. I am also grateful to James Miller, Richard Niemi, and Bert Rockman for their useful comments on earlier versions of this chapter.

199

> organizing principle for scientific meetings and lengthy
> conferences. Journals devote special issues to the theme.
> Texts and theoretical works in political science and
> monographs on the politics of many countries contain
> chapters on the topic. Scholarship has developed to the
> point that collections of articles are ready for the press,
> and the bibliography already runs to dozens of pages. . . .
> With this luxuriant scene before our eyes, it is hard to
> bring back to mind the barren vistas of the previous
> decade.

The outpouring of socialization research in the past decade
has greatly enhanced political scientists' knowledge of the preadult
political world. It has provided an increasingly clear picture of what
is learned and how it is learned. Yet this research has contributed
little to an understanding of adult political behavior or the opera-
tions of modern political systems. The reason for this is implicit in
almost all political socialization research. Researchers have been
content to assume that preadult political learning has important
consequences for both individuals and the political system. This
assumption has allowed them to avoid coming to grips with the
recalcitrant question which motivated students of politics to focus
on childhood socialization in the first place: what is the relevance of
preadult political learning for adult political behavior and, consequently, for political systems?*

If political socialization research is to continue to make important contributions to the study of politics, it must deal with these
linkage questions. I take some initial steps in that direction here by
outlining an explanation of a macropolitical phenomenon which
seems critical to the functioning of American politics—partisan
realignment. My explanation is grounded in theories of childhood
partisan socialization and adult partisan change. Taken together
these two theories provide a persuasive new explanation for past
realignments as well as for contemporary politics.

---

* One suspects that this linkage question has been ignored because
of the ease of collecting data from school children and the difficulty of
gathering data which tied adult political behavior directly to preadult
political learning.

Erosion of Childhood Partisanship

Of all the political orientations which develop in the pre-adult years, none promises to be more durable throughout an individual's life than partisanship. Psychological attachments to the Democratic and Republican parties emerge as early as grade two and become increasingly widespread among elementary school students with each passing year (Greenstein, 1965a, pp. 64–78; Hess and Torney, 1967, pp. 101–104). Although this partisanship appears to wane after elementary school (presumably as a result of nonpartisan influences in the school), high school seniors have been shown to be only about 10 percent less partisan than their parents (Jennings and Niemi, 1968b, p. 453). While childhood partisanship may represent little more than imitation of parental partisan orientations, there is little doubt but that it typically provides a strong foundation for adult partisan behavior (Campbell and others), 1960, pp. 146–149).

Partisan orientations normally develop early in the preadult years and persist throughout the life cycle. But during certain phases in American political history, inherited partisan orientations have been noticeably eroded. These periods of sharp change in the distribution of party loyalties in the electorate are termed *partisan realignments*. In the 1820s (before the emergence of the modern two-party system), the 1860s, the 1890s, and the 1930s, partisan changes have been of such force that they destroyed the previous balance of party power and inaugurated new lines of political conflict.

The aggregate characteristics of these realigning phases in American electoral politics are relatively easy to identify. Each has been accompanied by increases in electoral participation, sharp intraparty as well as interparty conflict, extensive geographical shifts in voting patterns, and unusually severe social or economic traumas (Burnham, 1970, pp. 6–9). Each has been preceded by a rise in electoral support for minor parties.

But individual changes during these realignments are difficult to identify. About the only source of data on such changes is the University of Michigan presidential election series, which sheds some light, though indirectly through recall of past voting behavior, on the realignment of the 1930s. Through analysis of the past and present partisan behavior of the respondents in these voter surveys, Campbell and his colleagues have been able to piece together a picture of individual change during this political upheaval (Campbell and others, 1960). In the following pages, I elaborate upon this picture—buttressing it with data drawn from a wider temporal interval and placing it into a broader theoretical context.

The realignment of the 1930s seems in retrospect to have been wrought principally by the new voters during the New Deal realigning phase, not by those who had voted in earlier years. As is demonstrated in Table 1, the first votes of these new voters were cast

Table 1.

REPORTED PRESIDENTIAL VOTES, 1924–1940

| | | *Percent Democratic of Two-Party Vote* | |
Election	All Voters	"Coming-of-Age" Voters	"Delayed" First Voters
1924	35	29	20
1928	41	38	53
1932	59	80	93
1936	62	89	77
1940	55	69	72

Source: Campbell and others (1960, p. 155).

overwhemingly in support of Franklin Delano Roosevelt. This behavior reflects the tendency for new voters to be swayed more heavily than their elders by the short-run forces in a particular election. It suggests also that the voting dispositions of these young voters were not wholly predetermined by their childhood partisan socialization. Given the likelihood that a majority of these first voters came from Republican homes (Republican identifiers were a majority prior to the 1930s), this first-time voting behavior signifies wholesale defections from inherited partisanship.

Before moving on, Table 1 warrants more careful examination. New voters are divided into two separate categories: those who were voting for the first time because they had just attained majority and those who were of age previously but had not voted. The behavior of these two groups of new voters is similar in all but one election—that of 1928. The nomination of a "wet" Catholic, Al Smith, by the Democrats in that year may well have attracted voters to the presidential contest who had been uninterested in presidential politics in previous years.* But on the whole, these two groups of new voters are virtually indistinguishable in terms of their voting behavior. The "delayed" voters were undoubtedly young adults moved by the same forces governing the "coming-of-age" voters.

Voting defections of the type portrayed in Table 1 are hardly sufficient to spawn a realignment. Realignments occur only when either inherited or active partisan allegiances are changed, producing large-scale shifts in the partisan loyalties of the voting public (Burnham, 1970, p. 6). While the electorate usually contains enough independents to allow some change in the distribution of partisanship, a shift of the magnitude of a realignment seems unlikely without many voters changing their partisan attachments.†

Experienced voters in the 1930s seem to have returned to relatively stable partisan loyalties. They support the theory that partisanship progressively hardens over an individual's life cycle, becoming more resistant to change with each passing year (Converse, 1969). Partisan shifts in a realignment are better explained by the recent entry of new age cohorts into the electorate. These young people are probably moving away more from a *nominal* inherited partisanship than from any deep-seated partisan orientations.

---

* One could infer from these data that Key's (1955) evidence of a realignment in 1928 in the industrial Northeast was, in reality, evidence of substantial defections only among older voters. These defections could probably not have forged a realignment by themselves without the subsequent depression of 1929.

† There is a possibility that a realignment could be produced without any partisan changes through the conversion of independents to a partisan disposition. This possibility was unlikely, however, as long as independents were few in number and the least knowledgeable and politically involved of all voters as was the case in the 1950s (Campbell and others, 1960, pp. 142–145). In more recent times, the characteristics of independents seem to be changing, and one can speculate that the absence of realigning forces in an electorate ripe for realignment has created a growing number of knowledgeable, involved independents—particularly among the young. This trend may well differentiate contemporary American electoral politics from those of any previous era. Discussion of the implications of such a trend is left until later.

This theory of individual change during realignments cannot be tested adequately until a new realignment occurs. It is based on the assumption that adult partisanship is much deeper, and hence less subject to change, than that articulated by a child or even a young adult. Support for this assumption can be found in a panel study comparing young adults and their parents (Jennings and Niemi, 1973). Adult partisan orientations have been reinforced by voting. Childhood partisan identifications, on the other hand, have received little of this behavioral support and, as socialization research has shown, are rarely buttressed by a well-developed sense of the policy differences between the parties. Although many adults see no difference between parties and although children clearly manifest partisan orientations that are likely to be reinforced in adulthood, nonetheless the weakest link in the transgenerational partisan chain within any family lies in the preadult years.

Circumstantial evidence can be marshaled to support the notion that this weakest link is most likely to be broken during the transition years between childhood and full adulthood—the first time childhood partisanship is tested. Young voter cohorts which supported Roosevelt so overwhemingly in 1932 and 1936 were overwhelmingly Democratic in their partisanship as well. Their break with tradition to cast a Democratic vote became a permanent rather than temporary defection. This is demonstrated in Figure 1: the major discontinuity in the division of party identifiers is found between those who were in their twenties when the Depression of 1929 struck and those who were over thirty at that critical watershed.* This change in the distribution of partisanship is both sharp and durable, preordaining the emergence of a new Democratic majority as the process of population replacement worked its inexorable magic.

* This figure parallels one reported in *The American Voter* (Campbell, and others, 1960, p. 154), but it is based on a much wider time interval and is restricted to presidential elections to ensure equivalency. Slightly different conclusions may be drawn from these two distributions of party identification by age cohort. Generational discontinuity in Figure 1 is not as sharp as that which appears in the figure from *The American Voter*. One reason is surely that independents have been excluded from the latter figure, but a second reason may be that the passage of time has dulled the apparent effects of the New Deal realignment.

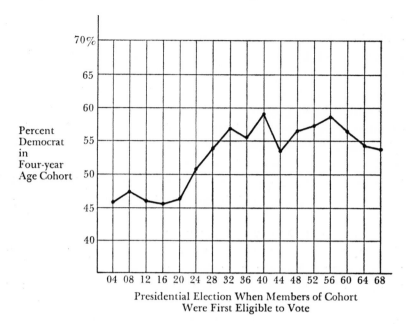

FIGURE 1. Party identification by four-year age cohort. These are the Democratic identifications of each four-year age grouping—including those who classified themselves as independents on first response but later admitted leaning toward the Democratic party—that were cumulated over every presidential election from 1952 through 1968, using the Survey Research Center election study data. The total N is approximately 9000 and the N is not less than 100 for any age cohort.

Given these data, however tentative they might seem, one must doubt that preadult political socialization fully determined the adult partisan orientations of these Depression generations. It seems much more likely that preadult orientations gave way under the impact of strong political forces for those who were in the transition years between childhood and full adulthood. Not yet habituated to a partisanship by actual electoral decision-making, these new voters were mobilized in new partisan directions. In the process, a new Democratic majority was formed.

The newest members of the electorate provide the dynamic element to American electoral politics. They are the ones most likely to break the partisan continuity between past and future and to force comprehensive changes in the policy agenda. Inherited partisan orientations are not always subjected to the intense pressures of a realigning phase, however. The excitement which pervades such a period, caused by the critical battle over agenda-setting for the future, cannot be sustained for long. Realignments phases then give way to the long periods of "normal politics," in which the party coalitions and policy agenda remain relatively stable. Normal politics promotes a high degree of intergenerational continuity in partisan orientations. Politics is simply too unexciting and too repetitious to continually subject the inheritances of new voters to severe pressures. Such pressures may be present in individual cases for idiosyncratic reasons, but they are unlikely to cumulate across an entire age cohort.

The study of political socialization has matured and prospered during a normal phase of American electoral politics. Thus it is not surprising that socialization theorists have seen more continuity than change in preadult political orientations and in the political system. It should now be obvious, though, that theories of socialization erected on a normal politics data base—especially those concerning partisanship—are misleading.

Cycles in Partisan Socialization

If it is true that the politics of realignment are intense enough to cause large numbers of voters to desert their childhood partisanship, it is also likely no other generation has more deeply entrenched partisan orientations and that, as a result, no other generation will transmit partisan orientations as successfully to its offspring as this realignment generation. These two assumptions combine to produce a new and powerful theory of preadult partisan socialization and the dynamics of realignment.

Three different groups of voters are involved in this theory. The members of group one adopt their enduring partisan orientations as emerging adult participants in a realigning phase. The partisanship of these realignment generations should have stronger intellectual underpinnings—a firmer grounding in rational responses to operative political realities—than that of any other age group. Group two includes all individuals who receive their preadult partisan socialization from members of a realignment generation. These "children of realignment," while lacking direct adult exposure to intense partisan conflict, are likely to receive much of the flavor of such conflict "across the dinner table" from their parents. Most group two individuals may be expected to carry into adulthood a partisanship which is supported by visceral if not intellectual underpinnings. Their childhood partisan orientations should be well insulated against change-inducing forces.

The third group of partisan learners is comprised of the individuals of the next generation. Their childhood political experience is gained during a period of normal politics; their parents were not direct participants in a realignment. The childhood partisan learning of these "children of normal politics" should provide little insulation from the short-term political forces they encounter as young adults.

A clear similarity exists between groups one and three—the realignment generation and the children of normal politics—even if they are sharply differentiated by age. Both receive relatively weak childhood partisan socialization, but the members of group one experience strong partisan socialization during their years of transition into adulthood, while the members of group three have not passed through this transition period yet. Even though the children of normal politics have become a realignment generation in every previous instance, there also exists the possibility that no such transformation will occur. This distinction is critical: in it lies the difference between political instability (when large numbers of voters reject partisanship) and political change (when large numbers of voters accept new partisanship).

Regular cycles of partisan stability and change have dominated American politics for more than a century. Realignments have occurred at roughly three-decade intervals, and each realignment has been followed by a long period of stable normal politics. This previously puzzling regularity in partisan politics is explicable when change is conceptualized in terms of the movement through the electorate of the realignment generation, the children of realignment, and the children of normal politics. Through the process of population replacement, the relative weight of each of these groups changes continually. Furthermore, the potential for sweeping partisan change depends on which of these groups is just entering the electorate.

This explanation can be grasped more readily if accompanied by a look at the century of American politics postdating the emergence of the modern two-party system. Three realignments have been identified in this time period. The first was associated with the political conflicts over slavery and civil war, the second with the urban-rural conflict of the late 1800s, and the third with the class conflicts of the New Deal. Each of these realignments occurred at a time when the children of normal politics were entering the electorate in full force. These voters seem to have been mobilized during their early adult years and subsequently became a realignment generation.

The fundamental population replacement process which underlies this theory is represented in Figure 2. Underlying the visible precision of this figure are several operational assumptions. First, the delimiting of each generation depends upon the location of clear initial and terminal points for every realignment phase. Such precision is difficult because of the very nature of realignments. At times they have emerged nationwide only gradually because of their uneven development in different parts of the nation (such as during the Civil War and the New Deal). The task of specifying the realignment phases is made even more difficult by the fact that each has been preceded by a period of partisan instability which appears, on the surface, to be "of a piece" with the subsequent realigning phase. (Nonetheless, a graphical depiction of my theory of realignment dynamics requires precise delimitation of these rather imprecise phenomena, and thus I have attempted to determine initial and terminal points as carefully as possible by weighing the relevant historical evidence. At the same time, I must reiterate that this is an artificial precision and that these points may be moved within reasonable bounds without disturbing the essential features of the theory.)

The Civil War realignment phase seems to have begun with southern secession from the Union in 1861, not with the long period of partisan instability which preceded it, as is often supposed. The basic structure of this Civil War party system seems to have been

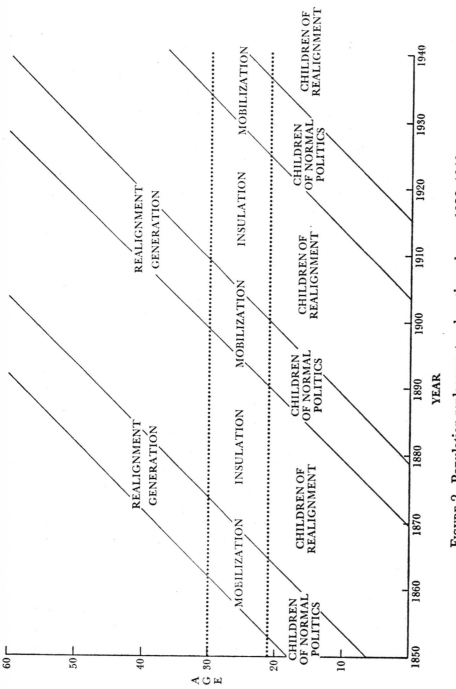

FIGURE 2. Population replacement and partisan change, 1850–1940.

set by the peace at Appomattox four years later. A number of scholars (Burnham, 1970; Sellers, 1965; Sundquist, 1973) contend that the Civil War realignment was completed by the beginning of the 1860s. Sundquist (1973), for example, concludes: "By 1858 the new alignment was firmly in place throughout the North" (p. 71). Yet, in retrospect, this assessment seems to overestimate the importance of this time period for the development of long-term partisan orientations. As Sundquist adds: "The heightened polarization of the war years etched the slavery-secession-war-reconstruction-Negro-rights line of cleavage more deeply into the political pattern until old lines dividing the electorate were obliterated. More and more voters made their party choices on the basis of the new line of cleavage rather than the old, especially the new generation of voters just coming to political maturity" (p. 87).

The period prior to the 1860s seems more an era during which the old party system was eroding rather than the new one forming. Pomper (1970) argues that the 1864 election, not an earlier election, first registered "the definite break with traditional sources of party support" (p. 114) even in the North; he supports his contention by reporting low correlations between that election and the average of the four preceding presidential elections and high correlations between it and the average of the four subsequent elections. Furthermore, Lipset (1960, chap. 11) shows that the realignment in the South postdated the 1860 election, coming with the referenda over secession several months later.

Scholars agree that the Panic of 1893 initiated the next realignment phase. Sundquist (1793) and Burnham (1970) ascribe to the Panic of 1893 the responsibility for the initial urbanite movement away from the Democrats. This movement was surely crystallized by the Democrats' choice of an agrarian populist as their presidential candidate three years later. Bryan's nomination countered these losses partially by attracting rural, particularly western, voters to the Democratic party. Pomper's (1970, p. 107) correlational analysis shows that the 1896 election was most unlike those that preceded and consistent with those that followed. This realigning phase had clearly runs its course by the reelection of McKinley over Bryan in 1900.

While Key (1955) identifies the beginnings of a realignment

in New England during the 1928 election, it seems doubtful that the New Deal realignment was fully initiated throughout the nation, and even in that region, prior to the Depression of 1929. The changes in voting patterns in the 1928 election were probably tied to the candidacy of Al Smith and would not have been permanent had the Depression of 1929 not reinforced the short-run lines of cleavage. As Sundquist (1973) puts it: "The heavy movement across party lines in presidential voting in the cities in 1928 was obviously caused by the issues that dominated public discussion in that election—religion and Prohibition. These were not the dominant issues of 1932 and 1936. The minor realignment of 1928 in the cities can therefore be considered an episode in American politics distinct from the realignment of the 1930s" (pp. 181–182). The realignment started by the Depression of 1929 and continued in the election of 1932 was probably not consummated until the 1936 election.

The second important assumption underlying Figure 2 is that the period during which adults are most likely to change their partisan attitudes comes between the age at which they are first eligible to vote (twenty-one before 1970 and eighteen since) and age thirty. Both are arbitrary bounds for the "adult formative years" and serve only as a first approximation until more is known about the formation of political attitudes in adults.

A third assumption is that the average age differential between parents and children is the conventional twenty-five years. This assumption plays an important role in the spacing of the mobilization phases in Figure 2. The generations available for mobilization are, by definition, those whose parents were not adults during the previous realigning phase. Thus, the children of normal politics begin to enter the electorate twenty-five years after the end of that phase. The mobilization phase begins twenty-five years after the termination of the preceding period of realignment and ends with the denouement of the new realignment phase. The children of normal politics may be in the electorate for some years (but no more than nine) before they are realigned.

This theory of realignment suggests that the prior disengagement of young voters from the established party system is a necessary precondition for realignment. The purportedly weak childhood partisan socialization of the children of normal politics only nurtures the "ripeness for realignment," however; a societal trauma, often a depression, seems from past experience necessary to deteriorate the actual realignment. It is clear in retrospect that traumatic events will not have this effect if they are not set in the context of an electorate "ripe for realignment." Other traumas of at least equal magnitude —the economic depressions of 1873 and 1907, two world wars, and the anticommunist hysteria of the early cold war period, for example —had no more than short-lived impacts on partisan behavior.

Manifestations of a decline in the importance of parties are apparent *prior* to each of the realignments in the past. Third party movements were unusually successful in electoral politics in the 1850s, the early 1890s, and the 1920s. Split-ticket voting also seems to have peaked during the 1920s (Cummings, 1966, p. 37) and may well have risen in the earlier periods if the pre-1900 electoral system had not made ticket splitting virtually impossible (Rusk, 1970). The decline of parties during each of these periods was arrested abruptly by the advent of a traumatic realignment-producing event and the consequent resocialization of young voters to provide a realignment generation.

This theory cannot stand without substantial qualification. First, a certain tentativeness is inevitably involved in any theory which purports to explain a macropolitical phenomenon using micropolitical behavior, without much more than circumstantial evidence linking the two. Second, the operational assumptions incorporated in Figure 2 are crude. The time interval between generations, the adult formative years, and the length of each realignment phase all resist precise quantification. Third, individuals in age-defined political generations do not necessarily share experiences during both childhood and the early years of adulthood. Political learning and experience are far too complex to be common for age-related individuals who differ substantially on other fundamental variables. The theory can withstand this qualification, however, because partisan realignments require only partial reshufflings of the electorate.

The most critical qualification to this theory is that it is grounded on assumptions about past individual-level political behavior which cannot be tested empiricially. We simply cannot determine whether the partisan orientations of previous realignment generations were more deeply rooted than those of other generations of voters. Furthermore, we know virtually nothing about the relative intensities of partisan socialization when performed by realignment versus normal politics generations. Precise answers to these questions must await another realignment phase in American electoral politics. Partial answers, on the other hand, may be suggested by contemporary political behavior, if they are researched. Even these answers, though, will not be forthcoming unless political socialization researchers recognize the importance of the early adult years for the formation of enduring political orientations and realize that substantial variations may exist in the success with which each successive generation socializes its young.

Contemporary American Electoral Politics

Recent American electoral politics has been marked by unusual instability. After a landslide victory of historic proportions in the 1964 presidential election, the Democratic party descended into bitter internecine strife and electoral defeat, followed by electoral disaster in 1972. During the same time period, pollsters plotted an increase in self-identified independents in the electorate, at the expense of both parties (see Figure 3). This change in the distribution of partisan orientations has been paralleled by a remarkable increase in split-ticket voting, particularly in the two most recent presidential elections—1968 and 1972.

Some observers conclude that recent events in American electoral politics signal a new realignment phase. Phillips (1970) trumpets the emergence of a new Republican majority coalition. Burnham, on the other hand, is more cautious: "It is particularly doubtful . . . that a new majority would be 'Republican' in any well-defined, party-identified sense of the terms; but such a majority, if derived from the 'great middle,' would surely be profoundly conservative" (1970, p. 141). If there has been any realignment, he concludes, its direction has been conservative, even though the dynamics of that realignment may well have set in motion a liberal-to-radical realignment to come in the future. A few political commentators have even perceived the birth of a new liberal majority in the politics of the sixties (Dutton, 1971), although they have been virtually silenced by the Nixon landslide in 1972.

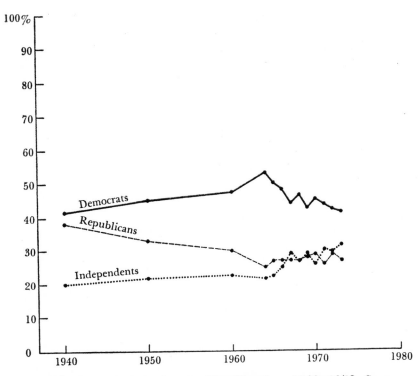

FIGURE 3. Distribution of party identification, 1940–1973. Source: The Gallup Opinion Index, Report No. 95, May 1973 (recent figures represent yearly averages).

Burnham (1969, 1970) also expresses considerable doubt that a realignment is possible any longer in American politics. This important mechanism of electoral change has been rendered inoperable, he maintains, by the "depoliticizing and antipartisan" electoral reforms enacted by the Progressives at the turn of the century. To Burnham, the decline in the importance of party loyalties (and, hence, parties) to the electorate is a long-term trend which was briefly slowed, but not reversed, by the New Deal realignment.

It seems to me that neither the theory of realignment nor that of the decline of parties provide adequate explanations for contemporary electoral politics. Nor does Burnham's (1970) combination of the two theories in a single explanation seem satisfactory. The best clues to the state of present politics are found in the political orientations of the youngest generation of voters. Change should be clearest, as well as most prophetic of the future, in this generation. Two logically interviewed characteristics of these maturing voters are conspicuous in recent years. First, this generation is much more heavily independent than older generations were at similar stages in the life cycle,* and there is every indication of increased independence among the young. (Data from the University of Michigan congressional election study in 1970 and from the Gallup Poll show that the generations which entered the electorate after 1968 were, if anything, more independent than their immediate predecessors.) Second, the heightened indepedence of this generation represents an erosion of support for both the Democrats and the Republicans.

Thus not only has there been no aggregate shift in a partisan direction, but there has been no tendency for young voters to flock to the banners of either party. Republican presidential victories in 1968 and 1972 were registered in spite of, not because of, the voting tendencies of this generation. McGovern's showing among these voters in 1972 does not augur well for an emerging Democratic majority. In the absence of changes in the distribution of partisan loyalties in the electorate and of a noticeable disproportionate mobilization of young voters into one party, realignment explanations for present politics seem inadequate.

Recent changes in partisan orientations, principally the increase in independents, appear, on their face, to be explained better by the theory of the decline of parties. Upon closer examination, though, this theory too is found wanting. It fails to explain a signal characteristic of the increase in independents: its suddenness. (Sundquist [1973, p. 353] has made this same point but with a different explanation for it than mine.)

As conceptualized by Burnham (1969, 1970), the decline of parties has been inexorable since the beginning of the twentieth century. Only the onset of the New Deal realignment slowed the spread

---

* In the past twenty years, young voters have continually identified themselves more as independents than have their elders. The common interpretation of this relationship is that it reflects life-cycle differences and that generations would become more partisan as they aged (Campbell and others, 1960, p. 162). While it is too early to determine whether the phenomenon will persist throughout the life cycle, the life-cycle differences in partisanship which have been common in past years appear to have been joined recently by pervasive generational differences.

of this fatal cancer in the party system, but it hardly effected a cure of it. Given this view, it is puzzling why the pace of the decline of parties accelerated so quickly in the sixties.

Beyond the theories of realignment and decline of parties lies an explanation of contemporary electoral politics. The socialization theory of realignment offers an explanation which fits both the present and the past. The 1960s and early 1970s bear striking resemblance to eras in American political history which preceded realignments. The electorate in each case—in the 1850s, the 1890s, the 1920s, and the present—contains a generation of young voters who, as children of normal politics, were (and are) ripe for realignment. The current ripe-for-realignment generation began to enter the electorate in full force in the 1960s (see Figure 4), and the decline of parties has been manifest ever since.

What differentiates the present from the earlier mobilization periods is that almost a decade has passed without an event with sufficient force and direction to destroy the old party alignment and mobilize young voters in new partisan directions. A second differentiating feature, making the current decline of parties all the more pronounced, is that a higher proportion of the electorate is in the under-thirty age group than has been the case in the recent past. One of the more subtle effects of the post-World War Two "baby boom" and the recent reduction of the voting age to eighteen has been to quicken the pace of partisan decay.

The Future of American Electoral Politics

While my socialization theory of realignments can explain both the periodicity of past realignments and the current drift away from parties, it yields no clear predictions about the future. Several alternative future scenarios may be suggested, each of which seems plausible.

The first scenario assumes that some critical, realigning event is "just around the corner." As in the past, this event may be economic in nature, though the major role government now plays in managing the economy would seem to preclude economic dislocations of the magnitude of past depressions. Current economic problems are sure to make their mark on political dispositions. But it is

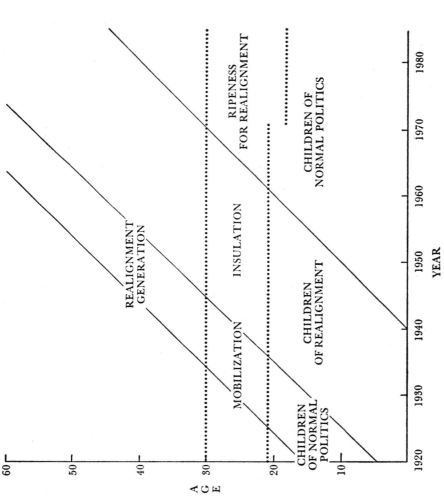

FIGURE 4. Population replacement and partisan change, 1920–1980.

doubtful that they will catalyze a realignment, particularly since they reflect current partisan cleavages. Another potential realigning event may be the Watergate affair. Past revelations of political wrong-doing have never tiggered a realignment, but one cannot be certain whether this is explained by their timing (none occurred when the electorate was ripe for realignment) or by the general nonpartisan "fallout" of such issues over the long run.

The conflict over civil rights for blacks may constitute a re-aligning issue. But unless there is considerable lag in the impact of events on partisanship, this issue does not seem to have generated the kind of traumatic force necessary to mobilize voters towards a new partisan alignment. Even though it seems premature to write an ending to the importance of this conflict and its realigning po-tential, there is little evidence that it will produce a realignment, especially since the major questions underlying this conflict are now juridical in nature and outside of the electoral arena.

An alternative scenario portrays a future almost wholly in-congruous with the past. In the absence of a catalyzing traumatic event, the current ripeness for realignment may continue, contribut-ing to an increasingly severe decline of party. Some voters in the generation ripe for realignment have already passed their thirtieth birthday and may no longer be available for partisan mobilization. This may lead to the increasing influence of "Madison Avenue politics" and to a perceptible decline in popular influence over public policy because, for all their faults, political parties are valu-able instruments of democracy, and no institutions have yet emerged which can supplant them as vehicles for popular control.

A variation on this theme assumes that independence rarely constitutes a meaningful long-run partisan orientation and that in-dependents over thirty will remain available for mobilization. If this assumption is valid, then we may expect a far more sweeping re-alignment in the future than his ever appeared in the past. Such a realignment could well endanger partisan competition in America by virtually vanquishing the party not favored in the realignment.

Whatever happens in the future, the socialization theory of realignment should considerably enhance our understanding of past and present electoral politics. Ripe for realignment in a system which has failed to generate any mobilizing forces in partisan directions, younger voters are drifting away from both parties to a haven of political neutrality. This drift could fundamentally alter the dynamics of American electoral politics by terminating the century-old cycle of realignments and normal politics. It could culminate in a paralysis in the making of public policy if confidence declines in political parties—the major forces for the policy coordination that occurs in American politics—and if no other institutions arise to take their place.

Bibliography

ABRAMSON, P. "Political Efficacy and Political Trust Among Black Schoolchildren: Two Explanations." *Journal of Politics,* 1972, *34,* 1243–1275.

ACHEN, C. "Issues and Intensity." Unpublished doctoral dissertation, Yale University, 1974.

ADELSON, J., AND O'NEIL, R. "Growth of Political Ideas in Adolescence: The Sense of Community." *Journal of Personality and Social Psychology,* 1966, *4,* 295–306.

ADORNO, T., FRENKEL-BRUNSWIK, E., LEVINSON, D., AND SANFORD, R. *The Authoritarian Personality.* New York: Wiley, 1950.

AGGER, R., GOLDSTEIN, M., AND PEARL, S. "Political Cynicism: Measurement and Meaning." *Journal of Politics,* 1961, *23,* 477–506.

ALMOND, G., AND VERBA, S. *The Civic Culture.* Princeton, N.J.: Princeton University Press, 1963.

AMIDON, E., AND HOUGH, J. (Eds.) *Interaction Analysis: Theory, Research and Application.* Reading, Mass.: Addison-Wesley, 1967.

Arsbok för Sveriges Kommuner. Stockholm: Statistika Centralbyran, 1969.

Austin Independent School District. *Government Curriculum Guide.* Austin, Tex., 1966.

BACHMAN, J., AND VAN DUINEN, E. *Youth Look at National Problems.* Ann Arbor, Mich.: Institute for Social Research, 1971.

BARR, R. (Ed.) *Values and Youth.* Washington, D. C.: National Council for the Social Studies, 1971.

BEM, D. Beliefs, Attitudes and Human Affairs. Monterey, Calif., Brooks/Cole, 1970.

221

BILLINGS, C. "Black Activists and the Schools." *High School Journal,* 1970, *54,* 96–107.

BILLINGS, C. "Black Student Activism and Political Socialization." Paper presented at the Annual Meeting of the American Political Science Association, Chicago, 1971.

BROPHY, J., AND GOOD, T. *Teacher-Child Dyadic Interaction: A Manual for Coding Classroom Behavior.* Research and Development Center for Teacher Education, University of Texas at Austin, 1969.

BROWN, R. *Social Psychology.* New York: Free Press, 1965.

BURNHAM, W. "The End of American Party Politics." *Transaction,* 1969, *6,* 12–22.

BURNHAM, W. *Critical Elections and the Mainsprings of American Politics.* New York: Norton, 1970.

BUROS, O. *Fifth Mental Measurements Yearbook.* Highland Park, N.J.: Gryphon, 1959.

BUTTON, C. "Teaching for Political Efficacy." *Theory into Practice,* 1971, *10,* 340–345.

BUTTON, C. "The Development of Experimental Curriculum to Effect the Political Socialization of Anglo, Black, and Mexican-American Adolescents." Unpublished doctoral dissertation, University of Texas at Austin, 1972.

BUTTON, J. "The Political Socialization of Children's Developing Orientations Toward the International System." Unpublished paper, University of Texas at Austin, 1971.

CAMPBELL, A., CONVERSE, P., MILLER, W., AND STOKES, D. *The American Voter.* New York: Wiley, 1960.

CAMPBELL, A., CONVERSE, P., MILLER, W., AND STOKES, D. *Elections and the Political Order.* New York: Wiley, 1966.

CARMICHAEL, S., AND HAMILTON, C. *Black Power: The Politics of Liberation in America.* New York: Vintage Press, 1967.

CARTER, T. *Mexican-Americans in School: A History of Educational Neglect.* New York: College Entrance Examination Board, 1970.

CONNELL, R. "Research and Thought on the Development of Political Beliefs in Children: A Critical Survey." Paper presented at the Annual Meeting of the Australasian Political Studies Association, 1969.

CONNELL, R. "On the Origins of Ideology: An Essay in the Integration of Psychological and Social Theory." Unpublished paper, University of Sydney, 1970.

CONNELL, R. *The Child's Construction of Politics.* Melbourne: Melbourne University Press, 1971.

CONVERSE, P. "The Nature of Belief Systems in Mass Publics." In D. Apter (Ed.), *Ideology and Discontent.* New York: Free Press, 1964.

CONVERSE, P. "Of Time and Partisan Stability." *Comparative Political Studies,* 1969, *2,* 139–171.

CONVERSE, P. "Attitudes and Non-Attitudes: Continuation of a Dialogue." In E. Tufte (Ed.), *The Quantitative Analysis of Social Problems.* Reading, Mass.: Addison-Wesley, 1970.

CUMMINGS, M. *Congressmen and the Electorate.* New York: Free Press, 1966.

DAHL, R. *Pluralist Democracy in the United States.* Chicago: Rand McNally, 1967.

DAHL, R. *After the Revolution.* New Haven, Conn.: Yale University Press, 1970.

DAVIES, J. *Human Nature in Politics.* New York: Wiley, 1963.

DAVIES, J. "The Family's Role in Political Socialization." *Annals of the American Academy of Political and Social Science,* 1965, *361,* 10–19.

DAWSON, R., AND PREWITT, K. *Political Socialization.* Boston: Little Brown, 1969.

DENNIS, J., AND MC CRONE, D. "Preadult Development of Political Party Identification in Western Democracies." *Comparative Political Studies,* 1970, *3,* 243–263.

DOLBEARE, K. (Ed.) *Power and Change in the United States.* New York: Wiley, 1969.

DOMHOFF, G. *Who Rules America?* Englewood Cliffs, N.J.: Prentice-Hall, 1967.

DREYER, E. "Change and Stability in Party Identification." *Journal of Politics,* 1973, *35,* 712–722.

DUTTON, F. *Changing Sources of Power.* New York: McGraw-Hill, 1971.

DYE, T., AND ZIEGLER, H. *The Irony of Democracy.* Belmont, Calif.: Wadsworth, 1970.

EASTON, D. *A Framework for Political Analysis.* Englewood Cliffs, N.J.: Prentice-Hall, 1963.

EASTON, D. "The New Revolution in Political Science." *American Political Science Review,* 1969, *63,* 1051–1061.

EASTON, D., AND DENNIS, J. "The Child's Acquisition of Regime Norms:

Political Efficacy." *American Political Science Review,* 1967, *61,* 25–38.

EASTON, D., AND DENNIS, J. *Children in the Political System.* New York: McGraw-Hill, 1969.

EASTON, D., AND HESS, R. "The Child's Political World." *Midwest Journal of Political Science,* 1962, *6,* 229–246.

EHMAN, L. "Political Socialization and the High School Social Studies Curriculum." Unpublished doctoral dissertation, University of Michigan, 1970.

FEY, W. "Acceptance by Others and Its Relation to Acceptance of Self and Others: A Reevaluation." *Journal of Abnormal and Social Psychology,* 1955, *50,* 274–276.

FISHER, F. "Influence of Reading and Discussion on the Attitudes of Fifth Graders Toward American Indians." *Journal of Educational Research,* 1968, *62,* 130–134.

FISHMAN, J. (Ed.) *Language Loyalty in the United States.* The Hague: Mouton, 1966.

FISHMAN, J. (Ed.) *Socialinguistics.* Rowley, Mass.: Newbury, 1971.

FOX, K. "The Junior High School Activists." *High School Journal,* 1970, *54,* 119–125.

FRANCO, J. "A Description of Project Beacon: A Program Designed to Improve Self-Concept and Academic Achievement in Negro Children." Unpublished doctoral dissertation, University of Rochester, 1971.

GARCIA, F. "An Inquiry into the Development of Political System Values Among Mexican-American Children." Unpublished paper, University of New Mexico, 1972a.

GARCIA, F. "The Political World of the Chicano Child." Paper Prepared for the Elementary Education Task Force, Political Science Education Project of the American Political Science Association, 1972b.

GARCIA, F. "Mexican Americans and Modes of Political Participation: Regime Norm Development." Paper presented at the Annual Meeting of the Western Political Science Association, San Diego, 1973a.

GARCIA, F. "Orientations of Mexican-American and Anglo Children Toward the U. S. Political Community." *Social Science Quarterly,* 1973b, *53,* 814–829.

GARCIA, F. *The Political Socialization of Chicano Children.* New York: Praeger, 1973c.

GEORGSSON, A. "Den unge väljaren och politiken." Unpublished licentiat-dissertation, University of Gothenburg, 1973.

GLAZER, N. "The Process and Problems of Language Maintenance: An Integrative Review." In J. Fishman (Ed.), *Language Loyalty in the United States*. The Hague: Mouton, 1966.

GOSLIN, D. (Ed.) *Handbook of Socialization Theory and Research*. Chicago: Rand McNally, 1969.

GOUGH, H. "Studies of Social Intolerance." *Journal of Social Psychology*, 1951, *33*, 237–269.

GRANNIS, J. "The School As a Model of Society." *Harvard Graduate School of Education Bulletin*, 1967, *12*, 15–17.

GREBLER, L., MOORE, J., AND GUZMAN, R. *The Mexican-American People: The Nation's Second Largest Minority*. New York: Free Press, 1970.

GREENBERG, E. "Children and the Political Community: A Comparison Across Racial Lines." *Canadian Journal of Political Science*, 1969, *2*, 471–492.

GREENBERG, E. "Children and Government: A Comparison Across Racial Lines." *Midwest Journal of Political Science*, 1970a, *14*, 249–275.

GREENBERG, E. "Black Children and the Political System." *Public Opinion Quarterly*, 1970b, *34*, 333–345.

GREENBERG, E. "Orientations of Black and White Children to Political Authority Figures." *Social Science Quarterly*, 1970c, *51*, 561–571.

GREENBERG, E. *Political Socialization*. Chicago: Aldine-Atherton, 1970d.

GREENBERG, E. "Black Children, Self-Esteem, and the Liberation Movement." *Politics and Society*, 1972, *2*, 293–302.

GREENFIELD, P., AND BRUNER, J. "Culture and Cognitive Growth." In D. Goslin (Ed.), *Handbook of Socialization Theory and Research*. Chicago: Rand NcNally, 1969.

GREENSTEIN, F. "The Benevolent Leader." *American Political Science Review*, 1960, *65*, 353–371.

GREENSTEIN, F. "Sex-Related Political Differences in Childhood." *Journal of Politics*, 1961, *23*, 353–371.

GREENSTEIN, F. *Children and Politics*. New Haven, Conn.: Yale University Press, 1965a.

GREENSTEIN, F. "Young Men and the Death of a Young President." In M. Wolfenstein and G. Kliman (Eds.), *Children and the Death of a President*. Garden City, N.Y.: Doubleday, 1965b.

GREENSTEIN, F., AND TARROW, S. *Political Orientations of Children: The Use of a Semi-Projective Technique in Three Nations.* Beverly Hills, Calif.: Sage, 1970.

GUSTAFSSON, G. "Strukturomvandling och politisk socialisation." Unpublished doctoral dissertation, University of Umeå, 1972.

GUTIERREZ, A., AND HIRSCH, H. "Political Maturation and Political Awareness: The Case of the Crystal City Chicano." Unpublished paper, University of Texas at Austin, 1972.

GUTIERREZ, A., AND HIRSCH, H. "The Militant Challenge to the American Ethos: 'Chicanos' and 'Mexican-Americans'." *Social Science Quarterly,* 1973, *53,* 830–845.

GUZMAN, R. "The Political Socialization of the Mexican-American People." Unpublished doctoral dissertation, University of California, Los Angeles, 1970.

HASTINGS, P. "The Non-Voter in 1952: A Study of Pittsfield, Massachusetts." *Journal of Psychology,* 1954, *38,* 301–312.

HASTINGS, P. "The Voter and the Non-Voter." *American Journal of Sociology,* 1956, *62,* 302–307.

HEISE, D. "Separating Reliability and Stability in Test-Retest Correlation." *American Sociological Review,* 1969, *34,* 93–101.

HESS, R. "Political Socialization in the Schools." *Harvard Educational Review,* 1968, *38,* 528–536.

HESS, R. "Political Attitudes in Children." *Psychology Today,* 1969, *3,* 24–28.

HESS, R., AND EASTON, D. "The Child's Changing Image of the President." *Public Opinion Quarterly,* 1960, *24,* 632–644.

HESS, R., AND TORNEY, J. *The Development of Political Attitudes in Children.* Chicago: Aldine, 1967.

HIRSCH, H. *Poverty and Politicization.* New York: Free Press, 1971.

HIRSCH, H. "Political Scientists and Other Camaradas: Academic Myth Making and Racial Stereotypes." In R. de la Garza, Z. Kruszewski, and T. Arciniegra (Eds.), *The Territorial Minorities: Chicanos and Native Americans.* Englewood Cliffs, N.J.: Prentice-Hall, 1973.

HIRSCH, H., AND GUTIERREZ, A. "The Socialization of Political Aggression and Political Affect: A Subculture Analysis." Unpublished paper, University of Texas at Austin, 1972.

HORTON, J., AND THOMPSON, W. "Powerlessness and Political Negativism: A Study of Defeated Local Referendums." *American Journal of Sociology,* 1962, *67,* 485–493.

HOSTETLER, J. *Amish Society*. Baltimore: Johns Hopkins University Press, 1963.

HOSTETLER, J. "Socialization and Adaptation to Public Schooling: The Hutterian Brethren and the Old Order Amish." *Sociological Quarterly*, 1970, *11*, 195–210.

HUSÉN, T. *Adolescensen*. Uppsala: Almqvist and Wiksell, 1944.

HYMAN, H. *Political Socialization*. New York: Free Press, 1959; rev. ed., 1969.

JAROS, D. "Children's Orientations Toward the President: Some Additional Theoretical Considerations and Data." *Journal of Politics*, 1967, *29*, 368–387.

JAROS, D. *Socialization to Politics*. New York: Praeger, 1973.

JAROS, D., AND CANON, B. "Transmitting Basic Political Values: The Role of the Educational System." *School Review*, 1969, *77*, 94–107.

JAROS, D., HIRSCH, H., AND FLERON, F. "The Malevolent Leader: Political Socialization in an American Sub-Culture." *American Political Science Review*, 1968, *62*, 564–575.

JENKINS, J. "The Acquisition of Language." In D. Goslin (Ed.), *Handbook of Socialization Theory and Research*. Chicago: Rand McNally, 1969.

JENNINGS, M., AND NIEMI, R. "The Transmission of Political Values from Parent to Child." *American Political Science Review*, 1968a, *62*, 169–184.

JENNINGS, M., AND NIEMI, R. "Patterns of Political Learning." *Harvard Educational Review*, 1968b, *38*, 443–467.

JENNINGS, M., AND NIEMI, R. "Continuity and Change in Political Orientations: A Longitudinal Study of Two Generations." Paper presented at the Annual Meeting of the American Political Science Association, New Orleans, 1973.

JENNINGS, M., AND NIEMI, R. *The Political Character of Adolescence*. Princeton, N.J.: Princeton University Press, 1974.

KENISTON, K. *Young Radicals*. New York: Harcourt Brace Jovanovich, 1968.

KENYON, S. "The Development of Political Cynicism Among Negro and White Adolescents." Paper presented at the Annual Meeting of the American Political Science Association, New York, 1969.

KEY, V. O., JR. "A Theory of Critical Elections." *Journal of Politics*, 1955, *17*, 3–18.

KNOWLES, L., AND PREWITT, K. *Institutional Racism in America.* Englewood Cliffs, N.J.: Prentice-Hall, 1969.

KNUTSON, J. "Psychological Deprivation and Its Effect on School Behavior." *Bulletin of the Oregon School Study Council,* 1967, *11.*

KNUTSON, J. *The Human Basis of the Polity.* Chicago: Aldine, 1972a.

KNUTSON, J. "Some Problems of Assessment in Political Psychology." Paper presented at the Annual Meeting of the American Political Science Association, Washington, D.C., 1972b.

KNUTSON, J. "Long-Term Effects of Personality on Political Attitudes and Beliefs." Paper presented at the Annual Meeting of the American Political Science Association, New Orleans, 1973a.

KNUTSON, J. "Personality in the Study of Politics." In J. Knutson (Ed.), *Handbook of Political Psychology.* San Francisco: Jossey-Bass, 1973b.

KNUTSON, J. "The New Frontier of Projective Techniques." In J. Knutson (Ed.), *Handbook of Political Psychology.* San Francisco: Jossey-Bass, 1973c.

KNUTSON, J. "The Political Relevance of Self-Actualization." In A. Wilcox (Ed.), *Public Opinion and Political Attitudes.* New York: Wiley, 1973d.

KNUTSON, J. *Personality Stability and Political Belief.* San Francisco: Jossey-Bass, 1974.

KOLKO, G. *Wealth and Power in America.* New York: Praeger, 1962.

KOLSON, K., AND GREEN, J. "Response Set Bias and Political Socialization Research." *Social Science Quarterly,* 1970, *51,* 527–538.

KRUG, M., POSTER, J., AND GILLIES, W., III. *The New Social Studies.* Itasca, Ill.: Peacock, 1970.

LABOV, W. "The Logic of Non-Standard English." *The Florida FL Reporter,* 1969, *6,* 60–74.

LABOV, W., AND ROBINS, C. "A Note on the Relation of Reading Failure to Peer-Group Status in Urban Ghettos." *The Florida FL Reporter,* 1969, *6,* 54–57.

LANGTON, K. *Political Socialization.* New York: Oxford University Press, 1969.

LANGTON, K., AND JENNINGS, M. "Political Socialization and the High School Civics Curriculum in the United States." *American Political Science Review,* 1968, *62,* 852–867.

LANGTON, K., AND KARNS, D. "A Cross National Study of the Relative Influence of School Education: A Causal Analysis." *ERIC ED 034 320,* 1969.

LAURENCE, J. "White Socialization: Black Reality." *Psychiatry,* 1970, *33,* 174–194.

LESLIE, L., LESLIE, J., AND PENFIELD, D. "The Effects of a Student Centered Special Curriculum Upon the Racial Attitudes of Sixth Graders." *Journal of Experimental Education,* 1972, *41,* 63–67.

LIEBSCHUTZ, S. "Peer Influence and the Acquisition of Political Attitudes." Unpublished doctoral dissertation, University of Rochester, 1971.

LIPSET, S. *Political Man.* Garden City, N.Y.: Doubleday, 1960.

LITT, E. "Civic Education, Community Norms and Political Indoctrination." *American Sociological Review,* 1963, *28,* 69–75.

LYONS, S. "The Political Socialization of Ghetto Children: Efficacy and Cynicism." *Journal of Politics,* 1970, *32,* 288–304.

MC CANDLESS, B., AND EVANS, E. *Children and Youth: Psychosocial Development.* Hinsdale, Ill.: Dryden Press, 1973.

MC CLOSKY, H., AND DAHLGREN, H. "Primary Group Influence on Party Loyalty." *American Political Science Review,* 1959, *53,* 757–776.

MACCOBY, E., MATTHEWS, R., AND MORTON, A. "Youth and Political Change." *Public Opinion Quarterly,* 1954–1955, *18,* 23–39.

MC WILLIAMS, C. *North from Mexico.* New York: Greenfield, 1948.

MARVICK, D. "The Political Socialization of the American Negro." *The Annals of the American Academy of Political and Social Science,* 1965, *361,* 112–127.

MASLOW, A. *Motivation and Personality.* New York: Harper and Row, 1954.

MASSIALAS, B. (Ed.), *Political Youth, Traditional Schools.* Englewood Cliffs, N.J.: Prentice-Hall, 1972.

MATTHEWS, D. *The Social Background of Political Decision-Makers.* Garden City, N.Y.: Doubleday, 1954.

MEAD, M. *Culture and Commitment: A Study of the Generation Gap.* Garden City, N.Y.: Doubleday, 1970.

MEHLINGER, H., AND PATRICK, J. *American Political Behavior.* Rev. ed. High School Curriculum Center in Government, Indiana University, 1968.

MERELMAN, R. "The Development of Policy Thinking in Adolescence." *American Political Science Review,* 1971, *65,* 1033–1047.

MERELMAN, R. "The Structure of Policy Thinking in Adolescence." *American Political Science Review,* 1973, *67,* 161–166.

MILBRATH, L. *Political Participation.* Chicago: Rand McNally, 1965.

MILLER, G., AND MC NEILL, D. "Psycholinguistics." In G. Lindzey and E.

Aronson (Eds.), *The Handbook of Social Psychology*, Vol. 3. Reading, Mass.: Addison-Wesley, 1969.

MITCHELL, W. "The Ambivalent Social Status of the American Politician." *Western Political Quarterly*, 1959, *12*, 683–698.

MOORE, J. *Mexican-Americans*. Englewood Cliffs, N.J.: Prentice-Hall, 1970.

MURRAY, H. *Thematic Apperception Test Manual*. Cambridge, Mass.: Harvard University Press, 1943.

MUSSEN, P., AND WYSZYNSKI, A. "Personality and Political Participation." *Human Relations*, 1952, *5*, 65–82.

NATIONAL ADVISORY COMMISSION ON CIVIL DISORDERS. *Report*. Washington, D.C.: Government Printing Office, 1968.

NIEMI, R. "Political Socialization." In J. Knutson (Ed.), *Handbook of Political Psychology*. San Francisco: Jossey-Bass, 1973.

NIEMI, R. *How Family Members Perceive Each Other*. New Haven, Conn.: Yale University Press, 1974.

PATELLA, V., AND KUVLESKY, W. "Situational Variation in Language Patterns of Mexican-American Boys and Girls." *Social Science Quarterly*, 1973, *53*, 855–864.

PATRICK, J. "The Impact of an Experimental Course, 'American Political Behavior,' on the Knowledge, Skills, and Attitudes of Secondary School Students." *Social Education*, 1971, *36*, 168–179.

PHILLIPS, K. *The Emerging Republican Majority*. Garden City, N.Y.: Doubleday, 1970.

PIAGET, J. *The Moral Judgment of the Child*. London: Kegan Paul, 1932.

"Political Education in the Public Schools: The Challenge for Political Science." *Political Science*, 1971, *4*, 434–446.

POMPER, G. *Elections in America*. New York: Dodd, Mead, 1970.

PONDER, G., AND BUTTON, C. "Student-Initiated Classroom Interaction Among Anglo, Black, and Mexican-American Twelfth Graders Experiencing an Experimental Government Curriculum: The Relationship Between Frequency of Student Initiations and Measures of Political Attitudes." Paper presented at the Annual Meeting of the American Educational Research Association, New Orleans, 1973.

PROTHRO, J., AND GRIGG, C. "Fundamental Principles of Democracy: Bases of Agreement and Disagreement." *Journal of Politics*, 1960, *22*, 276–294.

RATHS, L., HARMON, M., AND SIMON, S. *Values and Teaching.* Columbus, Ohio: Merrill, 1966.

ROCHESTER CITY SCHOOL DISTRICT. *Beacon Lights.* Rochester, N.Y., n.d.

RODGERS, H. *Community Conflict, Public Opinion, and the Law.* Columbus, Ohio.: Merrill, 1969.

RODGERS, H., AND TAYLOR, G. "The Policeman as an Agent of Regime Legitimation." *Midwest Journal of Political Science,* 1971, *15,* 72–86.

ROMANO-V., O. "The Anthropology and Sociology of the Mexican-Americans." In O. Romano-V. (Ed.), *Voices.* Berkeley: Quinto Sol, 1971.

ROSENBERG, M. "Misanthropy and Political Ideology." *American Sociological Review,* 1965, *21,* 690–695.

ROSSI, P. "Four Landmarks in Voting Research." In E. Burdick and A. Brodbeck (Eds.), *American Voting Behavior.* New York: Free Press, 1959.

ROTTER, J. "Generalized Expectancies for Internal Versus External Control of Reinforcement." *Psychological Monographs,* 1966, *80,* (609).

RUSK, J. "The Effect of the Australian Ballot Reform on Split Ticket Voting: 1876–1908." *American Political Science Review,* 1970, *64,* 1220–1238.

SANCHEZ, G. "History, Education, and Culture." In J. Samora (Ed.), *La Raza: Forgotten Americans.* South Bend, Ind.: University of Notre Dame Press, 1966.

SCHATTSCHNEIDER, E. *The Semi-Sovereign People.* New York: Holt, Rinehart, and Winston, 1960.

SCHUMAN, H., AND CONVERSE, J. "The Effects of Black and White Interviewers on Black Responses in 1968." *Public Opinion Quarterly,* 1971, *35,* 44–68.

SEARS, D. "Political Socialization." In F. Greenstein and N. Polsby (Eds.), *Handbook of Political Science.* Vol. 2: *Theoretical Aspects of Micro-Politics.* Reading, Mass.: Addison-Wesley, forthcoming.

SEARS, D., AND MC CONAHY, J. "Racial Socialization, Comparison Levels, and the Watts Riot." *Journal of Social Issues,* 1970, *26,* 121–140.

SEARS, D., AND TOMLINSON, T. "Riot Ideology in Los Angeles: A Study of Negro Attitudes." In J. Van Der Slik (Ed.), *Black Conflict with White America.* Columbus, Ohio: Merrill, 1970.

SEASHOLES, B. "Political Socialization of Negroes: Image Development of Self and Policy." In W. Kravaceus and others, *Negro Self-Concept*. New York: McGraw-Hill, 1965.

SELLERS, C. "The Equilibrium Cycle in Two-Party Politics." *Public Opinion Quarterly*, 1965, *29*, 16–37.

SIGEL, R. "Assumptions About the Learning of Political Values." *Annals of the American Academy of Political and Social Science*, 1965a, *361*, 1–9.

SIGEL, R. "An Exploration into Some Aspects of Political Socialization: School Children's Reactions to the Death of a President." In M. Wolfenstein and G. Kliman (Eds.), *Children and the Death of a President*. Garden City, N.Y.: Doubleday, 1965b.

SIGEL, R. "Political Socialization: Some Reactions on Current Approaches and Conceptualization." Paper presented at the Annual Meeting of the American Political Science Association, New York, 1966.

SIGEL, R. "Image of a President: Some Insights into the Political Views of Children." *American Political Science Review*, 1968, *62*, 216–226.

SIGEL, R. *Adolescence and Political Involvement*. North Scituate, Mass.: Duxbury Press, 1973.

SIMPSON, E. *Democracy's Stepchildren*. San Francisco: Jossey-Bass, 1971.

SKOLNICK, J. *The Politics of Protest*. New York: Ballantine Books, 1969.

SOMIT, A., TANENHAUS, J., WILKE, W., and COOLEY, R. "The Effects of the Introductory Political Science Course on Student Attitudes Toward Personal Participation." In R. Sigel (Ed.), *Learning About Politics*. New York: Random House, 1970.

SMITH, F., AND COX, B. *New Strategies and Curriculum in Social Studies*. Chicago: Rand McNally, 1969.

STEINER, S. *La Raza: The Mexican-American*. New York: Harper and Row, 1970.

STOKES, D. "Popular Evaluations of Government: An Empirical Assessment." In H. Cleveland and H. Lasswell (Eds.), *Ethics and Bigness*. New York: Harper and Row, 1962.

STOUFFER, S. *Communism, Conformity, and Civil Liberties*. New York: Wiley, 1955.

SUNDQUIST, J. *Dynamics of the Party System*. Washington, D.C.: Brookings Institution, 1973.

Svenska Institutet för Opinionsundersökningar. "Svensk Ungdom."

Mimeographed. Stockholm, 1955. Reported in H. Hyman, *Political Socialization.* New York: Free Press, 1959.

TAJFEL, J. "Social and Cultural Factors in Perception." In G. Lindzey and E. Aronson (Eds.), *Handbook of Social Psychology,* Vol. 3. Reading, Mass.: Addison-Wesley, 1969.

THOMPSON, W., AND HORTON, J. "Political Alienation as a Force in Political Action." *Social Forces,* 1960, *38,* 190–195.

TOLLEY, H., JR. *Children and War.* New York: Teachers College Press, 1973.

TRIANDIS, H. *Attitudes and Attitude Change.* New York: Wiley, 1971.

United States Commission on Civil Rights. *Hearing Held in San Antonio, Texas.* Washington, D.C.: Government Printing Office, 1968.

United States Commission on Civil Rights. *The Excluded Student.* Washington, D.C.: Government Printing Office, 1972.

VAILLANCOURT, P. "The Political Socialization of Young People: A Panel Study of Youngsters in the San Francisco Bay Area." Unpublished doctoral dissertation, University of California, Berkeley, 1972, 373–387.

VAILLANCOURT, P. "The Stability of Children's Socialization Survey Responses." *Public Opinion Quarterly,* 1973, *37.*

VERBA, S., AND OTHERS. "Public Opinion and the War in Vietnam." *American Political Science Review,* 1967, *61,* 317–333.

WARSHAUER, M. "Foreign Language Broadcasting." In J. Fishman (Ed.), *Language Loyalty in the United States.* The Hague: Mouton, 1966.

WESTBY, D., AND BRAUNGART, R. "The Alienation of Generations and Status Politics: Alternative Explanations of Student Political Activism." In R. Sigel (Ed.), *Learning About Politics.* New York: Random House, 1970.

Westinghouse Learning Corporation. "Evaluation of the Head Start Program." In *The Effectiveness of Compensatory Education: Summary and Review of Evidence.* Washington, D.C.: Department of Health, Education, and Welfare, n.d.

YOUNG, D. "The Socialization of American Minority Peoples." In D. Goslin (Ed.), *Handbook of Socialization Theory and Research.* Chicago: Rand McNally, 1969.

ZELLMAN, G., AND SEARS, D. "Childhood Origins of Tolerance for Dissent." *Journal of Social Issues,* 1971, *27,* 109–136.

ZIMBARDO, P., AND EBBESEN, E. *Influencing Attitudes and Changing Behavior.* Reading, Mass.: Addison-Wesley, 1970.

Index